CHANGING POLICY AND PRACTICE FOR PEOPLE WITH LEARNING DISABILITIES

Also available from Cassell:

H. Daniels and J. Anghileri: *Secondary Mathematics and Special Educational Needs*
S. Hegarty: *Meeting Special Needs in Ordinary Schools* (2nd edition)
G. Hornby: *Working with Parents of Children with Special Needs*
D. Johnstone: *Further Opportunities*
P. Mittler and P. Daunt (eds): *Teacher Education for Special Needs in Europe*
B. Norwich: *Reappraising Special Needs Education*
J. Sayer: *Secondary Schools for All* (2nd edition)
J. Stone: *Mobility for Special Needs*
B. Walters: *Management for Special Needs*
S. Wolfendale: *Primary Schools and Special Needs* (2nd edition)
S. Wolfendale (ed.): *Assessing Special Educational Needs*

Changing Policy and Practice for People with Learning Disabilities

Edited by

Peter Mittler with Valerie Sinason

CASSELL

*This book is dedicated with love and gratitude to the memory of
Professor Stanley Segal (1919–1994) – the greatest advocate of all*

Cassell
Wellington House
125 Strand
London WC2R 0BB

215 Park Avenue South
New York
NY 10003

First published 1996

British Library Cataloguing-in-Publication Data
A catalogue record for this book is available from the British Library.

ISBN 0–304–33398–0 (hardback)
     0–304–33399–9 (paperback)

Typeset by York House Typographic Ltd, London.
Printed and bound in Great Britain by Redwood Books, Trowbridge, Wilts

Contents

PART III   CHANGING ATTITUDES

PART IV   ADVOCACY IN ACTION

Preface

This book records the struggle to achieve basic human rights and a better life for people with learning disabilities over the last 50 years. It provides firsthand, eyewitness accounts of a number of attempts to influence policy and practice, some successful, others still continuing, as well as a parallel series of synoptic overviews of progress and problems in various areas of service provision. The book is dedicated with love and admiration to Stanley Segal, the greatest advocate of all: his daughter Valerie Sinason writes a personal account of his advocacy from its earliest origins to the time of his death in June 1994.

The contributors have all been engaged in advocacy over a period of years and are well placed to look back on what has been achieved and what still remains to be done. Part I is a historical record of their campaigns; Part II includes a number of overviews of progress in some key areas of service provision, such as education, day and residential services. Part III includes chapters on changing public attitudes and influencing the media.

Peter Mittler
University of Manchester
August 1995

Contributors

Lewis Carter-Jones, former Member of Parliament

Patrick Daunt, former Head of Bureau of Action in Favour of Disabled Persons, European Commission

David Felce, Professor of Research in Learning Disabilities, University College, Cardiff

Jean Garnett, formerly Head of Special Needs Support Services, Coventry; President, National Council for Special Education

John Garrett, former member of Her Majesty's Inspectorate of Education

Charles Getliffe, former Principal of Ravenswood Village and Special Education Centre, Crowthorne, Berks

Gus Gray, East Berkshire NHS Trust

Peggy Jay, former Chair, Committee of Enquiry into Mental Handicap Nursing and Care

Roy McConkey, Brothers of Charity, Melrose, Scotland

Peter Mittler, Professor of Special Education, University of Manchester

Philippa Russell, Director, Council for Disabled Children

Ann Shearer, former journalist, now practising psychotherapist

Valerie Sinason, Consultant Psychotherapist, Tavistock and Portman Clinics

Derek Thomas, Director, National Development Team

John Tizard, Strategic Planning Manager, SCOPE (formerly The Spastics Society)

Dame Mary Warnock, former Chair, Committee of Enquiry into the Education of Handicapped Children and Young People

Klaus Wedell, Professor of Educational Psychology (Special Educational Needs), Institute of Education, University of London

Andrea Whittaker, Project Officer, King's Fund Centre

Part I

Changing Policies

Chapter 1

Advocates and Advocacy

Peter Mittler

WHO ARE THE ADVOCATES?

People with learning disabilities have not lacked advocates who have been prepared to speak out against abuse and for human rights and better services. Courageous individuals have always been ready to make a public protest about inhuman or degrading conditions to which people with learning disabilities have been – and still are being – subjected. Sometimes they are individuals such as Stanley Segal or Peggy Jay with clear vision and with their sights set on a specific objective. They may be journalists such as Ann Shearer making the public aware of inhuman conditions in which people were living. Increasingly they are people with learning disabilities speaking for themselves and demanding to be heard.

GOVERNMENT INITIATIVES

Sometimes it is government or a particular minister that provides leadership, as in the case of Richard Crossman or Barbara Castle, or there may be a particularly timely report, such as that on Ely Hospital or the Audit Commission reports of the early 1990s on the need to revise the 1981 Education Act.

Although most contributors write from an English perspective, Patrick Daunt, formerly in charge of the EC Bureau of Action in Favour of Disabled Persons, provides an overview of the parallel struggles, campaigns and lobbies in Continental and Eastern Europe (see also Daunt, 1991; 1993a; 1993b)). The UK has much to contribute to its European partners but also much to learn about advocacy for people with learning disabilities.

The role of legislation

Legislation clearly has a major contribution to make to the development of better services, as long as it is effectively implemented and resourced. Lewis Carter-Jones, who, together with Alf Morris and Jack Ashley, piloted the 1970 Chronically Sick and

Disabled Persons Act through Parliament, gives a graphic account of the manoeuvres and intrigues that were necessary to persuade reluctant ministers to lend their full support to this and indeed all subsequent legislation designed to secure the rights of disabled people and to combat discrimination. The events of 1994 and 1995 demonstrate that no government has up to now been prepared to accept effective anti-discrimination legislation and that ministers will stop at nothing to prevent such legislation being passed or implemented. This at least unites disabled people and their supporters in a fierce determination to ensure that the next attempt to secure legislation is more successful than the last.

Mary Warnock writes equally frankly about the background to the work of her Committee of Enquiry, how they arrived at their recommendations and the factors which they failed to take into account in their deliberations. She also summarizes the disagreements within the committee on the issue of integration and the future of special schools and how these uncertainties were reflected in the 1981 Education Act and again in the 1993 Act which simply repeats the same escape clauses concerning 'efficient use of resources' and the risk of 'interfering with the education of other children in the school', clauses which can be regarded as discriminatory since they could not be applied to children without special needs or statements.

Although the 1981 Act might now be seen to have been flawed both by internal contradictions and by lack of resources, much was achieved at LEA and school level which would not have been possible without the Act and the Circulars and Regulations which followed. Klaus Wedell's chapter documents both the negative and the positive effects of the avalanche of educational legislation which engulfed education between 1988 and 1993. The special needs parliamentary lobby with which he has been closely associated has been remarkably successful in influencing Parliament and officials and in ensuring that, as far as possible, the interests of children with special educational needs were at least safeguarded and even enhanced.

Whatever may be the limitations of the 1993 Education Act as a whole, there can be no doubt that Part 3 is a considerable improvement on the 1981 Act. The UK is now one of the countries where special needs forms an integral but distinct element of mainstream legislation, in contrast to the 1981 Act which was essentially a separate 'special' Act for a small section of the population. The *Code of Practice* in particular marks a new point of departure in providing detailed guidance on the roles and responsibilities of ordinary schools and in tightening the procedures for the drawing up and review of statements. The *Code of Practice* is the product of months of intensive consultation in which there was a genuine dialogue between officials and the 'special needs constituency'. We can only hope that the honeymoon period and goodwill engendered by this consultation will survive the intrinsic problems of funding at the level of the school and the LEA.

Philippa Russell writes from the outside as well as the inside about the 1989 Children Act which is probably even more important than the 1993 Act in spelling out the rights of the child and in developing its own distinctive approach to the definition of 'children in need'. The task now is to achieve a working integration between the Children Act and the 1988 and 1993 Education Acts at local level. This is the responsibility of the local authority as a whole, not just Social Services or Education acting singly.

The National Development Group and the National Development Team

The setting up of the National Development Group (NDG) and the National Dev₋
ment Team (NDT) and the simultaneous launch of the Jay Committee in 1975 reflecte₋
the high degree of priority given by ministers to people with learning disabilities at this
time.

The NDG and the NDT represented new departures for a government department.
The NDG was described as 'in the machine but not part of it'. In other words, it was not
part of the bureaucracy, nor was it a traditional government committee, but it had a
considerable degree of autonomy and access not only to ministers but also to the
normal process of policy development and implementation. Its members were drawn
from all relevant disciplines, and included a parent, as well as people knowledgeable
about relevant research findings. Stan Segal's appointment as a representative from
education caused bureaucratic flurries in Whitehall; as the NDG reported to the
Secretary of State for Social Services, civil servants were nervous about the appointment of a member whose loyalties were to a different Secretary of State. However, the
fact that he was working in the voluntary and not the maintained sector finally
reassured them. Our insistence on appointing a parent was only successful when we
used our right of access to ministers.

The NDG was also well supported by officials and professional advisers from
psychiatry, nursing and social work. It wrote all its own publications which were then
disseminated with a positive ministerial foreword on a large scale and free of charge.
This was a convenient device to enable advice to be given to the field for which the
DHSS did not have to take direct responsibility, either from a policy or from a financial
point of view.

The NDG played an influential role in the development of policies for joint planning
and joint funding as between Health and Social Services. Its recommendations for Joint
Care Planning Teams and for Community Mental Handicap Teams (NDG, 1976;
1977a) were further developed by the NDT, as described in this book by Derek
Thomas, its current director. The NDG also wrote an influential pamphlet on day
services (NDG, 1977b) and a more formal published report on the future of long-stay
hospitals (NDG, 1978), which laid out detailed plans for relocation of residents and for
the development of more structured learning and rehabilitation environments. Before
it was disbanded, it completed work on the development of a set of quality assurance
standards for all services for people with learning disabilities that fell within DHSS
responsibilities at the time, thus excluding education, housing and employment, except
in so far as joint planning mechanisms were meant to include all relevant agencies
(NDG, 1980).

Research findings

There are rare occasions when successful innovators persuade others to experiment
with new methods of providing services, as in the case of the Brooklands and Wessex
experiments. Research findings, if effectively disseminated and publicized, can also

create a climate of commitment to change and promote advocacy at many levels. In the UK, the work of Jack Tizard, Alan and Ann Clarke and Herbert Gunzburg in the 1950s and 1960s demonstrated that people with learning disabilities were able to learn and to benefit from education and training, provided they were given time to learn and were taught by qualified staff using appropriate well-researched methods. In the following decades, the Hester Adrian Research Centre at Manchester University put particular emphasis on the active dissemination of relevant research to practitioners, including parents (Segal and Varma, 1991). Since then, a number of other major research centres have been established in the UK and in other European countries, all of which have been involved to varying extents with developing research relevant not only to public policy but also to day-to-day work in service settings and in families. But the gap between research and practice still remains uncomfortably wide and needs to be narrowed as a matter of urgency.

PARENTS AND PARENT ORGANIZATIONS

The main impetus for change has often but not always come from the parents' movement and from their insistent demands for basic services to which their sons and daughters are entitled, including the right to life, the right to education, the right to housing and the right to employment. In short, parents have insisted on equal opportunities and rejected discrimination in all its forms.

The period following the Second World War witnessed the growth of parent societies at local and then at national and international level (Dybwad, 1990). These often started with just a few parents meeting in one another's homes to share ideas and experiences. The origins of MENCAP, for example, can be traced to a letter sent to a national newspaper by a parent (Judy Frydd) in which she simply asked other parents to write to her. In most countries, parents gradually organized themselves to demand access to local services for their children or to start such services themselves when they met with no official response. At the international level, the International League of Societies for Persons with Mental Handicap (now Inclusion International) regularly speaks for people with learning disabilities within the United Nations system and protests directly to governments when there are examples of infringement of fundamental human rights.

Some of these parent societies across the world are now large organizations employing hundreds of people. Sometimes they themselves provide services, such as schools, day services, sheltered workshops, sheltered housing, group homes or recreational facilities. They also stimulate the development of parent-to-parent mutual support groups. In most cases, the larger societies mount active campaigns to improve services or to oppose discrimination and abuse. To this end, they may organize lobbies and pressure groups to campaign on specific issues or merely keep a watching brief on the development of legislation or the implementation of policy. Some have parliamentary officers or an office in Westminster to make it easier to gain access to legislators and to seek to influence them. The chapter by Lewis Carter-Jones illustrates the powerful influence which non-governmental organizations (NGOs) can exercise on the parliamentary process, especially if they work together and can speak with a single voice, as happened in the 1986 Disabled Persons Act and again in the abortive anti-discrimination legislation debates of 1994 and 1995.

Philippa Russell traces the development of the parent movement in the UK, from its origins when parents were seen as 'patients' and as 'handicapped families' through the early struggles to achieve basic services for their children towards the current aims of empowerment and insistence on the rights of families to play a full and equal part in decision-making. Parents want to feel in control and are no longer prepared to play the role of passive and grateful recipients of whatever services happen to be available. Despite charters and a more militant consumerism, many families still feel disenfranchised and deprived of information; furthermore, the culture of commissioning and purchasing of services leaves many families at the mercy of market forces in which their needs are anything but a priority. It remains to be seen whether the full implementation of the 1989 Children Act and the *Code of Practice* (Department for Education, 1994) are really going to produce a sea change in facilitating a higher degree of family participation or whether such changes as do take place affect only a minority of the more articulate and determined parents.

THE GROWTH OF SELF-ADVOCACY

People with a learning disability are increasingly speaking for themselves. The chapter by Andrea Whittaker documents the growth of the self-advocacy movement in the UK and makes it clear that self-advocates are no longer prepared to let others speak on their behalf, whether they are parents or professionals.

The rapid growth of the self-advocacy movement raises a number of questions for the future which organizations of parents and of professionals have not yet faced. For example, what is the role of the family and of the school – and of both working together – in helping young people to lay the foundations of self-advocacy skills which they will need in the future (Mittler, 1995)? What, if any, should be the relationship between a parent society at local or national level and a self-advocacy group? How can the two work harmoniously together and respect each other's autonomy?

In some countries one or more self-advocates are full members of the executive boards of the parent organization. This is also true of Inclusion International and of many other bodies. The nature of the support required to make an active contribution to the work of such groups will vary from individual to individual; some will need a great deal, others relatively little. But the nature of the relationship between the individual and their support worker is critical. If the support workers are over-zealous, there is a risk that they will too readily interpret and 'speak for' the persons they are supporting, rather than ensuring that they are speaking with their own voice.

Similar issues are raised by the relationship of the individual self-advocate with their advocates; there is an inherent tension between these roles which can be resolved but which must be confronted and discussed. The greater the limitations of the person with a learning disability, the more tempting it is for the advocate (who may be independent, a professional or a parent) to speak for him or her.

Neither parents nor professionals, nor the organizations in which they work, have yet fully come to terms with the arrival of the self-advocacy movement and its implications for them in the present or the future. This is a key item on any future agenda.

THE 'ORDINARY LIFE' MODEL

Underpinning all the developments and changes described in this book, the most important single influence affecting advocates for human rights and for better services has undoubtedly been the fundamental philosophy of what in the UK has come to be called the 'ordinary life' model. Deriving from the principles of normalization and social role valorization, but written in much more accessible and user-friendly language, the 'ordinary life' model shows how people with learning difficulties should and can have access to ordinary services – health, education, housing, social services, employment, leisure. In a series of ground-breaking conferences and publications, the King's Fund Centre in London secured wide acceptance of the principles and practices consistent with the 'ordinary life' model. More recently, the emphasis has been placed on the concept of 'supported living', in recognition of the fact that some form of support relevant to the specific needs of the individual is essential.

These principles are closely related to the concept of equal opportunities which has much in common with the 'ordinary life' model but covers a much broader spectrum of people. The United Nations *World Programme of Action in Favour of Disabled Persons* defines equal opportunities as:

> *The process through which the general systems of society such as the physical and cultural environment, housing and transportation, social and health services, educational and work opportunities, cultural and social life, including sport and recreational facilities are made available to all* (United Nations, 1983).

A major task for advocates, therefore, is to ensure that all really does mean all.

Towards educational responsibility

The campaign to end the stigma of ineducability and to make education authorities responsible for the education of all children without exception was fought by Stanley Segal and others and is recorded here by John Garrett. This was an example of British leadership at its best. Many countries have followed the lead set by the UK example, though UNESCO studies show that there is still a minority where responsibility for education rests with health or social welfare agencies or with the voluntary sector.

Looking back to the England of the 1960s, it is difficult to understand the basis for the resistance to this transfer of responsibility. Not only were some health authorities or individual health professionals or managers convinced that they were offering a better service but there was at first little enthusiasm either from the Department of Education and Science or from LEAs to accept responsibility for a group of children whom they had officially declared ineducable. Furthermore, neither MENCAP nor some individual parents were initially convinced that such a transfer was necessarily in the interests of the children and preferred to stay with Health on the grounds of their existing experience in this field.

The strongest pressure for change came from a relatively small but highly articulate coalition of parents and professionals who were joined fairly late in the day by MENCAP and some of the professional associations. Richard Crossman, Secretary of State for Social Services at the time, openly stated that it was only parental pressure that led his department to agree to this transfer of responsibility.

No one can doubt that the decision to make education authorities responsible for the education of all children has been fully vindicated. The quality of education for children in the schools improved out of all recognition; improvements were made in initial and continuing professional development of teachers and the work of the special schools was praised by HMI and the Warnock Committee. The schools adopted systematic approaches to teaching and developed innovative methods of curriculum development.

Most recently, they have responded imaginatively as a group to the challenge posed by a National Curriculum which originally took no account of the needs of these children by developing ways in which the statutory curriculum could be made more accessible and meaningful. More publications have come from teachers of children with severe learning difficulties than from any other single group of teachers concerned with special needs. The Schools Curriculum and Assessment Authority has supported these developments by developing a less prescriptive and rigid curriculum and by providing greater scope for professional judgement both in teaching, assessment and in the setting of priorities.

But however good the work of special schools, there is increasingly strong advocacy for the inclusion of all children in ordinary schools. This comes from advocacy groups such as the Centre for Studies in Integrated Education, the Integration Alliance and many parent groups at local and national level. The case is made on moral and ethical as well as educational grounds. They argue that children have a right to attend an ordinary school, preferably their neighbourhood school, and that nothing that is currently provided in special schools could not be provided within the setting of an ordinary school. Indeed, the head of a special school has publicly stated that there can be no such thing as a good special school, since such a school, by definition, deprives its pupils of the possibility of living and learning alongside other children living in their neighbourhood.

This is not the place to rehearse the arguments for and against education of all children in ordinary schools (e.g. Hunt, 1994). But since advocacy is the theme of the book, we should note that advocacy for inclusive education is increasing in strength every year and will continue to do so in the light of the growing volume of evidence that it is both possible and effective.

There seems to be little open disagreement with the principle that all children, including those with severe learning difficulties, should attend ordinary schools. There are now many published and unpublished accounts of the successful inclusion of individual children and some areas have developed well-designed and effectively supported schemes. The difficulty lies in implementing such a policy for individual children in particular schools and LEAs, given highly variable levels of commitment and lack of funding.

Bringing children out of hospital

The battle to end the admission of children to long-stay hospitals, described here by Peggy Jay, was partly one of combating the traditional view, reflected in many official statements, that 'there will always be a minority of children whose needs are such that only the specialized facilities of a hospital can meet them'. Maureen Oswin's stark documentation (1978) of the actual day-to-day realities of a life on a long-stay children's ward, followed by the official reports of the NDT, highlighted the hollowness of such statements. Furthermore, parents voted with their feet, with the result that the number of children in hospital, which the 1971 White Paper estimated would need to remain at around 6,000 for 20 years, has long since dwindled to insignificance because parents simply refused to contemplate their children going into hospital for long-term care and also because better residential alternatives became available.

Towards hospital closures

David Felce's chapter documents in some detail how traditional assumptions about the role of long-stay hospitals came to be questioned and eventually discarded and how numbers in hospital were approximately halved in the period between 1980 and 1992. The number of community homes trebled to 3,600 between 1980 and 1992 and the number of places in them doubled to 40,000. The impetus in this sector came from a variety of sources but one of the most influential was the evidence from a number of examples of successful practice that change was not only possible but could also be shown to be effective.

Evidence from the famous Brooklands experiment that it was possible to develop a regime which was based on the best principles and practice of child care rather than on the traditional hospital regime was energetically promoted by the late Jack Tizard, one of the first and most inspirational examples of the researcher as advocate. This work in turn influenced the Wessex Regional Hospital Board to develop what they called small 'locally based hospital units' and to fund a research team to evaluate the experiment. Here again, it was Albert Kushlick's passionate advocacy of alternatives to traditional hospitals that influenced many others to follow the Wessex example by exploring options.

The wider campaign to run down and finally close long-stay hospitals for adults as well as for children was initially fought by the Campaign for the Mentally Handicapped in the late 1960s and throughout the 1970s and was given further weight by the report of the Jay Committee on the training needs of nursing staff and by a whole series of committees of inquiry and by the NDT drawing attention to impoverished environments and sometimes inhuman conditions, staff shortages and lack of clear rehabilitative programmes. It was increasingly accepted that many residents of long-stay hospitals had no need of these facilities and that the majority could be discharged into supported living environments in the community.

From the early 1980s, the government endorsed a policy of rundown of hospitals and relocation of residents to the community, funded by 'dowries' representing the cost of hospital care which were transferred to social services departments responsible for providing community services. This policy has been broadly accepted by health professionals and, unlike other countries, there has been no large-scale or systematic opposition from the nursing or medical professions or from care staff employed in hospitals, whatever reservations may have been expressed by individuals. But there are still major issues about the quality of life and the adequacy of services for former hospital residents, as well as those who have always lived in the community but who are not receiving additional funding.

A new movement of parents and family members of long-stay residents was created in the 1980s to draw attention to the lack of community resources to support people coming out of hospitals. This was RESCARE, which campaigned to halt the programme of hospital closure. Although this campaign has been ineffective, there has been growing advocacy to retain a wide spectrum of non-NHS residential provision, which is summarized in the chapter by Charles Getliffe. It is argued that parents should be able to retain the option of choosing a residential community if this is felt to be in the interests of their son or daughter.

There is an ethical issue here, in so far as it is usually the family that opts for residential communities such as Ravenswood; the individual concerned may or may not be consulted but even if they are, they are not always aware of the range of alternatives which may be available to them. Be that as it may, such communities include many people who are fairly competent and could live in the community with support but who appear to be well settled and may be reluctant to be 'resettled'.

As people began to be discharged from long-stay hospitals, the shortcomings of the care in the community initiative became apparent. Many of these are due to severe underfunding but others arose more from mismanagement and lack of planning. For example, Margaret Flynn's (1988) study of residents discharged from long-stay hospital showed that they tend to be rehoused in the poorest and most deprived inner city areas. Most experienced a profound loneliness and isolation, and sometimes victimization and abuse from neighbours. Professional support from social workers was limited or non-existent. There were few examples of care plans which had been drawn up jointly between hospital and community staff; as a result, there were not enough things for people to do during the day and too few leisure opportunities at any time.

Group homes and supported living

During the 1970s, a major influence on the development of thinking on residential options came from the Eastern Nebraska Community Office for Retardation (ENCOR) movement which was in turn influenced by Wolfensberger's work on normalization. A number of visits to and from Nebraska at that time resulted in many people with the whole range of learning disabilities living in ordinary houses with whatever degree of support they needed at any given time. This policy was actively promoted by the campaign for People with Mental Handicap, was widely disseminated and was adopted in part at least in many areas of the country, including large regions such as north-west England. The NIMROD project in Cardiff adopted this model as part of a comprehensive programme of community services from which no one was to be excluded on grounds of severity of disability or challenging behaviour.

Despite the quantitative progress that can be confidently reported, can we be satisfied about the quality of the provision available? As Felce points out,

> Small size does not guarantee quality and nor does community location, ordinary housing design or adequate staffing. They are certainly necessary to achieving high quality but the relationship between outcome and the nature of the environmental context is mediated by internal organisation, working methods and the procedures which shape *what staff do* [italics added].

The research on deinstitutionalization and supported living highlights the importance of matching policy initiatives with parallel programmes of staff training – a message promulgated clearly by pioneers such as Jack Tizard as long ago as the 1960s, but, tragically, one that has not been heeded by those responsible for planning and funding training (Hogg and Mittler, 1987).

Day services

If education and residential services have been helped by powerful advocates, this is unfortunately not the case for the 50,000 adults attending day services. Indeed, the story of day services, as summarized by Gus Gray, is a depressing one. The national picture here is one of stagnation and neglect, with isolated examples of forward-looking innovative practice. The publication of the NDG's Pamphlet No. 5, *Day Services for Mentally Handicapped Adults*, coming close on the heels of the first national survey of Adult Training Centres carried out by Whelan and Speake (1977), stimulated a number of changes but some of these were cosmetic rather than real. There was a flurry of conferences and reports in the mid- to late 1980s but these were not followed up by lobbying or pressure groups at national level. Since then, the advent of the purchase–provider principle has probably led to further fragmentation and underfunding of day services with the result that these may well lay claim to being the new Cinderella of the services for people with learning disabilities.

PUBLIC ATTITUDES AND PUBLIC EDUCATION

In the last analysis, the success of the care in the community initiative depends largely on public support or at least on public acceptance or the absence of open hostility.

This is why the language we use when we speak about people with learning disabilities is so important and why it is essential in the future to consult self-advocates and service users when contemplating yet another change in terminology. The large charities (with some exceptions) are rethinking both their names and how they portray disabled people; for example, the Spastics Society is now SCOPE and MENCAP has modified its posters if not its name.

Even more important is the language which parents and professionals use in public; this is not to be dismissed as 'mere political correctness'. Using a phrase such as '*the* mentally handicapped' reflects a stereotyped assumption that *they* are 'all the same'. For a while, it was customary to talk about 'people with disabilities' until it was pointed out by self-advocacy groups that if they have to be referred to *en masse* at all, their preference was for 'disabled people', since they saw themselves as ordinary people disabled by social barriers and institutions.

Roy McConkey's chapter sets the scene and the historical context by dispelling a number of myths about 'public education campaigns' for which there is no evidence or evidence which runs counter to what many well-intentioned people would like to believe. Instead, he summarizes a number of studies which have shown that change is most likely to result from positive and enjoyable interactions with disabled people: hence one of the strongest arguments for inclusive schools is that the next generation will have more positive attitudes to disabled people as a consequence of having gone to the same school and had the same friends. Similarly, there should be many more natural opportunities in the future than in the past for casual encounters with disabled people in employment, in places of sport and entertainment and in shops and in the street. Indeed, the mere presence of ramps, accessible public transport and dropped curbs reminds the public about the needs of people with physical disabilities; fostering positive attitudes about people with learning disabilities requires a different approach and one that takes longer to pay dividends.

His chapter includes many highly practical suggestions on community education and participation and the contribution which can be made to this process first and foremost by people with learning disabilities themselves, but also by their families and by the front-line professionals who work with them.

Ann Shearer writes as an experienced journalist who has also played a leading advocacy role in the Campaign for Mentally Handicapped People (now Values in Action) on ways of presenting a positive image of people with learning disabilities in the popular media which are heard and watched by millions of people whose attitudes to disabled people may be negative or neutral. The advice contained in her chapter should be on every sub-editor's desk as well as in the mind of anyone who prepares a press release about people with learning disabilities.

There are signs that the quality of media stories on radio, television and in the local and national press are now much more positive than they used to be and that public attitudes are somewhat more favourable, though it is impossible to judge whether this is a result of better media coverage or more personal experience. On the other hand, there are still many examples of gross discrimination against disabled people either as individuals or when there is a proposal to develop a group home or day centre in a neighbourhood.

CONCLUSIONS

Because the rights of people with learning disabilities remain unmet in every country of the world, and because their needs are always the last to be considered, the need for advocacy at every level is greater than ever. This book provides examples of many kinds of advocacy and illustrates a variety of campaigns to achieve a wide range of objectives. But the examples are mostly drawn from the UK or more specifically from England and Wales and what is permitted or possible by way of advocacy differs greatly from country to country.

Taking a global perspective by way of conclusion, a number of common patterns can be discerned.

First, the most powerful and the most convincing advocates for change are people with learning disabilities themselves. Their advocacy can be expressed by creating an organization through movements like People First; alternatively or additionally, self-advocacy groups can be formed wherever groups of people are already meeting for other purposes, such as a day centre or residential centre or even a school or it can be developed by people coming together from different settings to form local groups. Self-advocacy can remain at the level of the individual making choices and decisions where real alternatives are seen to be available – and this process can begin and be encouraged in early childhood.

At the other end of the scale from grass-roots self-advocacy, there is a pressing need in all countries for appropriate legislation which ensures that the rights and needs of persons with learning disabilities are met and which actively counters discrimination. Very few countries have achieved this and the UK has a shameful record of its government's blocking at least 15 attempts to put such legislation on the statute book. This record is particularly disappointing since support for such legislation has come from the majority of parliamentarians and is also supported by the general public and all the relevant professional associations.

However, much of the force behind lobbies such as those wishing to pass anti-discrimination legislation has come from people with physical and sensory impairments. People with learning disabilities are now beginning to make common cause with people with other disabilities and are uniting in a single lobby. But there is still a long way to go before organizations and lobbies in this field include all people with disabilities and before those with learning disabilities demand and are given their rightful place in this movement.

The United Nations has provided leadership in the field of disability by means of a series of declarations, legally binding conventions and, most recently, through the adoption of the *Standard Rules on the Equalization of Opportunities for Persons with Disabilities* (United Nations, 1994). These 22 Standard Rules are expressed in concrete language in order to make it possible to monitor and evaluate the extent to which they are being implemented in any country. A special rapporteur and an expert panel have been appointed by the Secretary General of the United Nations for this purpose. A letter has been sent to every government asking a small number of specific questions concerning the steps which the government proposes to take to improve the position of disabled people in their country. This international initiative needs to be supported through advocacy at national level.

This book is a tribute to advocates who have gone before: their achievements are with us. But it is also intended as an encouragement to the present and future generations to continue to fight for the rights and needs of people with learning disabilities.

REFERENCES

Daunt, P. 1991. *Meeting Disability: A European Response*. London: Cassell
Daunt, P. 1993a. Western Europe. In P. Mittler, R. Brouillette and D. Harris (eds) *World Yearbook of Education: Special Needs Education*. London: Kogan Page
Daunt, P. 1993b. The 'New Democracies' of Eastern and Central Europe. In Mittler *et al.*, *op. cit.*
Department for Education. 1994. *Code of Practice on the Assessment and Identification of Special Educational Needs*. London: DFE.
Dybwad, R. 1990. *Perspectives on a Parent Movement: The Revolt of Parents of Children with Intellectual Limitations*. Boston: Brookline Press
Flynn, M. 1988. *Independent Living for Adults with Mental Handicap*. London: Cassell
Hogg, J. and Mittler, P. (eds) 1987. *Staff Training and Mental Handicap*. London: Croom Helm
Hunt, M. 1994. *Planning and Diversity: Special Schools and their Alternatives*. Policy Options Series No. 5. Stafford: National Association for Special Educational Needs Publications
Mittler, P. 1995. Rethinking partnerships between parents and professionals. *Children and Society*, **9**, 22–40.

National Development Group for the Mentally Handicapped. 1976. *Mental Handicap: Planning Together*. London: DHSS

National Development Group for the Mentally Handicapped. 1977a. *Mentally Handicapped Children: A Plan for Action*. London: DHSS

National Development Group for the Mentally Handicapped. 1977b. *Day Services for Mentally Handicapped Adults*. London: DHSS

National Development Group for the Mentally Handicapped. 1978. *Helping Mentally Handicapped People in Hospital*. Report to the Secretary of State for Social Services. London: DHSS

National Development Group for the Mentally Handicapped. 1980. *Improving the Quality of Services for Mentally Handicapped People: A Checklist of Standards*. London: DHSS

Oswin, M. 1978. *Children Living in Long Stay Hospitals*. Oxford: Blackwell Scientific Publications

Segal, S. and Varma, V. (eds). 1991. *Prospects for People with Learning Difficulties*. London: Fulton

United Nations. 1983. *World Programme of Action in Favour of Disabled Persons*. New York: UN

United Nations. 1994. *Standard Rules on the Equalisation of Opportunities for Persons with Disabilities*. New York: UN

Whelan, E. and Speake, B. 1977. *First National Survey of Adult Training Centres*. London: National Association of Teachers of the Mentally Handicapped

Chapter 2

Expanding Opportunities: 1944 to 1970

John Garrett

INTRODUCTION

Each generation of teachers faces new situations, new challenges, new obstacles as well as new opportunities to continue to make progress. In few areas can the going have been harder than in the field of special education where the rate of progress over the years seems to have been determined by the drive and enthusiasm of individuals (Stan Segal and others) and the strengths of the pressure groups (voluntary associations of people concerned about handicapped children) which they were able to enlist in support, rather than as a result of society's growing knowledge and moral values. Indeed, to tell the story of these individuals and groups over the years is to tell, in some measure, the story of special education in the UK. They have developed in such close association that it is almost impossible to write of one without constant reference to the others.

PRE-1944 DEVELOPMENTS AND OPPORTUNITIES

Edouard Seguin was probably one of the earliest individuals to press for special educational facilities in the UK by coming over from France in 1837 to try to engender support for an organized system of education and care for 'mental defectives' in the UK. His efforts encouraged concerned members of the medical and teaching professions to begin pressing for different arrangements to be made for those children in elementary schools who were considered to be 'not normal'. This 'pressure group' finally persuaded the government of the day to appoint a Royal Commission in 1880 to look into the matter.

The Commission's recommendations led to the passing of 'The Education (Defective and Epileptic Children) Act 1899'. This Act empowered LEAs to establish special schools. However, as the power conferred by the Act was 'permissive' and not 'compulsory' many LEAs still did not make any provision in their areas. Even in those areas where the Act was implemented there were different opinions as to the teaching methods to be adopted and the grade of teacher to be employed. It was considered by many that a high degree of teaching skill was not required: all that was needed was someone who would be kind to the children, train them in habits of cleanliness and keep them quiet. For many years even more enlightened education authorities employed only uncertificated teachers in their special schools. (The head teacher of the first special school the writer served in after the Second World War was an uncertificated teacher.)

It is clear, therefore, that the early workers in the special schools had many problems to overcome if their efforts to meet the special needs of the mentally or physically defective children in their care were to be successful. So, early in 1903, headteachers of the four Liverpool special schools invited colleagues living within easy distance of the city to meet to discuss these problems and exchange views and ideas.

As a result of their initiative, teachers and other workers from Liverpool and adjoining districts later in that year met colleagues from Birkenhead, Birmingham, Bolton, Bradford, Burnley, Darlington, Leeds, Leicester, London, Manchester, Nottingham and Salford and unanimously passed the following resolution: 'That this meeting considers it essential to the welfare of Special Schools that an Association of Special Schools Teachers and Managers and all interested in the work should be organised at an early date.' The following main aims of this non-political association were approved at a later meeting:

1. To use every means to advance the methods of education of mentally and physically defective children.
2. To enlist the sympathy and active interest of the general public on their behalf.
3. To consider and evolve the best methods of training teachers for special schools.
4. To consider the after care of mentally and physically defective children.
5. To promote the interchange of experience by conferences and meetings, local and general, and to consider and adopt any other means which may be calculated to further the interests of mentally and physically handicapped children.

These aims still express the fundamental purpose of most of the special education associations which have developed over the years in the ever-widening field of special education, thus reflecting the wisdom and foresight of those early pioneers.

The official birthplace of this Special Schools' Union – the first special education pressure group in the UK – was the School of Technology, Manchester where, on 9 and 10 October 1903, a National Conference of Special School Teachers and Friends was held.

The printed report of this first conference numbered 183 pages and was published in 1904 at a cost of 2 shillings per copy. It was issued to the 379 members of the new Union. During the years immediately following its inception, the voluntary campaigning efforts of the members were concentrated on:

1. bringing pressure to bear on the authorities, both central and local, to promote or delay measures providing or preventing the education, care and control of defective children, and
2. convincing the general public as to the necessity of dealing with this serious and urgent problem.

Members were not only few in number but were widely scattered. But what was lacking in numbers was more than adequately compensated for by the missionary spirit and dedication of these pioneers.

In 1907 the Union launched its first campaign. Concern had been growing over a long period of time about the increasing number of authorities which employed not teachers but other quite unsuitable people for work in special schools. The position became acute because of the Board of Education's new regulations which countenanced the employment of unqualified teachers in special schools. Consequently, a strongly worded protest was sent to the Board deploring the employment of 'teachers' in special schools who were not qualified so that they would be acceptable to teach in state elementary schools. The protest ended with a statement insisting that children in special schools required the best teachers available.

It is also particularly interesting to note that, sixty years before any action was taken by central government, the Special Schools' Union was actively concerning itself with the plight of *children excluded* from special schools and who were *certified* as ineligible for admission to such schools.

A vigorous campaign by the Special Schools' Union against the setting up of a Board of Control in amalgamation with the Chancery Visitors and the Lunacy Commissioners resulted in the Mental Deficiency Act of 1913 which ensured the safeguarding of the interests of all *'improvable mental defectives'*. The Elementary Education (Defective and Epileptic Children) Act 1914 which followed also ensured that it was the duty of education authorities to make provision for the education of children whose age exceeded seven years and who were *ascertained to be defective* within the meaning of the Act. So the threat to the existence of special schools was removed.

Although the inter-war years saw little or no material advances in the provision of special education, a considerable amount of progress was made in the study of child development and in research into their intellectual growth by Burt, Duncan and Schonnell, who focused on the needs of backward children. They were supported and encouraged in their efforts by the organized campaigning of the Special Schools' Union and by concerned individuals.

By the end of the Second World War, the time was ripe for a new approach to the education of handicapped children and the campaigning efforts of the voluntary associations over the years were recognized by the government when the Education Bill 1944 was being prepared. Representatives of the Special Schools' Union, the National Institute for the Blind, the College of Teachers of the Deaf and the College of Teachers of the Blind were invited to the Special Services Branch of the Board of Education to discuss the amendments to the Bill which had been formulated at joint meetings of the four organizations and submitted to the Board. Some of the amendments were accepted and incorporated in the new, important and far-reaching 1944 Education Act.

THE 1944 EDUCATION ACT

The 1944 Act reflected a change of outlook and established a new attitude towards handicapped children by recognizing them as being ordinary children with disabilities rather than as defective children lacking normal qualities.

They were to be educated as far as possible in the mainstream of education and not to be treated as 'defectives' and cared for separately.

LEAs were reminded that as part of their obligation to provide primary and secondary schools to meet the varying ages, abilities and aptitudes of the children in their area, they should have regard to:

> The need for seeing that provision is made for pupils who suffer from any disability of mind or body by providing either in special schools or otherwise, special educational treatment, that is to say, education by special methods appropriate for persons suffering from that disability.

Writing in the 1944 Summer issue of the *Special Schools' Journal*, Sir William Alexander noted that special schools were to be given their rightful place in the educational programme:

> It will appear, that under the new structure these schools are not really Special Schools at all, but simply schools, as all other schools, providing education according to the 'age, aptitude and ability' of certain groups of children whose ability and aptitude show a wider deviation from average than in the majority of cases. In this sense they are no more Special Schools than the Grammar School itself, which in essence, provides education suitable for those children whose ability in academic fields varies too much from average to make it possible for them to be fully educated without special education. Indeed, all of the schools under the new Act have the same fundamental task.
>
> The organisation of each school depends fundamentally on the ability and aptitude of the pupils who attend it and the problem is so to organise the schools of an area that there is a place in one or other of them for every child in the community who is educable, to have an education suitable for him.

So the possibility of a great programme of expansion of the special school system lay ahead as the Act increased the number of recognized categories of special education from four to eleven (reduced to ten in 1953). These new categories included varying degrees of blindness or deafness, physical impairment and speech defects. The terms 'educationally sub-normal mild and moderate' (ESN–M) and 'educationally sub-normal severe', (ESN–S) were later used to distinguish between different types of subnormality. These children were deemed 'ineducable' on account of the severity of their handicaps and they were excluded from the education system.

Despite this exclusion, the members of the Special Schools' Union greeted the Act with delight. Overnight it seemed that all the hopes and dreams of the Special Schools' Union had come true.

The important concept in this Act and in later Regulations (Handicapped Pupils and School Health Service Regulations 1945, 1953 and 1959) was that the factor determining which children needed help was an *educational* one. All children failing in their school work would be given special help suited to their particular educational needs. Formal certification of defective children within the education system would no longer be required and any child who was considered to be educable would in future have access to schooling as of right. Although the less seriously handicapped children might now be catered for in ordinary schools, those with serious disabilities would continue to be educated in special schools.

Such ideas were seen by special school teachers as justifying their existence. These ideas also encouraged many teachers willing to accept the challenge of providing meaningful education to handicapped and less able children to join the ranks of special school teachers. Society's attitude to the education of handicapped children and to the status of teachers engaged in this work seemed about to change.

POST-WAR TEACHERS

Those who took up the challenge were often pre-war qualified teachers returning after war service or other ex-service men and women who had completed a shortened 'Emergency Teacher Training course'. These teachers generally were mature people. Many of the latter group were choosing to give up careers started before the war in order to become teachers. Some who had 'failed' to be selected for grammar school education at the pre-war 11-plus exam had proved during their war service that they were capable of carrying out responsible and demanding duties, requiring high levels of intelligence and ability.

These men and women had much to offer the teaching profession and many revealed a real understanding and awareness of the problems faced by children and young people with learning and other disabilities. This, and the reception given to the 1944 Education Act generally, suggested that attitudes towards the 'less able' were likely to be good. Prospects for handicapped children within the post-1944-Act school system had never looked brighter.

PAMPHLET NO. 5: *SPECIAL EDUCATIONAL TREATMENT*

The 1944 Education Act laid the responsibility for making special educational provision for each category firmly at the door of the LEA.

To provide guidance, in 1946 the Ministry of Education published Pamphlet No. 5, *Special Educational Treatment*. This pamphlet discussed the form of special educational '*treatment*' to be provided to meet the needs of children suffering from a 'disability of mind or body'. It suggested that pupils more than 20 per cent below average in educational attainment should be regarded as educationally subnormal and that the total ESN group could be divided into the following types:

1. children with backwardness due to limited ability and
2. children with backwardness due to other causes.

The former were considered to be 'true' ESN pupils whose needs would best be met in a special school. The difficulties of the latter were considered to be remediable, so they would be allowed to remain in a normal school. The most frequently used criterion to determine this distinction was the ascertained intelligence quotient (IQ). Experience has since shown that this division was too simplistic. Teachers in both normal and special schools have often said that mistakes were made in the categorization of these children. The belief, implicit in the 1944 Education Act, that educability can be related precisely to IQ was considered by some of the more enlightened members of the teaching profession as the root of many problems.

DEVELOPMENT OF SPECIAL EDUCATION

The medical model

The earliest forms of special provision were for children with physical and sensory difficulties which were clearly identifiable medical conditions. As a result, the decision to recommend 'special educational treatment' was based mainly on a medical diagnosis.

Apart from the categories of 'maladjustment' and 'educational subnormality', the disability categories identified in the 1944 Education Act could all be described in medical terms and their diagnosis was seen to be relatively clear-cut. Therefore, while the Education Act 1944 placed the duty to ascertain children in need of special education by categories of handicap on the LEA, the ascertainment process still continued to take the form of a full medical examination and a Stanford-Binet Intelligence Scale Test, both carried out by a medical officer from the Health Department. This emphasis on the role of the medical officer tended to support the belief that difficulties in learning arose because of basic characteristics of the child and that there was something wrong with him/her which could not be overcome.

This belief has been questioned by teachers in special schools who have shown over many years that by providing a curriculum relevant to the special needs of such pupils along with carefully structured teaching programmes, many of these pupils' difficulties could in fact be overcome.

The special education associations therefore urged that a full investigation of a child's disabilities should be carried out by a multi-professional team with greater emphasis being placed on the educational aspect.

Educational model

Intelligence tests in secondary school selection

The basic principle of the 1944 Act that the educational provision should be based on 'age, aptitude and ability' led to the use of intelligence tests of the 11-plus examination to predict which children would benefit from the different forms of secondary education.

It was made clear by intelligence-test enthusiasts at that time that the test would provide a more accurate prediction of potential ability than the pre-war 11-plus examinations. It was designed, they claimed, to assess *innate* aptitude and ability and would therefore determine accurately, regardless of previous teaching methods used, the type of secondary school education best suited to meet the genuine individual needs of the pupils. Many teachers accepted this theory and continued to provide a broadly based curriculum and did not even consider using verbal, general knowledge and intelligence-type tests (which could be purchased from bookshops) to give children practice in doing the tests.

Other teachers (and ambitious parents) saw these aids as a means of ensuring success. They encouraged their pupils/children to complete books of verbal and general knowledge tests both in school and at home. As a result, many pupils who had concentrated on completing these books gained good scores in the official 11-plus examination tests and were allocated places in grammar schools, whilst the others were placed in secondary modern or technical schools where a more vocationally-oriented curriculum was offered.

Later the problems resulting from relying on this method of predicting future achievement were recognized and comprehensive secondary education was introduced.

Intelligence tests and selection for special education

In the 1950s and 1960s, if a child failed to progress at a rate comparable to his peers, it was inevitably assumed that the fault lay with him. The usual explanation given was that the child's low intellectual capacity resulted in his inability to learn effectively. Severity of learning difficulty and level of intelligence were regarded as one and the same problem.

Thus, the belief in the use of intelligence tests as a means of accurately assessing innate ability resulted in the continued use of the IQ tests to ascertain which pupils should be offered places in a special school.

For example, Cyril Burt, the first educational psychologist to be appointed in the UK, used intelligence tests as the main assessment tool to identify which children should be withdrawn from mainstream education and placed in special schools. Children with an IQ of less than 70 were considered to be unlikely to make satisfactory progress in a mainstream school but to be likely to benefit from education in a special school.

Educational psychologists and special education

The number of educational psychologists steadily increased during this period and their role in the assessment of educationally subnormal children became increasingly important. However, although intelligence test results continued to be the major form of assessing children's learning potential, by the time the Summerfield Report (*Psychologists in Education Services*) was published in 1968, the primary emphasis of the educational psychologist's work had moved to early detection, assessment and diagnosis of learning difficulties. The report also suggested that the educational psychologist's services are best used 'for psychological assessment of children whose need for special education treatment is particularly uncertain'.

Unfortunately, as was also noted in the Summerfield Report, the detailed assessment of children's psychological and learning problems was not matched by the range of possible courses of action to solve the problems. The need, therefore for teachers and educational psychologists to work together to press for increased variety of special school and class provision and to develop different methods of special teaching within schools was made repeatedly by the special education associations.

TRAINING OF SPECIAL EDUCATION TEACHERS

In the years following the implementation of the 1944 Education Act, the number of children receiving special educational treatment increased. This created a need to increase the number of teachers required to meet their special educational needs.

Leading representatives of all the different volunteer special education associations pointed out that, although a sense of vocation was essential to the successful teaching of handicapped children, this alone was insufficient and training was needed in addition to that required for teaching 'normal' children.

However it was not until 1950, four years after the appearance of Pamphlet 5, that the first one-year Diploma Course in the Education of Handicapped (E.S.N.) Pupils was started at the University College of London's Institute of Education. Another four years were to pass before a second course was started at Birmingham University in 1954. A one-year course on backward children for experienced teachers was started by the University of Leeds' Institute of Education in 1955.

Over the years which followed, a small number of one-year courses were started in different parts of the country and some shorter courses were organized every year by the Ministry, by LEAs and by voluntary associations for teachers of most categories of handicap. In 1965, in an attempt to improve the situation, the Guild of Teachers of Backward Children began a campaign to establish a College of Special Education. Two important developments resulting from this were: (1) an annual conference on research relevant to the education of children with learning handicaps, and (2) the growth of a series of 'Guidelines for Teachers', resulting in publications which reached several thousand people.

In spite of all these efforts, Segal reported in his editorial comment in *Forward Trends* (1971) that there was, 'at best, an elite of not more than 2% of the profession inside the various organisations focused upon the handicapped and involved in what can be viewed as continuous training'. No one was more vociferous or determined about the need for training than Stan Segal. He noted that it was special school teachers themselves who had insisted that, as teachers of hearing and visually impaired children, they should be required to take a course of study and training on the teaching of visually or hearing impaired children to obtain specific professional qualifications additional to those which entitled them to the status of qualified teacher. Segal, in his editorials in *Forward Trends*, repeatedly urged that teachers working with children and young people with any form of special educational need should demand that sufficient training opportunities be made available to them so that appropriate qualifications could be required of and obtained by them to enable them to meet the specific needs of their pupils effectively and efficiently.

Notwithstanding all this effort and campaigning, half a century after the 1944 Act many children with special educational needs still do not have access to an appropriately trained teacher and, with so many of those early pioneering campaigners reaching the age of retirement, as well as financial cutbacks and the closing of special education courses in colleges and institutions of higher education, the future looks even bleaker

SPECIAL SCHOOLS

As a direct result of the 1944 Act, a number of special schools were opened in country mansions that had been vacated by the government after wartime use. Experience in one such mansion school which had been known locally as the 'Cripples School' made the writer determined to join those who were campaigning for better conditions for handicapped pupils. A hut in the school yard was still referred to as the 'Cobbler's Workshop'. The flagged ground floor of the school was bare and cold and the kitchen smells of cooking vegetables mixed with disinfectant, medical and urine smells could have discouraged new pupils, their parents and visitors.

Fortunately, in the 1950s, following pressures from parent and special school teachers' associations, local authorities replaced many such establishments with newly-built schools designed and equipped specifically to meet the needs of the category of pupil attending. Much innovative work carried out by teachers in these special schools prepared the ground for current thinking and ideas as well as for the changes in attitude towards children with disabilities and learning difficulties which has taken place over recent years. The residential schools (and some day schools) developed a 24-hour curriculum by using out-of-school activities to support and extend classroom work. For example, a day school for ESN–M pupils in downtown Leeds (Hunslet Lane Secondary Special School) obtained a cottage in the Yorkshire Dales for the sole full-time use of the school. Over many years the pupils spent a full week during holiday and term times as well as regular weekends, applying the basic skills learned in the classroom to practical real-life situations in the cottage and in the beautiful surrounding countryside.

A further example is the residential school for children with physical disabilities in South Wales (Ysgol Erw'r Delyn) which was sited on the same campus as a comprehensive school. Here the staffs of the two schools co-operated closely to provide the first three years of the secondary school's O Level curriculum to a number of selected pupils in the special school. At the end of the three years, two or three of these pupils then transferred each year to the secondary school to join able-bodied pupils taking the third year of the course. By repeating the third year, the special school pupils were able to make a good start and gain confidence as individual pupils in a mainstream class. Returning to the special school in the evening, each pupil received discreet caring, medical and educational support and encouragement from staff and friends as required. This controlled weaning of individuals from the so-called segregated special school to full genuine integration in a mainstream school was successfully carried out in that school during the 1960s because of the joint efforts of teachers in both the special and the mainstream schools.

There are lessons to be learned from this example for those who currently are pressing for integration at any cost. Society must ensure that the cost of the integration ideal is borne by the state and is not carried out at the expense of the pupils from either the ordinary or the special school.

Critics of special school education could have found similar initiatives taking place in many special schools throughout the UK during the 1960s. For example, two or three children from Borocourt and Smith Hospital Schools in South Oxfordshire were sent out to local primary and secondary schools in the early 1960s without any support in those days, except a telephone connection if the need arose (Mittler, personal communication).

One has to question whether the benefits of the 24-hour curriculum which was offered to pupils in the special schools of the 1960s will be available to pupils with special needs in mainstream day schools of the 1990s where staff and pupils are now subject to considerable pressure to gain a high place in the schools' examination league tables.

VOLUNTARY TEACHERS' ORGANIZATIONS

On returning to England from Australia in 1955, Stanley Segal noted that despite the 1944 Education Act and the better understanding of the needs of children with learning difficulties, there was still 'a distaste on the part of many teachers to teach backward pupils'. At that time there was less than 1 per cent of the teaching profession to be found in any of the voluntary teachers' organizations concerned with the needs of handicapped children.

In an effort to overcome this problem, Stanley Segal brought together a group of like-minded teachers who, with him, had successfully completed the Univesity of London's Diploma Course in the Education of Handicapped (ESN) Children, and formed the Guild of Teachers of Backward Children. The Guild aimed to bring parents and professionals closer together and to assert the existence and rights of backward and mentally handicapped children and to co-ordinate activities on their behalf. In 1955, and with the same aims, the Guild's journal *Forward Trends* started to be published, with Stan Segal as editor. In 1956 the Guild, assisted by Sir Cyril Burt and supported by leading members of a small force of researchers and educational psychologists, organized the first National Conference on the Backward Child.

Later, in 1960, the first International Conference on the Backward Child organized by the Guild was held in the UK. In spite of these initiatives and the change of name of the Special Schools' Association in 1962 to the Association for Special Education in an attempt to attract teachers of special children in mainstream schools, there was little response. Very few teachers from ordinary schools were drawn to these organizations. It was clear that at that time the task of making inroads into the ordinary schools was a most difficult one.

However, the situation was considerably improved when, in 1965, the need to develop expertise to overcome the learning difficulties of children requiring remedial help in ordinary schools led to a small number of teachers in the Midlands getting together to form the National Association for Remedial Education (NARE).

From 1966 onwards, the Guild, led by Stan Segal, campaigned energetically for a Plowden-type inquiry into the area of handicap with particular reference to children excluded from the school system. Such efforts backed up by other special education associations must have influenced the government to finally agree to set up the Committee of Enquiry into the Education of Handicapped Children and Young People chaired by Lady Warnock.

THE JOINT COUNCIL FOR THE EDUCATION OF HANDICAPPED CHILDREN

The major special education associations co-operated to persuade other smaller voluntary teacher organizations, each representing the interests of a different category of handicapped children, to come together in 1965 to form the Joint Council for the Education of Handicapped Children. Its aim was to unite the groups in the common aim of developing and improving the education and welfare of all handicapped children and young people. The Council began its work by listing the following six outstanding needs:

1. The early detection of handicap.
2. Improved provisions in ordinary schools.
3. Increased provision of ancillary services.
4. More help for the handicapped school-leaver.
5. More government money for research.

6. The transfer to the Department of Education and Science of complete responsibility for the education and training of ALL school age children, including the severely subnormal and the delinquent.

Its first policy statement – *Needs of the Handicapped Child* – was circulated amongst local authorities and other organizations early in 1968. The following points in the policy statement were considered to be of major importance in ensuring early detection of handicap:

1. The keeping of some form of observation and 'at risk' register as an essential initial stage.
2. Infant and primary school teachers to take their share in detection, through suitable training in observing and recording in the early school years.
3. A more widespread use of short screening procedures assisted by an improved school psychological service.
4. More interdisciplinary assessment units at the nursery and primary stages to help in preventing or minimizing the effects of handicaps and to make an accurate diagnosis of children's needs.

In pressing for the integration of more mildly handicapped children into ordinary schools, the Council laid down the following seven essential needs:

1. A planned system of special classes and remedial classes and services.
2. A realization of the special needs of educational priority areas.
3. Better buildings, equipment and apparatus.
4. A re-examination of methods and curricula in ordinary schools to determine whether they could meet the needs of 'special' children.
5. An extension of opportunities for teachers to receive specialist training and more encouragement given to students at colleges of education to study the needs of children with handicaps and/or learning difficulties.
6. The responsibility of the Department of Education and Science to continue up to the age of at least 18 years for handicapped young people, with a Youth Employment Service to be available for them to the age of 21.
7. An improved ancillary service to include the social worker–counsellor who should also give continuing help and advice to leavers and their families to help them adjust to the world outside school.

In July 1970 the Council's first national conference, 'Handicapped Children – Their Potential and Fulfilment', was held in Manchester.

NEWSOM REPORT

The Central Advisory Council for Education, under the chairmanship of Sir John Newsom, published its report *Half our Future* in 1963. It was concerned with the education of less able pupils in the secondary schools of England and Wales and its recommendations included:

1. raising the school leaving age to 16;
2. more appropriate curricula and examinations;
3. a new building programme;

4. new teaching methods; and
5. extra payments for teachers working in difficult areas.

The raising of the school-leaving age did not affect children attending special schools who could already stay to 16 years of age. However, in 1970 Sir William Alexander expressed reservations about the raising of the school-leaving age for pupils in mainstream schools regardless of their aptitude, ability and interest:

> What good does it do to raise the school leaving age to 16 when it means that the less able children simply have to endure another year at school ... Authorities have fulfilled the letter of the various Education Acts, but the spirit of real education is still lacking. Long ago these children would have had little or no schooling, but now they have it they do not want it because it is *not relevant* to their needs. The schools are wasting these children's time and their own – they blame the stupidity of their pupils and leave it at that.

The children with learning difficulties who are failing in the ordinary schools are different from and behave differently from the successful academic pupils who make up a quarter of the school population. The unsuccessful three-quarters will have left school by the age of 16 through disinterest, disgust, dismay or economic pressures. Like the boy of 13 wandering the streets when he should have been in school saying 'they don't teach what I want to know'.

Teachers in special schools in fact have always aimed to provide a curriculum relevant to the needs of their pupils by teaching what children with learning difficulties wanted (and needed) to know. In addition, their campaigning has continued to be concentrated on the need to ensure that their methods are extended into further education schemes and improved training facilities for employment.

THE PLOWDEN REPORT

Of the major educational inquiries which span the 1960s, perhaps none was more influential in stimulating, educating, mobilizing and directing both professional and public opinion than the 1967 report of the Central Advisory Council (England) on *Children and their Primary Schools* (the Plowden Report).

The report drew particular attention to the problems of schools in areas where family circumstances and social attitudes provided little positive assistance to children's progress and where a limited cultural background gave little preparation and continuing support for the process of being educated.

It called for the establishment of *educational priority* areas (EPAs) into which extra resources were to be put as a means of *positive discrimination* in favour of deprived children.

In the chapter on educational priority the report urged:

> Teachers must be constantly aware that their ideas, values and relationships within the school may conflict with those of the home, and that the world assumed by teachers and school books may be unreal to the children. There will have to be constant communication between parents and the schools if the aims of the schools are to be fully understood.

In the chapter on handicapped children, the report did not include comment on the education of primary-aged children in special schools. It simply accepted that handicapped children should be educated in ordinary schools wherever possible and highlighted the growing tendency to provide for groups of handicapped children in special classes and units. However, it did not consider very closely the form, organization and educational programme of these classes and units. Possibly recognizing this omission, it did make a specific recommendation for a detailed inquiry into the needs of handicapped children, including slow learners, and the provision to be made for them.

As the Guild of Teachers of Backward Children had been unsuccessful in pressing the government of 1966 to set up a Plowden-type inquiry into the entire area of handicap, including that of children then excluded from the school system, the Guild and the Association for Special Education were quick to highlight this recommendation in the Plowden Report and to again urge the politicians and the public to press the government to act on it.

Stanley Segal in his closing address at the second Stanley Segal Lecture in 1978 referred to a discussion he had had with Sir Edward Boyle in the House of Commons in 1968 when he had not needed to press him (the shadow spokesman for education) 'at all hard on the need for such a Plowden type enquiry into the entire area of special educational needs'. Although not claiming any personal credit, he suggested that this might have led to the significant pressure for such an inquiry by MPs of all parties which took place in the House of Commons in the course of the following years.

CHILDREN WITH SEVERE LEARNING DIFFICULTIES (SCOTT REPORT)

In response to pressures from campaigning parent and teacher organizations, the Ministry of Health set up, in 1959, a Mental Health Advisory Committee to consider the training and supply of staff working with mentally handicapped children and adults.

Its report (the Scott Report), published in 1963, made a number of recommendations aims at improving the training and status of teachers of mentally handicapped children. However, it did not recommend transferring responsibility for mentally handicapped children to the education services, thereby perpetuating the surprising anomaly that a director of education could not oversee the education of these children but a medical officer could try.

It was even reported that one minister in discussing the report suggested that bus drivers possessed adequate qualities to 'teach' mentally handicapped children in the junior training centres and that it would be premature and unnecessary to insist on educational qualifications for such workers.

However, in spite of such opposition, the government established the Central Training Council for Teachers of the Mentally Handicapped, chaired by Professor Alan Clarke, to supervise the training of teachers of children and instructors of the adults. This body acted as a kind of Council for National Academic Awards (CNAA) watchdog over qualifications such as National Association for Mental Health (NAMH) Diplomas for Teachers of Mentally Handicapped People.

It was a significant step forward on the route to full incorporation of the provision for mentally handicapped children within the education service and was used effectively by the special education associations generally and by Stan Segal and his Guild colleagues in particular in their successful campaigning to achieve the transfer of responsibility for all children from Health to Education.

'NO CHILD IS INEDUCABLE'

Another event which played an important part in persuading the government to transfer the responsibility of children categorized as ESN–S from the Health to the Education Department was the publication, in 1966, of Stan Segal's important book *No Child is Ineducable*.

This book made a clear philosophical statement which challenged attitudes based on the 1944 Education Act's implication that children with severe learning difficulties had a 'disability of the mind' which meant that they were incapable of profiting from education. At the time the book was published, such children were being placed in junior training centres (JTCs) which would not infrequently offer facilities that were often considered unsuitable by parents and other concerned people. These training centres at that time were thought of mainly as caring establishments and were overseen by health authorities.

Stanley Segal regarded this position as scientifically and professionally untenable and morally indefensible. This book and Segal's indefatigable campaigning played a major part in changing attitudes and eventually in persuading the government to agree to transfer the responsibility for the education of children with severe learning difficulties from Health to Education.

Although delighted, Stan Segal could not resist commenting wryly that those who shaped the great Education Act of 1870 could not have dreamt that it would take 100 years before the educational umbrella could be extended to all children of school age.

This extension was generally widely welcomed by special educators although the manner in which the transfer was to be brought about organizationally occasioned some misgivings amongst them. The problem was complex and could not be side-tracked. It was felt that merely to relabel a training centre as a special school, or to add the population to an existing special ESN school, could encourage a helpless or callous disregard of the real needs.

Concerns were also voiced that, no matter how severe their impairments, no children should be regarded as ineducable. This argument gathered considerable support, and in 1970 legislation was introduced whereby LEAs were required to make special educational provision for all types of disability. Although it was not stipulated that this provision should necessarily take the form of separate schools or classes, this became the predominant practice and, as a result, 'special education' tended to be regarded as that which occurred in special schools.

THE HESTER ADRIAN RESEARCH CENTRE AT MANCHESTER UNIVERSITY

Stanley Segal and the Guild of Teachers of Backward Children led a national campaign to establish a Kennedy Institute of Special Education as a memorial to the murdered President of the USA. Although wholehearted support was obtained from all sides of the Houses of Parliament and from the relevant state and voluntary professional organizations, the Franks Committee decided in favour of another kind of memorial.

In spite of this, the momentum was not allowed to stop. A new committee under the chairmanship of Lady Hester Adrian was set up to explore the possibility of the establishment of an institute with similar aims. The National Association for Mental Health (NAMH) and Hester Adrian herself played leading roles in bringing this second project to fruition.

The co-operation of the University of Manchester, assisted by a grant of £100,000 from the Sembal Trust, brought the Hester Adrian Research Centre into being in 1968 at the university under the leadership of Professor Peter Mittler. The name of the centre was determined following the death of Lady Hester Adrian. The purpose of the centre was to research the problems faced in training centres and hospital schools for children and adults with mental-handicapping conditions, the psychological, social and educational factors that affected their development and the services provided for them.

Professor Mittler was particularly keen to ensure that the best results from the research carried out at the centre would be disseminated to both staff and parents and be incorporated in staff training programmes.

The following extract from an early monograph highlights his aims for the centre:

> Research workers are usually criticised either because the problems that they choose to study seem artificial and irrelevant to teachers, or because the findings are not communicated. To make matters worse they are often unintelligible to all except fellow specialists. These criticisms have the ring of truth, and are only partly avoidable, but we shall do what we can to tackle the problem because we are very conscious of the need not merely to *tell* teachers what we are doing, but also to *ask* for their advice and guidance about our work. We want our research to be of some practical value to teachers and above all to their children, and we are asking for help to enable us to ask the right questions and to set about answering them the right way. (Mittler, 1970)

A wide range of research reports and other materials of considerable value to parents and professionals emanated from the centre and were published over many years.

SOCIAL SERVICES INVOLVEMENT (SEEBOHM REPORT)

In 1968 the report of the Committee on Local Authority and Allied Personal Social Services (the Seebohm Report) was published. This advocated a more positive approach to community care, recommending the creation of a new local authority department – a social services department – aimed to provide a community-based and family-oriented service. This department, it was suggested, would cut across existing boundaries between departments, do much to avoid divisions of responsibility and duplication of social work effort and lead to a more comprehensive, co-ordinated and flexible approach to families and individuals needing help. In theory, at least it would avoid administrative confusion and inefficiency.

Amongst numerous recommendations relevant to special education were suggestions that:

1. Social work in schools should become the responsibility of this new department, social workers being attached to a school or group of schools.

2. Greater co-operation should be developed between education and social services departments in the appointment and training of child care staff of boarding schools.
3. Increased provision should be made for maladjusted children.
4. There should be further development of social services for physically handicapped and subnormal children.
5. Greater provision of hostels for handicapped school-leavers should be made.

To implement the report's recommendations, the Local Authority Social Services Act 1970 established the new social services departments.

The Seebohm Committee also supported the demands from parent and professional associations that LEAs should take over responsibility for the education and training of ALL subnormal children and for the junior training centres to change their name to 'some variant of special school'.

Most special educators supported and approved this report at the time, looking forward to early action on the recommendations which they hoped would be of benefit to the handicapped children in their care.

Unfortunately, over twenty years later the view frequently expressed is that the social services departments have taken on too many roles for which they are not qualified or for which they are not sufficiently experienced. Perhaps they had bitten off more than they could chew.

For example, many parents and professionals concerned with adults with severe learning difficulties do not consider that the transfer of the former adult training centres (ATCs) from Health to Social Services as recommended in Seebohm has been as effective or as successful as the transfer of junior training centres to education departments.

Stanley Segal led many of the campaigns organized by volunteer parent and professional associations to urge that the responsibility for the ATCs should be given to Adult Education Services rather than to the Social Services. In the view of many concerned professionals and parents, it is unfortunate that the campaigns met with little success.

CONCLUSIONS

The Ministry of Education pamphlet No. 2, (1956) *Education of the Handicapped Pupil 1945–1955* – ends with the following paragraph:

> The record of what has been done since 1945 reflects the growing interest in the handicapped and of the need to give them every possible help to overcome their disabilities. It is a striking fact that local education authorities, at a time when they have been hard pressed in the primary and secondary field generally with the problem of providing school accommodation for the raising of the school leaving age and to deal with the growth of the school population as a result of the rise in the birth rate after the war, should have been able to expand the special school system more rapidly than in any previous decade. *Still more striking perhaps is the contribution made by voluntary bodies to these post-war developments. In this field, voluntary organisations clearly still have a big part to play in the partnership with the Ministry and the local education authorities.* [My emphasis]

The voluntary bodies referred to in the above paragraph must surely include the voluntary, non-political special education teacher associations. The paragraph illustrates how the special education opportunities offered during the decade following the Education Act of 1944 were expanding and how teachers and authorities developed them.

The years between the 1944 Education Act and the Education (Handicapped Children) Act 1970, when the responsibility for the education and treatment of children formerly considered ineducable was transferred from Health to Education, were certainly a continuing period of expanding opportunities for those involved in, and concerned about, the education and all-round development of children and young people with special needs.

It was the special education association and the parent-inspired bodies led by people like Stan Segal which took advantage of the opportunities by campaigning constantly for improved conditions for handicapped children in their care.

Stanley Segal concluded his closing address to the Second Stanley Segal Lecture (see Mittler, 1978) by urging people to continue campaigning:

> We have considerable and gathering reason for optimism, because we give each other skills and strength; because we wait for no one to implement what we ourselves must implement; and because in our activities we are further helping to improve the overall climate which affects life for each of us.

It should not be forgotten that current ideas on people with special needs are based on the innovative work and the campaigning efforts of such people and their supporting organizations. It is also of great importance that the good work done by them should not be lost by an unthinking response to emotively biased statements about 'segregated' special schools and the pressures for the 'integration' of ALL children with special needs.

A closer, cool and unbiased look should be taken at some of the benefits gained by disabled and less able children who attended good special schools since 1944. People like Stanley Segal and many other special school teachers believed that putting some handicapped children into the competitive atmosphere of the present day schools before they had developed a degree of independence and a sense of self-worth could create many continuing problems for the growing child.

There is much to be said for enabling the disabled and less able child to learn by mixing with others with similar but different problems; that it is acceptable to be different; that success can be achieved in areas different from those achieved by the majority; and that a sense of self-worth and of confidence can often be developed in the secure, stimulating, invigorating and demanding atmosphere of a good special school. From such a base, the likelihood of genuine integration later is possible.

Let us move forward confident that the efforts of Stan Segal and his generation shall not be wasted.

REFERENCES AND FURTHER READING

Central Advisory Council (England). 1967. *Children and Their Primary Schools* (the Plowden Report 1957). London: HMSO.

Gulliford, R. 1967. 'Plowden and Special Education'. *Special Education*, **55**

Holyroyde, C. 1964. Short History of the Association for Special Education (formerly The Special Schools' Association 1903–1963). Unpublished document held by NASEN

Ministry of Education. 1956. *Education of the Handicapped Pupil* 1945–1955. Pamphlet No. 2. London: HMSO

Mittler, P. 1969. The need to end uncertainty. *Special Education*, **58**, 4

Mittler, P. 1970. *Teaching and Training*, **8**, Monograph Supplem., 1–47

Mittler, P. 1978. *Teaching Children with Severe Learning Difficulties*. The Second Stanley Segal Lecture. Sevenoaks Costello.

Peter, M. 1967. Editorial: The Plowden Report. *Special Education*, **56**, 2, June 1967

Peter, M. 1968. Editorial: Seebohm Report. *Special Education*, **57**, 3

Peter M. 1968. Editorial: Summerfield Report. *Special Education*, **57**, 4

Norris, D. 1969. Forward from Isolation. *Special Education*, **58**, 1

Segal, S.S. 1970. Editorial: The Hester Adrian Research Centre. *Forward Trends* **14**, 3

Segal, S.S. 1971. Editorial: Forward to Where? *Forward Trends*, **17**, 2

Chapter 3

Lobbying Parliament: 1970 to 1995

Lewis Carter-Jones

Looking back 25 years to the autumn when Alf Morris won first place in the private members' ballot feels like entering another world. Indeed in parliamentary terms, the contrast could hardly be greater. A Labour Government with a majority of 100, far from attempting to stamp out reformist legislation from the back benches, was actually prepared on occasion to provide Government time. This is not to say that the Chronically Sick and Disabled Persons (CSDP) Bill was plain sailing. The Secretary of State, Dick Crossman, was aloof if not actually hostile; neither Alf nor the Bill even rates a mention in his famous diaries. Crossman was particularly scathing about our claim that hundreds of thousands of disabled people were totally unknown to and ignored by the NHS and local authorities. On one occasion, Alf and I cornered Crossman in the lobby and he tried to fob us off with the survey then being undertaken by the Office of Population Censuses and Surveys (the Amelia Harris Survey) which he assured us would allay our concerns. This tactic was used to much greater effect in the mid-1980s when a second OPCS survey was used to delay improvements in benefits for several years. One should always treat ministers with a healthy scepticism. Of course, when Amelia Harris published her report in 1971 we were wholly vindicated: she estimated over 3 million people with impairments in Great Britain including 1.2 million with appreciable or severe handicap. At that time local authority registers barely accounted for 200,000. By then Alf's Act was happily in place to identify and bring desperately needed help to the missing million.

Alf started with a blank piece of paper and in those days the disability lobby was practically non-existent. The Disablement Income Group had been formed a couple of years before; but its co-founder, Mary Greaves, said that it was the CSDP Bill that created the disability movement rather than the movement the Bill. The passage of the Bill through Parliament has been charted a number of times. Suffice it to say that at least the two most important clauses, which became sections 1 and 2, were drafted by senior parliamentary counsel and have proved more durable than their many critics in local government. The Bill passed through both Houses without a division and the only peril it faced was caused by Harold Wilson's decision to call an election in June 1970. The Cabinet, however, decided to give it priority and it was practically the last measure to receive Royal Assent before the dissolution. The apple of Crossman's eye, his National Superannuation Bill, did not survive.

I may be permitted a little partisan regret in lamenting that it was left to a Tory Government to bring the new Act into force. Yet that Government, with Sir Keith Joseph as last of the big spenders, was unrecognizable to students of the Thatcher years. Section 2 was brought into force in August and section 1 a year later. Although section 2 has received most attention, perhaps section 1 was the more radical, requiring as it did local authorities to ascertain the number and needs of disabled people in their areas. This ensured that disability would never again slip off the local or national agenda. Nevertheless the Circulars issued could be said to be somewhat lacking in enthusiasm and it was apparent that at that time disabled people had no real friend within the DHSS.

By the time Labour was back in power and Alf Morris was installed as the world's first ever Minister for the Disabled, the problems with section 2 were becoming clearer. This section listed a number of services which, apart from the provision of a telephone, were culled from an ancient welfare circular. The difference was that now the local authority had a duty to assess need for each service and if need was accepted they had a duty to make the appropriate provision. Unfortunately it was not immediately apparent how these duties were to be enforced. The Secretary of State had default powers under the old National Assistance Act but it was not clear how they would work in relation to the 1970 Act; and in February 1975 I introduced a Disablement Commissioner Bill which suffered the usual parliamentary fate of objection on a Friday afternoon by an anonymous Government whip. Many disabled people wanted direct access to the courts. Unfortunately one famous case which reached the Court of Appeal in 1978 appeared to direct them back to the Secretary of State (although subsequent judgments have modified this).

The speed with which the 1970 Act had to be rushed through the Lords left a number of obvious gaps and in 1976 a modest Bill added places of employment to the access provisions. These sections were widely regarded as being little more than exhortatory but an attempt to use planning law to give them more teeth was fiercely resisted. One civil servant neatly expressed traditional attitudes when he stated: 'it is the use to which the land is put that is important not who uses it.' Happily five years later the Scottish Office accepted that planning law was appropriate to ensure people with disabilities could actually get into buildings and the Department of the Environment was forced to follow suit. Moreover, a few years later it finally came round to the idea that access facilities should be included in building regulations which MPs and voluntary organizations had been saying was glaringly obvious for a decade.

Parliament now seems an increasingly grim place but in those days it was not without its humour. Alf was very keen to see his Act extended to Northern Ireland and persuaded a willing Gerry Fitt to sponsor a Bill. The Northern Ireland Office was not nearly so eager on the grounds (1) that it would cause them a lot of work, (2) that they could do everything in the 1970 Act without legislation and (3) if they wanted legislation they could do it by Order in Council. Poor Lord Melchett came to the All Party Disablement Group to explain all this and Jack Ashley, its long-standing Chairman, was predictably not too impressed. The Bill was introduced with myself as a co-sponsor.

Very few MPs know much about parliamentary procedure and I am sure Gerry would not claim to be amongst them. Unfortunately his other sponsors were excellent friends and colleagues but it was well said at the time that none, despite years in Parliament, even knew where the Committee corridor was – and they were all automatically selected to serve on the Committee. So on the fateful morning we were sitting as the minutes ticked away waiting for one more MP to make up a quorum. Finally the door opened and Robert Bradford walked in. 'I never thought I'd be happy to see a Unionist!' exclaimed Gerry. Shortly afterwards Bradford added to his discomforture by congratulating him on introducing a Unionist Bill. As Gerry rose to expostulate I managed to grab his shoulder and hiss in his ear that he could say what he liked when he had got his Bill, but not before.

The most important Government Bills for people with disabilities in that Parliament were concerned with benefits. In 1973 a revolt in the Lords (to whom then and now we owe much of the progress in this field) required the Government to publish a review of benefits for disabled people. This duty fell to the incoming Labour Government and the result was frankly disappointing. It led directly to the formation of the Disability Alliance, in the words of Colin Low 'united in fury at the poverty of the proposals'. Despite this welcome outcome which over the last twenty years has become a key resource for disabled people and MPs alike, at the time those of us fighting for improvements in Parliament were almost totally dependent on one adviser in the form of Peter Large.

It was he who drafted an amendment for me which circumvented the Money Resolution and forced the Government to include married women in the new non-contributory invalidity pension. This victory was, however, less than it seemed at the time. The Government delayed introduction of HNCIP for a further two years and implemented the so-called 'household duties test' in a way which caused anger and distress to disabled married women throughout the country. It was eventually declared contrary to European law and abolished in favour of the severe disablement allowance.

Perhaps the Government had learned a lesson because shortly afterwards the legislation for mobility allowance – arguably the most important innovation since the war – was slipped into Parliament the day we rose for the Whit recess to be debated two days after our return. At this time Peter Mitchell gave tremendous support to MPs of all parties with an interest in disability issues. He was an indefatigable and effective adviser and researcher on all problems relating to disabled people. By sheer chance he was in the House on the Friday afternoon to listen to the adjournment debate and heard the Minister mention that mobility allowance amendments had been tabled to the Pensions Bill. He rang me at home and I asked him to draft amendments to cover all the issues that he knew I was concerned with. Nevertheless the Money Resolution was so tightly drawn that only a couple of my amendments were in order and to include all the material I had been given I enthralled a bemused House with the urgent mobility problems of agoraphobic 4-year-olds!

In the dying days of the Callaghan administration Eddie Wainwright won a second reading for a Bill to make the 1970 Act enforceable in the courts. It had the support of the Government and apparently of the Opposition. It fell at the election and all subsequent attempts to resurrect it were firmly stamped on. In response, a group of charities launched a project aimed at enforcing the Act through the Secretary of State. This certainly had the effect of publicizing the requirements of the law; but the reluctance of the Secretary of State to proceed at even a snail's pace often vitiated the whole procedure in individual cases. I know of at least two references of his conduct to the Ombudsman for maladministration which evoked some of the strongest language of rebuke I have ever known from the Parliamentary Commissioner – but all, of course, to no avail.

The International Year of Disabled People coincided with the depths of Thatcherite retrenchment. Happily one of our foremost protagonists, Dafydd Wigley, had won a place in the ballot and produced a Bill which had some fairly mild provisions in relation to access but included a clause which required local authorities to keep their information on disabled people up to date. There was no time for debate at second reading and the Government arranged for an objection to kill the Bill. For the first time, but by no means the last, the Government felt the wrath of people with disabilities unleashed on a national scale. This was their year and the Government was kicking them in the teeth. MPs were inundated with letters and 329 – over 50 per cent of the House – signed a motion in favour of access legislation along the lines of the report of the Silver Jubilee Committee on Improving Access for Disabled People which had been published in January 1979. Ironically the recommendations were far stronger than the Bill that had been killed. The Government gave way and drafted a useful Bill for Dafydd, but lacking the key enforcement mechanisms he wished to see. The new Bill passed all its Commons stages without discussion.

Other things being equal that would have been the end of the story; any attempt to improve the Bill in the Lords would have led to its death. Indeed, assurances were sought from the 'mobile bench' that they would not press amendments unacceptable to the Government. By a stroke of good fortune, however, a Scottish Bill was passing through the Commons and, as I mentioned earlier, the Scottish Minister took a rather more rational view of the use of planning consent to make buildings accessible. Moreover, when the Scottish Bill reach the Upper House their Lordships felt no compunction about strengthening it – the promise exacted only applied to the Disabled Persons Bill. To cut a long story short, the Government produced amendments to both Bills which, although they were somewhat bizarre and never in fact brought into force, led inexorably to the eventual incorporation of the Code of Practice for Access for the Disabled to Buildings into Building Regulations.

In 1981 there was, of course, a very important Government Bill to implement the report of the Warnock Committee. Since the Warnock Report and the Education Act 1981 are covered in detail elsewhere, I will only mention here that it was one of the most interesting committees I have ever sat on since the Bill was committed to a Special Select Committee which allowed us to take evidence from all interested parties before the normal Committee stage. I believe I am right in saying that this experiment has never been repeated. Despite the Committee being as a consequence one of the best informed ever, I do not think the Government accepted a single amendment. The major flaw, however, was the failure to provide adequate resources for the Act's implementation.

Throughout the International Year there were increasing demands from the grass roots for anti-discrimination legislation. Shortly before leaving office in 1979, Alf Morris had appointed a successor body to the Silver Jubilee Committee, again under the chairmanship of Peter Large, called CORAD (Committee on Restrictions against Disabled People). The new Government did not kill it off, although they increasingly starved it of resources, and its report was published in the Summer of 1982.

Unsurprisingly its first recommendation was that 'there should be legislation to make discrimination on the grounds of disability illegal'. Jack Ashley immediately introduced a Bill which had an unopposed first reading but inevitably died through lack of time. In December Donald Stewart used his place in the ballot to reintroduce it but it was 'talked out' at second reading, as the Bill's supporters had failed to rally 100 MPs to close the debate.

In retrospect it is clear that at that time not nearly enough background work had been done amongst MPs. It must be remembered that in strictly legal terms the Race and Sex Discrimination Acts had not proved an overwhelming success and many people genuinely felt that the additional complications of legislating in the area of disability would render any Act a dead letter. Nevertheless the 1973 Rehabilitation Act in the USA was slowly beginning to make its mark and some of the Australian states which had adapted UK race and sex legislation to their needs had also successfully incorporated discrimination against people with disabilities.

Thanks to the general election in May 1983 the private members' ballot was held in June, which allowed Bob Wareing five months to rally support before his Bill's second reading in November. This produced the fiercest lobbying by disabled people seen to that date. The year 1981 had also seen the birth of the British Council of Organisations for Disabled People which increasingly demanded the right to speak for disabled people in place of the established charities. These charities were themselves also becoming more democratic and, for example, the Spastics Society arranged a series of conferences around the country for disabled people to give their views. These came out unanimously in favour of the legislation.

At the Bill's second reading, well over half the Commons was present, a very rare event on a Friday afternoon. Although the Bill's supporters mustered 166, the 'payroll vote' numbered 212; although there was no official 'whip', a letter in no uncertain terms had been sent by the DHSS to all ministers. The Bill was reintroduced in the Lords by Lord Longford where, quaintly, it received a third reading but was defeated on the motion 'that this Bill do now pass'!

There is no doubt that Bob Wareing's Bill politicized people with disabilities to an even greater extent than Dafydd's in 1981. 'Equal rights' was a much more effective banner around which to rally than details of building regulations or enforcement procedures, as more recent events have clearly shown.

Two years later Tom Clarke won first place in the ballot. Some disabled people were no doubt hoping that he would take up the Wareing Bill and ride to another glorious defeat. However, he was convinced that even with a hostile Government there was a number of important measures that he could achieve. He was particularly concerned to do something for people with learning disabilities whose special needs had never really been addressed in previous legislation.

Unlike 1969, there was a vast number of voluntary organizations willing to provide advice and assistance. Very soon agreement was reached on the main principles of the Bill: greater involvement of disabled people in decisions which affected them, both generally and individually; and an attempt for three key groups to substitute crisis prevention for crisis management by requiring comprehensive assessment of need before disabled children leave school, before mentally ill or handicapped people leave long-stay hospital and before informal carers can no longer cope unaided. The first principle was to be achieved by: giving disabled people the right to appoint a representative (or advocate); giving them more say in the services provided for them under the Chronically Sick and Disabled Persons Act 1970; and giving voluntary organizations of people with disabilities more weight on a variety of committees and requiring disabled people to be consulted and their needs taken into account in devising local structure plans.

In three short weeks before Christmas the Bill went through a series of drafts as a result of lengthy discussions amongst the voluntary organizations and with officials at the Department of Health. Some ideas to which the Government strongly objected on principle were dropped and several amendments were made which did not damage the principles of the Bill. There was a general determination to push the Government as hard as possible but not to sacrifice the whole Bill over one or two minor issues; on the other hand, some desirable, but not essential, features were deliberately included in order to facilitate a compromise later if concessions were required on both sides.

I think it is probably fair to say that perhaps for the first time both sides were evenly matched. The voluntary organizations worked in almost perfect harmony, with each taking on responsibility for what it could do best, whether it was detailed drafting and negotiation, press contacts or organizing a nationwide lobby.

At second reading the Government maintained a 'sceptical neutrality' but did not oppose the Bill which was a major strategic victory for Tom Clarke since he was assured as long a Committee stage as he needed and a full afternoon on Report. Some cynics have suggested that this success owed more to the Westland crisis than to the power of the disability lobby; if that is true one can only be grateful for a fortuitous coincidence.

The Minister's main arguments against the Bill were that it was too expensive and too bureaucratic. He almost turned the Committee stage into a farce by announcing that the Government amendments were not ready but he would seek to remove key sections of the Bill at Report. Also in an unprecedented step he undertook to produce a consultation document on its amendments and obtain the views of the relevant public and professional bodies as well as of voluntary organizations.

If the Government made a strategic mistake in failing to oppose the second reading, this consultation document was a grave tactical error. Tom's supporters were already in close touch with the local authority associations and the latter, surprisingly, were, generally speaking, more in favour of the parts that the Government was seeking to excise than those it was agreeing to retain. Despite the Minister's criticisms, many of his own proposals were seen as retaining the bureaucracy without providing much advantage to disabled people. Only three weeks were allowed for comment which was far too short a time for bodies who were approaching the subject cold. For the voluntary organizations to organize a massive response in favour of the original Bill was comparatively simple with the active help of the All Party Disablement Group. The result was that the vast majority of the bodies – local and health authorities as well as voluntary organizations which responded by the deadline – expressed support for the original Bill and were highly critical of the Government proposals.

The way the consultation had backfired put the Department in rather a defensive mood, but they still insisted that they had no more to offer and would be printing their amendments on the Thursday before Easter. Now, finally, the unremitting labours of the Spastics Society press officer began to bear fruit and media interest started to take off. Two days before the Report Stage there was a massive lobby of Parliament by people with disabilities followed by a meeting with ministers at which it was clear the pressure was beginning to tell.

During the following day television coverage reached its peak and the Prime Minister was questioned three times by the Leader of the Opposition on her attitude to the Bill. By then the Government was aware of the strong support for the Bill on its own back benches and it is apparent that during that evening and night senior ministers were desperate to reach a compromise. Sensing the turn of the tide, Tom Clarke and Dafydd Wigley (acting as his 'whip') stood firm and waited for morning.

Although 99 per cent of the time Government comes first and backbenchers nowhere, Standing Orders happily decree that the sponsor's New Clauses take precedence; so it was Tom, rather than Tony Newton the Minister for the Disabled, who was appearing for the first time, who could set the agenda. One after the other, Government backbenchers stood up to support him and the same story continued all afternoon. He estimated that by the third reading, of the four key issues in contention he had won three and a half. The Bill went to the Lords with almost all its basic principles intact and far more detail than anyone would have thought possible four months earlier. Once the political battle had been won civil servants competed with each other to improve the Bill and two important new sections were added. On its return to the Commons, Tony Newton said that the Government had finally 'clutched it to their hearts with considerable enthusiasm'.

This was, however, the high point. Only a handful of sections were implemented the following April and it was left almost entirely to the voluntary organizations to tour the country explaining the Act and encouraging local authorities and local associations to work together. Eight years later four key sections are still not in force, including the two of most significance to people with learning disabilities, those which would allow them to appoint a representative or have one appointed for them. Despite continuous campaigns inside and outside Parliament we have proved once again an old maxim of mine that it is far easier to pass legislation than to get it implemented.

I left Parliament at the 1987 election so have been less closely involved with subsequent campaigns and legislation. Undoubtedly the most significant legislative action taken this decade which will prove of immense significance to people with disabilities worldwide was when President Bush signed the Americans with Disabilities Act in 1990. No longer would a Conservative Government be able to object to anti-discrimination legislation on ideological grounds. In 1991 Alf Morris once again won a place in the ballot. The Labour Party was now committed to anti-discrimination legislation and he decided to discard previous models in favour of an anglicized version of the US Act.

The voluntary sector rallied round again and a far more substantial Bill than previous versions was available for second reading early in the new year. Whatever happened the Bill stood no chance of becoming law since an election in late spring was no longer at the discretion of the Prime Minister. Nevertheless the Bill lived up to expectations in embarrassing the Government in a way which, despite the long history of weird parliamentary events that I have related, I do not think anyone could have foreseen. Previous Private Members' Bills had been filibustered to reduce the time available to less than one and a half hours, which by tradition is the minimum time a debate must run before the Speaker will accept a closure motion. Shortly before the debate was due to finish a Tory MP rose to speak. He was challenged as to whether he intended to talk the Bill out and he said he would not. Alf had well over one hundred MPs at his back but the Deputy Speaker refused to accept a closure and the Tory MP was still on his feet at 2.30 when the debate was automatically adjourned.

Of course, all hell broke loose. Angry remonstrations are customary when Bills fail on a Friday but this was of a different order. A few weeks later the offending member made a personal apology to the House which was widely believed to have been demanded by the Speaker, an event for which I cannot recall a precedent in my time in Parliament. The issue was naturally a key issue in the subsequent general election when he was defeated by the Labour candidate, Dr Roger Berry.

It was therefore entirely appropriate that last year Dr Berry should win a place in the ballot and reintroduce Alf's Bill. This time it received a second reading but, just like the Tom Clarke Bill, the Government, though profuse in general criticism, offered no amendments in Committee. Suddenly just before Report Stage five MPs who had previously shown no interest in the Bill tabled about 80 amendments and proceeded to talk it out. At first the Minister denied his department had assisted with the amendments, but later withdrew his denial. One of the Tory MPs involved received a very fierce rebuke from the Speaker and considerable vilification from the media. Every conceivable parliamentary opportunity was taken to bring the subject back to the House and on subsequent occasions it is hardly surprising that the Minister for the Disabled was left to plough his furrow all alone. Poor Nick Scott who was always a very good personal friend and a good friend of disabled people was thus condemned to terminate his ministerial career on a sad note in circumstances which he did not deserve.

At the time of writing, a discussion document is out for consultation. (August is always a favourite month for such exercises!) I do not doubt, however, that the anti-discrimination legislation which people with disabilities want will be enacted sooner rather than later even if we do not see the return of a Labour Government within a couple of years. The disability movement is now irresistible. Whilst the Executive undoubtedly has more powers than a medieval tyrant it has shown itself quite incapable of ending up without egg on its face each time it seeks to frustrate the will of disabled people.

Chapter 4

EXODUS: Bringing Children Out of Hospital

Peggy Jay
in association with John Tizard

British social policy contains some sad, ugly and shameful chapters in its history. The plight of so many children with mental handicaps who have been incarcerated in hospitals since the welfare state was formed in 1945 is one of the worst chapters. It demonstrates a combination of ignorance, lack of will, marginalization, protection of vested staff interests, and failure by government and the wider community.

We should all share some of that shame.

Equally we should be proud of what has been achieved, especially in the last few years. This is a story of hope and achievement. It is a story about what has happened and more importantly what can and what must happen.

It is the story of some brave crusaders – namely Maureen Oswin, Stan Segal, Derek Ricks, Ann Shearer and many others.

It is also the story of some careless and indifferent politicians, civil servants and health service 'professionals' and administrators.

As late as 1980 the *Observer* was able to report on a visit by the National Development Team for the Mentally Handicapped to Queen Mary's Hospital for Children, Carshalton in the following terms:

- Refuse bins from the wards were only emptied twice a week, and patients have been eating from these bins.
- There was a chronic shortage of clothing for patients; what clothing there was quickly became ruined in the hospital laundry.
- The laundry failed to provide enough clean linen; some wards received five to ten sheets a day when they had asked for fifty; bath towels were rare.
- Patients received a maximum of 50p a week pocket money whilst the rest of the money they were entitled to (allowances) was allowed to accumulate to a total of £12,000.
- We were shown a ward for disturbed boys aged 15 to 23. The behaviour of these adolescents was indeed very disturbed. We saw head banging, running up and down and masturbation, and one lad kept throwing himself at nurses and visitors.
- Some of the lavatories were very tiny and many did not have doors on them.

- The lavatory smells pervaded the wards. (*Observer*, 1980)

This report was meant to be confidential. It was to be very hotly contested by nursing and medical staff and their representatives.

This was Britain – an NHS hospital in 1980 not a Romanian orphanage at the height of Ceausescu's reign.

Maureen Oswin (Oswin, 1971; 1978a; 1978b; 1984) and others had chronicled the problems of lack of resources, inadequate staff training, and environments built around constraint, containment and drugs rather than development, stimulation, education and care – that is, not built around the needs of the child.

It seemed as if these children – the forgotten thousands – were not to be regarded as children simply because they had a mental handicap.

In 1948 the NHS was born. Its aims and aspirations should never have allowed this intolerable situation to occur some thirty years later.

Successive ministers had already recognized the needs of such children and had sought to take appropriate action but somehow it never happened.

*   *   *

Following the report of the Curtis Committee, the 1948 Children Act transformed the conditions and quality of life for thousands of deprived children in local authority care. The Act specifically omitted the needs of children who were in the care of the NHS. It most certainly ignored and was meant to ignore the needs of those children who had been banished to live their lives in long-stay subnormality hospitals. The NHS knew what was best for them – and even today there is an element of this thinking remaining.

In the 1960s I became active in health service matters. I had already been a leading member of the London County Council's Children's Committee. I was appointed as a member of the Secretary of State's Advisory Council, as a member of a regional hospital board, and later as Chairman of Camden Community Health Council. Having seen dramatic and progressive improvements in residential local authority child care – though now one realizes that there was still room for improvement – I was saddened and amazed to find conditions for the country's most deprived children living in long-term NHS care so archaic and anti-child.

Proper appropriate standards of child care, small family groups in domestic settings, attempts at family placement – fostering and adoption, and individual-child-focused care – seemed to be unknown and alien to practice and professional thinking. The children lived in isolated, large, stark hospital wards, without appropriate or adequate staffing and without toys and other stimulants.

I became totally involved in this issue and determined to find a solution in the mid-1960s when a report came before the North West Thames RHA Board. It was by Ann Shearer and described conditions at Harperbury Hospital in Hertfordshire. She described children lying naked on the ward floors, rows of beds, no toys and staff who were untrained in the needs of children. I vowed that action was required. No ounce of energy should be spared in pursuit of change.

Many of my board colleagues were more concerned about the 'evil' of journalists writing about such matters than they were about the needs of the children. I went immediately to Harperbury. Ann Shearer's account was right. I felt as if I had travelled back in a time machine to a Victorian or at best a 1920s children's orphanage.

In the 1960s, children in hospital care were being bypassed by the 1948 Act and experiencing conditions that would have been unacceptable in a local authority home. Maureen Oswin had chronicled conditions in hospitals like Harperbury and Queen Mary's (these were not isolated instances) in very graphic and heart-stopping detail. This was a national scandal. I was determined that action should be taken. The board decided to appoint a consultant paediatric psychiatrist to take charge of the children's wards at Harperbury.

Dr Derek Ricks, a consultant at Great Ormond Street and University College Hospital, was appointed. A man of genius, he proceeded to empty the ward. He set up and ran clinics for parents and children in their own local areas in London, ran a bed-backed service and pioneered small family-scale care units supported by fostering initiatives.

It was not an easy task. There was tremendous resistance to be overcome – resistance from junior and senior staff, from the trade unions and from the NHS establishment.

However, we demonstrated what could be achieved and what should be done.

I was later appointed by Barbara Castle, Secretary of State for Social Services, to Chair the Committee of Enquiry into training for Mental Handicap Nursing and Care. I realized that there had to be a common approach to care across local and health authority provision. The simple and common-sense recommendations of the Jay Committee created an incredible furore and attacks from COHSE (Confederation of Health Service Employees) and other vested groups which at times seemed to have no or minimal concerns for the patients in their care.

The National Development Group under the chairmanship of Professor Peter Mittler began to consider and to report on these issues but would its voice be listened to and heeded?

There was little movement. More pressure; more action was required.

In the mid-1970s a group of voluntary organizations led by the Spastics Society and MENCAP was formed to campaign for the rights of children living in or likely to live in long-stay mental handicap hospitals. EXODUS was born. Its committee was soon joined by professional experts including Derek Ricks. Its aim was simple and clear: To ensure that no child lived inappropriately in long-term hospital because she/he had a mental handicap. EXODUS argued then, as it does now, that children are children irrespective of any disability they might have. The campaign wanted a closure pro-gramme for all such hospital provision and the development of alternative community-based provision, including respite and family placement services.

The campaign had some immediate achievements. Awareness was awoken through the revelations at Queen Mary's, Borocourt and other hospitals. There were press reports and television programmes. The public and some politicians were amazed at what they now discovered was happening to children in their own NHS. They wanted change. They wanted rapid progress. The level of public opinion led to the government making clear statements of intent and voting some money to tackle the problem. The intent was all too often no more than pious words and the money far too little!

In 1980 I was to write:

The placing of the mental handicap services within the National Health Service in 1948 has given rise to a continuing series of problems of which we are only now beginning to see the full implications. At the time, it is to be understood, great emphasis was laid on the importance of aiming to reduce distinctions between 'mental ill health and physical ill health'. The fact, however, remains that if one does not regard mental handicap as an illness, an institutional Health Service is not an appropriate provider of care and accommodation for them. It has to be remembered, to quote from the Report 'That after 100 years in which educators, philanthropists, doctors, and social workers had all tried to deal with the problem, the care of mentally handicapped people in residential accommodation was handed over to the health professions in 1948. Local authorities, however, retained some interest in that they were responsible for aftercare and day facilities for mentally handicapped people.

We ask the question then, who should be responsible? Clearly for the foreseeable future, the provision of residential care must be a combined responsibility, with certain provision coming from health and certain from local authorities. If, however, we look back to the 1946 Curtis Committee Report and consider particular problems and interests of mentally handicapped children, it will be seen that the basic decision in 1948 must have been a wrong one. The Curtis Committee, in its Report, stated that the group of, at that time, more than 10,000 mentally handicapped children growing up in wards of long-stay mental handicap hospitals were 'the most deprived group of children in the whole community'. To the eternal shame of those responsible for the final form of the 1948 Children Act, these children, despite the recommendation of Curtis, were excluded from the provisions of that splendid and historic Act on the grounds that 'they must be all right because they were in hospital'. Now, 30 years later, with report after report raising causes of the utmost anxiety in relation to these children, we begin to see the full implications of that disastrous omission. The recently leaked NDT report on conditions at Queen Mary's Carshalton are but the latest in a series of reports which focus inevitably on the broad spectrum of concern for adults, but highlight the particular problems of children in these hospitals.

We come then to the issue of which authority is really best suited to offer long-term residential care to the handicapped whether adult or children. The late Professor Jack Tizard, was in no doubt in his famous Brooklands work in the 1950s that the hospital structure of hierarchies, staff training needs, departmentalism and so forth, while probably suited to the needs of curing acute physical illness, was highly unsuitable for the provision of home-like conditions, particularly essential in the case of children. To quote from that report, we are reminded 'that because of the nurses' preoccupation with duties which have to be completed, it is very easy for the children and human needs of the patient to be given a low priority. The role of a nurse is very different from that of a house mother, and that difference is profoundly reflected in what one can call the ideology of the two types of institution. By the ideology of an institution we mean the system of beliefs and values which govern its practices, the ends it aims to serve. The ideology of the child care services was, in England, authoritatively stated by the Curtis Committee 20 years ago. It is to protect children, to keep them with their families whenever possible. While they are in residential care the object of the service is to give them an environment which as closely as possible resembles that of an ordinary home, with ordinary standards of affection, companionship, security, good physical care and adequate education'. This was written 25 years ago. Still there are voices who say the philosophy remains to be proved.

The evidence which Maureen Oswin sent to the DHSS on behalf of EXODUS encapsulates the reasons why we must look to see the responsibility for care of the mentally handicapped, particularly for children, progressively being transferred to a local authority base. 'The tragedy has been that children in mental handicap hospitals have not fully benefited from the past reforms because the 1948 NHS organisation placed them under hospital services instead of under local authority social service departments.' The staff in the social services departments have the professional expertise to deal with the residential care situation. Clearly there will have to be, and will be, every kind of opportunity for medical back-up in resource based units with experts with a medical background to assist and advise the staff.

The 1971 White Paper 'Better Services for the Mentally Handicapped' is now in process of being re-written and updated. In recently published statistics on local authority community care developments for the mentally handicapped, a more encouraging picture is seen. The fact however remains that some 40 local authorities have as yet provided no residential accommodation for children. We know in fact, if each local authority took responsibility for some 30 mentally handicapped children, and this is an outside figure, the present 3,800 children in the long-stay wards could be transferred to a small locally home-based unit.

One of the major problems is that of finance. The National Health Service is financed in a totally different way from the local authorities, one example of which is that when comparing costs per place, the health service does not take capital costs into account, whereas the local authority is obliged to do so. A major request coming forward now to government is the need to set up a high-powered study group to try to improve upon the joint funding/joint financing provision so that the transfer of individuals from the care of the health service to that of the local authority may be actually encouraged and facilitated, as opposed to too often being frustrated. A word of praise for the joint financing/joint planning provision must be said. This initiative taken by Barbara Castle in 1974 when she set up the committee of enquiry into Training Staff (as well as the late lamented Quango, the National Development Group for the Mentally Handicapped) has in fact given a tremendous shot in the arm to our thinking, and indeed in many cases to action on behalf of mentally handicapped people and above all children.

There is no doubt whatever that the future must see a progressive transfer of responsibility from the residential care of mentally handicapped people from the health service to the local authority field. The recently published Working Party's report on the Management of Psychiatric Hospitals (including mental handicap hospitals) stresses yet again the need for care to be offered on a district, i.e. a local basis. We must accept that the huge extra-territorial hospitals which history has bequeathed us are a great encumbrance to the development that we must see in the near future.(Conference paper, 1980)

I make no apology for quoting this piece at length because even in 1995 some of the key issues remain.

Significant progress has been made over the last decade. Credit must be given for this to government, health authorities, local authorities and individual professional staff. It must also be given to pressure groups such as EXODUS, individual voluntary organizations and individual people including Maureen Oswin.

In 1980 Patrick Jenkin, then Secretary of State for Health and Social Services, told a MENCAP conference that: 'The long stay hospital is no place for a child to grow up in.' It should also be stated that a hospital is no place for short-term care. All too often such care can be provided only on a 'revolving door' basis. This provision is better carried out at home in the family.

Was this clear government policy implemented? The answer has to be, not whole-heartedly. Indeed, some children still live their lives in hospital wards; others are forced to spend respite periods on them; others are placed on the wards of specialist hospitals when they require acute care in an acute hospital setting.

The NHS has developed a range of domestic-style community-based services. These are to be welcomed. Local authorities have developed a range of alternative provision, as have many voluntary organizations. However, the fact remains that there is much still to be done.

* * *

Over the last decade the number of children in hospital long term has been greatly reduced. The quality and appropriateness of the care and provision in general has been

Table 4.1 *Children (aged 0–14) resident in hospitals and units for people with learning disabilities, by duration of stay, 1983–93*

Duration of stay	Year at 31 December			
	1983	1984	1985	1986
All durations	931	846	652	584
Under 1 year	309	315	292	273
1 year –	102	76	44	74
2 years –	87	89	43	31
3 years –	116	100	95	89
5 years and over	337	270	160	130

Duration of stay	Year at 31 March						
	1987	1988	1989	1990	1991	1992	1993
All durations	not available		340	520	270	230	150
Under 1 year			200	230	150	130	100
1 year –			80	90	30	10	20
2 years –			10	100	30	40	10
3 years –			10	50	30	20	10
5 years and over			30	50	30	30	20

Source: Letter to writer from John Bowis MP, Parliamentary Under-Secretary DoH, August 1994. Figures are not consistent but are reproduced as received.

much improved (see Table 4.1). The concern that too much respite care was being provided in a hospital setting has also lessened. All too often families had no alternative provision in this much-needed service than a hospital placement. In the late 1980s there were 12,000 short-term admissions for such care to long-stay hospitals per annum. This was intolerable. Often it was the same children being admitted, re-admitted and re-admitted – the 'revolving door syndrome'. For some it was a form of near-permanent care. Thankfully more enlightened approaches led to community- and family-based alternative provision. Respite is and always will be a vital service to preserve families and to underpin community care.

EXODUS would wish to claim much credit for what has been achieved and the significant process over the last decade – particularly the concerted effort by ministers to ensure that health authorities stop admissions for children into long-stay subnormality hospitals.

The 1989 Children Act has and can make a contribution to the welfare of these children. If a child is provided with accommodation by a health authority or an NHS trust for more than three months on a consecutive basis or the intention is that this will happen, the health authority or NHS trust has a duty to notify the responsible social services department. The responsible social services department must take all reasonably practical steps to enable it to decide whether the child's welfare is adequately safeguarded and promoted whilst he/she stays in the accommodation and to decide whether it is necessary to exercise any of its functions under the Children Act.

Health authorities may invite the Social Services Inspectorate to participate in inspections of their services (or of services registered by them) as they relate to children. This is good but it does not go far enough.

The Department of Health is pledged to continue to work towards further improvements in the services available for children with learning disabilities. In 1991 the Department published its policy on the admission of children to hospital. The guidance contained in *The Welfare of Children and Young People in Hospital* is based on the cardinal principle that children should be admitted to hospital *only* if the care they require cannot be as well provided at home, in a day clinic or on a day basis in hospital.

The Children Act 1989 is probably the single most important initiative directed at improving services for children. In May 1993, the Social Services Inspectorate inspected four local authorities to determine progress being made in implementing the new duties of the Children Act in relation to disabled children. The inspection focused on services planned, provided or purchased by the local authority, through the social services department. It did not inspect health or education services, but it did look at the interface and collaboration between these authorities.

In February 1994, the Social Services Inspectorate published its report of this inspection under the title *National Inspection of Services to Disabled Children and their Families*. This highlighted both progress and concerns. Such inspections and reporting can contribute to the achievement of this goal.

Such inspections will become a regular feature in this field. The Department of Health will continue to monitor progress through both the inspection programme and the new statistical returns currently being developed.

In addition, the Children Act requires that information about children's services should be co-ordinated and planned. Some local authorities have produced comprehensive plans and these are welcomed.

Ministers have promised to look at the experience of community care plans (introduced in 1992), which are compulsory, joint and published, to see if there are lessons to be learned from these plans that could improve the planning system for services for children.

In June 1994 the Audit Commission published its report *Seen But Not Heard*. It argues for better co-ordination of services and the publication of joint plans to improve services. Why in 1994 is such a report necessary?

EXODUS now believes that the time has come for one final push to end this sad chapter in the social history of the UK. Its agenda for action includes:

- an end to all long-stay hospital placements for children on the grounds of learning disability and/or profound multi-disability
- an end to respite care provision for these children in hospital or other institutional settings
- a statutory responsibility on the Social Services Inspectorate and local authority social services inspection units to monitor all NHS, local authority and independent sector provision for children with learning disabilities
- the creation of an independent inspection service – evaluated by an independent agency – independent of the NHS and local authorities
- clear national minimum standards for the quality of care; assessments; staff training and competence; and parental support and involvement in service planning and commissioning
- a transfer of all responsibility for the commissioning of the care, accommodation and support needs (non-medical) of children with learning disabilities
- clear statements relating to services for children with learning disabilities and their families in local authority community care plans
- the development of appropriate respite and family placement services
- sufficient earmarked funding for local authorities within their community care resource allocations for developing and sustaining services for these children and their families
- an annual report to Parliament by the Secretary of State for Health on progress on a national programme on these issues
- involvement of voluntary organizations, specialists, families and advocates for the children in the national and local planning for these services
- the provision of information, advice and support services for parents
- new integrated multidisciplinary training programmes for staff, building on the new care, social work and nursing schemes and competencies

I am confident that the original aim of EXODUS ('To ensure that no child lived in inappropriate long-term hospital because she/he had a mental handicap.') can and now will be realized.

Stan Segal was one of those who awakened the nation to the needs of these special children. His work, his philosophy and his commitment have to be continued.

I have raised these matters with successive Secretaries of State and Ministers of Health including Enoch Powell, Dick Crossman, Keith Joseph (who actually cried 'something must be done'), Barbara Castle, Patrick Jenkin, Norman Fowler, Kenneth Clarke and Virginia Bottomley. The message has not been lost on any of them. It lies now in the present Secretary of State's or her immediate successor's power to take the necessary action and to resource it so that the UK can be described as a compassionate and civilized society.

This is an achievable goal. EXODUS will continue its campaign until it is realized – that would have been the wish of Stan Segal and it is the wish of thousands of children and their families. Let no one deny them their rights.

REFERENCES

Audit Commission. 1994. *Seen But Not Heard*. London: HMSO
Department of Health 1994. *The Welfare of Children and Young People in Hospital*. London: HMSO
Observer. (1980)
Oswin, M. 1971. *The Empty Hours*. London: Allen Lane
Oswin, M. 1978a. *The Holes in the Welfare Net*. London: Bedford Square Press (National Council for Social Services)
Oswin, M. 1978b. *Children Living in Long Stay Hospitals*. Oxford: Blackwell Scientific Publications
Oswin, M. 1984. *They Keep Going Away*. London: King Edward's Hospital
Social Services Inspectorate. 1994. *National Inspection of Services to Disabled Children and their Families*. London: HMSO

Chapter 5

The Work of the Warnock Committee

Mary Warnock

The Committee of Enquiry into the Education of Handicapped Children and Young People was proposed by a Conservative Government in 1973, when Margaret Thatcher was Secretary of State for Education. In 1974 there was a general election which the Conservatives lost, but the committee came into existence none the less. The reason for its being set up was that it was only relatively recently (since 1970) that all children, whatever their disabilities, had been entitled to education; more important, there was intense pressure on government to take seriously their obligation to provide education for all, not least from Stanley Segal, who lobbied tirelessly on the theme that no child was ineducable.

It was, looking back, a great advantage to the committee that, because of this change of government, we felt ourselves to be entirely politically neutral. It is almost impossible to conceive such neutrality in any educational inquiry today. The committee was large. It consisted of 24 members, plus, it seemed, innumerable observers from England, Scotland and Wales. It must have been a difficult task for civil servants to select the members. The world then, as now, was full of people interested in and knowledgeable about children with different disabilities; but then, far more than now, they tended to be narrow in their interests and even jealous of competition and defensive of their own patch. Obviously not all interests could be represented on the committee, and there was a certain amount of complaining about those who had been left out. It took some time to get the committee to recognize that we had a wide and common purpose and that members were there for the general, not the particular, expertise they could bring. But we came, after four years, to work well together and to recognize the common educational goals we shared. This meant that, when it came to the actual writing of the report in 1978, we could allocate chapters to members with particular expertise, and then discuss them in the whole committee, with minimum adaptation to what came to be a house style. This method, which was economical of time, failed only in the case of one chapter, which, when the draft was presented to the whole committee, turned out to be entirely unintelligible, and had to be rewritten from scratch.

The most influential and knowledgeable non-member of the committee was John Fish, who worked as an adviser throughout our existence as a committee. It was difficult at the time, and is still difficult, to determine how much in our final report came from within the civil service and how much from members; how much was descriptive of existing good practice, how much truly new. Certainly all the professionals, whether civil servants or those concerned with special schools, assumed that children with disabilities, however severe, should be educated, not merely cared for. But some members, including myself, held that this could not be taken for granted: it had to be argued for, or at least placed in a framework of the general justification for education, if resources were to be expended. Many people still thought that there were children who could not benefit from 'real' education (which, they held, meant learning to read and write); and that attempting education at all for the most disabled was inevitably expensive and ineffective. Such children could gain nothing from education, would never contribute to the economy, and had therefore better, and more economically, be left alone, even if, by law, in some sort of school. Some children, we were told, were, after all, 'vegetables'.

And so we felt it necessary to enunciate the principle that education had a common purpose for everyone. Hitherto it had been widely assumed by non-professionals that special education was what went on in special schools: a different kind of activity, and with different goals from those of 'real', or 'normal' education. We, on the contrary, drew a picture of education as a shared journey, all children on the same road, leading towards independence, competence and enjoyment. Some children would not get as far as others on this journey, but the only difference between the education of the handicapped and that of the rest was that those with handicaps had greater obstacles in their way along the road, and needed help if they were to overcome them.

This was, in effect, a moral picture, and one that came to have enormous importance for the committee. I clearly remember the visual image I formed of this common road; and it was from this picture, shared by all the committee, that there rose the concept of 'special needs', later to be enshrined in the 1981 Education Act. For a need must be identified relative to some end. I need a spade *if* I am to dig my vegetable plot; I need professional lessons *if* I am to become a singer. Thus *if* a child with disabilities is to progress towards the identified goals, increasing independence, increasing competence and increasing enjoyment of the complexities of the world and of relationships with others, then he or she will need to have access to the curriculum, will need to be able to communicate, and will need reassurance that progress is indeed possible. All these are the ingredients of special education, the help required to meet the specific needs a child may have.

One of the main reasons why this picture appealed to us, the picture of the common educational road, beset by obstacles along the way (though for many children clear and smooth enough), was that it seemed to get us away from the medical model of educational handicap. Hitherto, like people suffering from specific diseases, children with handicaps had been classed according to what was wrong with them: they were 'Spastic'; they were 'Educationally sub-normal'; they were 'delicate'; and so on. Special schools were set up to deal mainly with one or other of these defects, though it was acknowledged that this did not always work, many children suffering from more than one disability.

We wanted instead to identify what it was that a child would need if he or she were to make progress. Of course this need often related to a specific condition. A deaf child's educational needs were different from those of a blind child, for example. The needs of a child who had particular difficulty with reading were different from those of a child whose problem was that of physical access to the classroom.

We thought the first and most important thing was to identify what *provision* for a child would make educational progress possible. As was the fashion of the time, we were opposed to 'labelling'. This led to certain absurd difficulties and circumlocutions, which have, if anything, increased since the days of our report. For example, we retained the expression 'maladjusted', because we could not think of a better way to describe those children whose special needs were emotional. These children are now inelegantly referred to as EBD children, meaning those with emotional and behavioural difficulties. I cannot think that this is much of an improvement. Nor are parents much enlightened when they are told that their child has 'specific learning difficulties' when what they correctly believe is that he is dyslexic (not, incidentally, that dyslexia was a recognized 'handicap' in those days, at least not recognized by the Department of Education). However, the intention to move away from the idea of what is wrong with a child towards the idea of what he needs if he is to function properly (never mind the *cause* of his difficulty) was, I think, on the whole beneficent. It led, for one thing, to the notion that there might be a continuum of needs, some permanent, some temporary, some easily supplied, once identified, some requiring considerable expertise and expense to supply.

This notion of a continuum of needs, now incorporated in the 1993 Act, and in the *Code of Practice* which followed, meant that we had vastly widened the scope of 'special education', or rather of special educational needs. For at one end of the continuum there would be children who, let us say, had become temporarily deaf, following an infection, or who had for some reason missed a lot of school, and were therefore behind the others in their class. Both these kinds of children would need special help; and if they did not get it, they would fall further and further behind until they could never catch up with the rest of the class. But such help could well be given them, and their need would thereby be met. Or it might be that a child had a need which could be met only by a specialist teacher, but which could be fully met, if it was identified early enough, and the specialist brought in, so that after a time that child would be on equal terms with his contemporaries. This would be the case for most of those suffering from mild dyslexia; and provided that identification occurred early, they might suffer no lasting educational disability. At the other end of the spectrum would be children who were severely and multiply disabled, who, perhaps, could not speak, and, without educational help, could not even make known their preferences, could not move or exercise any autonomy of any kind. Such children need intensive education, and even with this help they will not progress far down the common road. But they will progress a little way. And for them, every inch of progress makes a vast difference to their quality of life. All this we gradually learned, on the committee, often by seeing children at both ends of the spectrum, and in the middle, actually receiving the teaching they needed – and sometimes, memorably, by seeing them not receiving it.

By including all these very different children within the scope of the concept of special needs, we had, of course, enormously increased the number of those hitherto thought of as candidates for special education. Special education, as I have said, was thought of as that which was provided in special schools; and in 1974, when the committee of inquiry was set up, about 2 per cent of all school-age children were in special schools. But we held that up to 20 per cent of all school-age children would have a special need in our newly expanded sense; that is to say that, at any one given time, five or six children in a class might have a special need.

This figure of 20 per cent was a kind of guess. But it has become enshrined in the literature. It is, however, a very misleading figure. The idea of special needs, and the widening of the scope of the notion of meeting needs, was most attractively flexible. I, for one, was attracted to it partly because one could embrace within it the needs of children who were specially gifted in, particularly, mathematics or music, and who needed extra help if they were not to become frustrated and bored, with no possibility of exercising their talents. But this is, partly at least, a different story.

The widening of the scope led to another consequence that was, in a way, welcome. The committee, though unanimous in its view of common educational goals, and unanimous in its enthusiasm for the 'real' education of all children, whatever their disabilities, was deeply divided about the question of 'integration'. This was one of the issues of the time. There were those amongst us who thought that integration of all children who were in any way disabled into the normal school was a straight matter of equality, or fairness. These people held that the ultimate goal of the reform of special education was a kind of extension of the comprehensive ideal, and that we should not be satisfied until all special schools had been abolished. Such an aim, they held, was the logical continuation of the abolition of selection by the 11-plus examination. Others amongst us, of whom I was one, were more sceptical, not about the possibility but about the desirability of such an outcome. There are, for example, deaf children whose life, both immediately and in the future, will be made totally miserable by the attempt to force them to integrate with the hearing world. (This is not true of all deaf children, but of some.) Again, and perhaps more crucially, it may be asked how one can insist on the integration into the ordinary classroom of children whose difficulties had first arisen because they could not adjust to the classroom, who were either disruptive, violent and damaging to other children, or who were totally withdrawn – who were, in fact, maladjusted to ordinary school. Our differences on these matters were ideological, and therefore extremely difficult to settle. For evidence and argument have little impact on ideology. In fact, the question of integration was the only ideological difficulty that we encountered, except the closely related issue of boarding education.

On the question of boarding education, the difficulty was that there were members of the committee, I think the same members who felt so strongly about total integration, who regarded the whole idea of boarding school as a kind of madness of the English upper and middle classes. No one, they held, should ever be separated from their families. No one, they said, should be deliberately sent away from home, a fate that was inevitably interpreted by a child as a kind of banishment or punishment. And no one, they argued, would wish to punish a child for being disabled, or having special educational needs.

The weakness of such arguments in the context of children with special needs bore crucially on the proper way to educate those children whom we continued to refer to as maladjusted. For such arguments took no account of two important facts. The first was that in the case of many, if not most of such children, it was precisely their family situation that was at the root of their emotional and behavioural difficulties and disabilities. There was, then as now, a tendency to glorify the family as the source of all wisdom, support and security. But it was perhaps less well recognized then than it is now that many families are not merely inadequate to supply children's emotional needs (and, I would add, their linguistic and social needs as well), but are positively harmful to children, on account of the physical, sexual or verbal abuse or severe neglect to which the children are subjected by their families. Our psychiatrist member was insistent that often the only hope for a severely disturbed child was to get him away from his family, at least for a time, so that the ground could slowly be prepared for him to become capable of education. For such children, moreover, the regimen of a boarding school, the 24-hours-a-day education, the routine and the security, was itself essential, if any educational progress was to be made.

This last point, about the actual necessity of boarding schools for some children, was in the end acknowledged (though, alas, many such schools have since closed though lack of funds). The first point, about integration as the absolute ideal, was not conceded. The only thing we could do in our chapter on this issue in the report was partially to evade it. This was done by distinguishing between various different things that could be meant by 'integration', and between different degrees of integration – a useful enough exercise, and indeed an essential one, if talking at cross-purposes was to be avoided.

However, the impact of this disagreement was very much lessened by the fact that we had, as I have already explained, so enormously widened the scope of the concept of special educational needs from 2 per cent of all children at school to 20 per cent that it was inevitable that most children with special needs would already be, and have always been, in ordinary mainstream schools. So when people asked whether the committee was in favour of teaching children with special needs in the ordinary classroom, the truthful answer was 'Yes, of course. That is where most of such children are, and will remain.' The question whether or not all of such children's needs should be met in the mainstream classroom became less urgent. There was enough work to be done on meeting the needs of 20 per cent of all schoolchildren to make the abolition of special schools an extremely distant goal, even if it was a goal at all. Nevertheless, at the time the issue of integration was thought to be of immense, even if not of immediate, importance, and I was often told that our committee had been a committee 'about' integration. To this day it is often assumed that our main message was that all children with special needs should be taught in the ordinary classroom. It is a matter of some complexity to explain what we actually said.

The 1981 Act, based on the 1978 report of the committee, shows the same evasiveness about the issue of integration, and for the same reasons. It was an ideological hot potato. The Act lays down that children should be educated in mainstream schools, or classes, wherever possible. This is repeated in the 1993 Act. What would render such education impossible would be if it proved to be unduly expensive or unduly disruptive for other children in the class. This seems a reasonable compromise, but it does not answer the direct question of whether or not there is a future for special schools.

I believe that the widening of the scope of 'special education' was one of the most important outcomes of the Committee of Enquiry. However, I also believe that we should have widened it still further, and I greatly regret that we did not do so. We had been instructed, in being given a gloss on our terms of reference, not to include amongst those with handicaps those who were deprived or disadvantaged by factors which could broadly be called social; and in particular we were told not to include children whose first language was not English (a form of this injunction is to be found in both the 1981 and the 1993 Acts).

That we were obedient to these instructions shows that, whatever our intentions, we had not wholly avoided the old medical model of handicap. We still thought that children who had special educational needs were children with something the matter with them, at least from the standpoint of their teachers. Of course, as I have already suggested, *some* children with special needs do have things the matter with them: they may be blind or suffer from various forms of dysfunctions of the brain. But these are not the only children with special needs. We were not true to our vision. We had seen that an educational need must be identified by considering what help a child must have if he or she is to make progress along the educational road, whatever the cause of the need for help. We should have been more ready to insist on what we all knew (but which is perhaps more generally acknowledged now than then), namely that some kinds of social deprivation produce, by themselves, special educational needs, which can and must be met.

The obstacles that lie along the educational road for children who, for example, have virtually no conversation with their parents or parent, who think of grown-up people as essentially hostile and abusive, who spend more hours watching television even than playing with their contemporaries, for whom the intrinsic disciplines of listening and learning are totally unknown ... these obstacles are formidable indeed. We should have laid more emphasis (though we did lay some) on nursery education, and on early identification of potential educational needs. We should also have done more to identify the commonest causes of 'maladjustment' to school (that is of disruptive behaviour, aggression and truanting, as well as of criminality). The 'maladjusted', though even then they constituted the second largest class of all children with special needs, and we knew this (and their numbers have almost certainly proportionately increased since then), were not thoroughly investigated by the committee. We did not take nearly enough thought about prevention. And this is another sign that we were concentrating too exclusively on special needs arising out of conditions themselves beyond prevention, or at least beyond educational prevention, that is on roughly medical rather than social conditions.

The committee was not criticized at the time for this omission, though I believe it should have been. We were, however, understandably criticized for our neglect of the financial and resource implications of what we recommended. And of course it was therefore easy for government to allocate no extra resources at all for the implementation of the 1981 Act, which incorporated most of our recommendations.

There were, I think, two reasons for this neglect, or I should say one cause and one reason. The *cause* was that in 1974, when we started our deliberations, and even, to some extent, in 1978 when we reported, there was a certain optimism still in the air, to which we were not immune. I remember, for example, that with absurd *naïveté*, as it now seems, we believed that since the numbers of children of school age were declining, there would be more money to be spent on each child in future. More important, we believed that our main task was to point to the needs children had, educationally, and that thereafter action would be taken by LEAs, backed up by new legislation, to satisfy these needs. We were still living, that is to say, in the shadow of the welfare state, though at the very last end of its shadow. For the philosophy of welfarism was based on the proposition that needs, genuine needs, would be met for everyone, whether these needs were in the field of housing, of social support, or health or of education. Moreover, within education itself, we were accustomed to the idea that government would fund institutions, notably the universities, according to the needs they could foresee would arise in the next five years – the old quinquennial grant system. The educational 'cuts' did not really begin to be felt until the early 1980s. The climate, in short, was the climate of paradise, even though, as it turned out, a fool's paradise.

Our *reason*, on the other hand, for neglecting costing (and we did discuss at length whether or not to include it) was that we wanted to be seen to be concentrating not on details but on principles. The whole philosophy of special educational needs seemed to us then immensely exciting. There were many principles that we wanted to emphasize – for example, the importance of parental involvement and the essential collaboration between different government departments and different local services without which our great ideas could not be implemented: above all, our vision of all children involved in the enterprise of education together, marching towards the same goals. We could, of course, have put all this in our report and then produced appendices to show how much we estimated it would all cost. But we thought that LEAs, would turn to the appendices first, and rubbish the whole report because they disagreed with these details. The comfort now is, perhaps, that if we had put all these sums in, they would almost certainly have been wrong to start with, and in any case out-of-date in a few months.

However, our insouciance about money had one consequence that I regret. The committee specified in some detail the stages of assessment that a child would go through in the course of his special needs being determined. At each stage more experts from outside school would be involved, always with parental involvement as well. The final stage of assessment, which only a small number of children would reach, whose needs were especially complex, would result in the issuing of a statement of needs, and, as part of the statement, the provision, specific to the child, that must be made to meet these needs. At the point of the issue of a statement for a child, the local authority would have an obligation to make the provision specified in the statement. All this was incorporated in the 1981 Act, and again in Part 3 of the 1993 Act.

The outcome has, in my view, been, if not disastrous, at least very bad. And we should have foreseen it. For we should have reflected that since only that provision mentioned in a statement was mandatory, there might come a time when a local authority would perforce have to cut back on all other provision that was not mandatory, in order to fulfil its legal obligations to children with statements. Moreover, though we assumed that only about 2 per cent all children at school would go through to the end of the assessment programme and get a statement, this was not, and could not be, laid down. So since parents could ask that a further assessment of their child be made, with a view to the issuing of a statement, and since the worse the financial stringencies of local authorities became, the more firmly parents believed that only a statement would result in any special provision for their children, so the number of statements issued crept up. Local authorities varied enormously in the number of statements they issued. But, as times got harder, this did not necessarily mean that the children with statements did better. For it became increasingly obvious that the authorities were specifying provision no longer according to the needs of the child, but according to what they could afford. There were long delays in the issuing of statements, and even longer delays before parents could express their dissatisfaction at tribunals. Because local authorities had a legal duty to provide what the statement specified, the whole system became increasingly litigious. Parents, encouraged to some extent by the issuing of government handouts about their rights, began to turn automatically to the courts, when they were dissatisfied with the provision for their child, as increasingly they were.

The new 1993 legislation has attempted to cut down the delays and parental frustrations which have come to be associated with the business of issuing statements. Statements must be produced within six months of the assessment; there must be an annual review; parents are entitled to question a decision not to issue a statement. And a new, and supposedly more friendly form of tribunal has been established.

But all this, though well-intentioned, seems to me to be mere tinkering. The real evil is the system of statements itself. Not everyone agrees with this judgement. There are probably some members of the committee of inquiry who do not. We introduced statements in the first place to protect the interests of those who were worst off. We wanted to ensure that no local authority could argue that for the most severely handicapped, education of a serious, still more of an expensive kind was inappropriate. We also wanted to ensure that if the parents of a severely disabled child moved into a different area, the statement would go with them, and the provision would continue.

There are those who argue that these considerations are still so strong that they outweigh all the disadvantages that flow from the issuing of statements. I do not accept that argument. I believe that, on the contrary, by ensuring that more is done for those children with statements, we are also ensuring that less is done for those children who have been assessed as having special educational needs, but whose needs are not deemed to be so acute that they deserve a statement. And this constitutes the enormous majority of children with special needs. As I have said, the committee estimated (relying on figures provided by the then Department of Education and Science) that about 20 per cent of all children at school would, at some time or other in their school career, be identified as having a special educational need. We thought that about 2 per cent of all children would be so severely disabled, or their needs so complex, that they would merit a statement. That leaves 18 per cent of all school-age children who will be identified as having special needs, who will have no statement yet who have to be educated, their special needs as far as possible met. And, as I have suggested, these figures are extremely misleading. In some schools the numbers of children with special educational needs is far more than 20 per cent; whether or not some proportion of these have statements is almost irrelevant to the provision for the rest.

Although the existence of the 18 per cent of children is recognized in the new *Code of Practice*, issued to schools after the 1993 Act was passed, there is no real guarantee that money will be spent specifically on their education, nor is there any certainty that in schools where there are large numbers of disadvantaged children, whose needs are great, all will be identified as having special needs. Moreover, LEAs, as long as they still exist, have direct responsibility only for those children who have statements. If more schools opt out of local authority control, as is the wish of government, it is likely that education and social service committees will be amalgamated. This may have certain advantages, but I fear that it may at the same time make it less likely that education, as distinct from care, will remain a top priority, even for the 2 per cent for whom the LEAs are at present responsible. And the rest, the so-called 18 per cent, are to be the responsibility not of the local authority, under whatever guise, but of the school itself. In my view, this constitutes too great a distinction between those children with and those without statements.

Indeed it may seem that we have moved back to the days before the idea of a continuum of ability and disability gained acceptance. For we are now faced with the possibility of 2 per cent children of school age, approximately the same number as those who used to attend special schools, being targeted for special help, whilst others, the rest of the continuum, may increasingly have to sink or swim in the ordinary school, their needs perhaps identified, but not necessarily met. It is true that under new legislation every school has to publish its policy with regard to children with special needs. But it is one thing to have a policy, another for that policy to be effective, specific and workable. I deplore, too, the fact that those parents whose children have statements may be able to demand provision as of right, whilst those whose children have no statement may call in vain for a generalized policy to be so implemented that their children get the help they need.

I very much hope that my fears are without foundation. It has to be remembered, however, that the 1981 Education Act, based as it was on the report of the Committee of Enquiry, was in many ways already a fish out of water, an anachronism, a last-gasp assertion of the philosophy of the welfare state. For it presented the meeting of educational needs as a proper aim for government legislation. Seven years later, the 1988 Act might have come from a different world. In this Act the driving force of education was to be the market, and parental choice of school. Parents would, it was assumed, choose schools which prepared their children for employment, and which were well-run and cost-effective. A successful school was one whose output met quality standards, dictated by the needs of the national economy, and which, by these standards, offered to government value for money. Moreover, in order to help parents to choose successful rather than unsuccessful schools, there were to be competitive 'league tables' setting out how well or badly schools had succeeded with their pupils in public examinations, especially GCSE and A level, and, later, in the tests of the National Curriculum. There is no place for welfare under this new regime; nor is there any suggestion that resources will go where needs are greatest. Competition between schools and value for money are the key concepts, and the whole vocabulary of education has suddenly been borrowed from that of manufacturing industry. No one within the management of a school will be willing to allow money to be spent on anything but that which will enhance the market-value of the school.

Some of the measures proposed in the 1988 Bill (arrogantly referred to by its authors as the 'Great Educational Reform Bill'), were beneficial. I believe, for example, that the National Curriculum, when at last it settles down, will prove to have been of benefit to all pupils, whatever their abilities. And since the enactment of the Bill it is probably true that the most educationally ineffective schools have either improved or closed. Nevertheless there was immediate anxiety amongst those who saw how uneasily children with special needs would fit with the new atmosphere of cut-throat competition. There are many children whose education will inevitably be expensive, of infinite value to them, but of little or no value to the national economy; and 'quality assurance' in the new school/factories did not include assurance that education should benefit the individual child, or improve his life, except in so far as it made him employable. The education of the most severely disabled could not meet these standards.

Part 3 of the Education Act of 1993 was designed to allay these fears. And that Act, with the *Code of Practice* added to it, may indeed afford some hope.

My remaining fear may seem unduly philosophical. The most that has been offered by recent governments to those whose needs are greatest is that there should be a 'safety net', so that, if they fall, they will not actually kill themselves. The provision of a safety net, though admittedly better than nothing, is a pretty negative kind of provision. The philosophy of the market necessarily carries with it the implication of danger to the losers, of 'devil take the hindmost'; and the safety net is simply a concession to decency, so that this implication should not be too blatantly offensive to morality. The Committee of Enquiry, reporting ten years before the 1988 Act, based its recommendations on totally different moral principles. It assumed that the state had a duty to educate all children, for the sake of improving their lives, in the ways we specified. That assumption lies behind Part 3 of the 1993 Act. But very different assumptions underpin the rest of the Act. I fear that no legislation can work well when it is based on contradictions of principle. My fears are thus not wholly laid to rest.

Chapter 6

Education Legislation: 1988 to 1994

Klaus Wedell

Although ideas and practices in special needs education have inevitably moved on, the aims enunciated by the Warnock Committee still stand. They form a rallying call whenever there is a threat to the hard-won progress which has been achieved since its report (Department of Education and Science, 1978) was published. My task in this chapter is to describe some of the efforts of those who were campaigning to maintain the direction of special needs development threatened by the terms of the 1987 and 1992 Education Bills.

The late 1980s marked the end of the era during which the Warnock Report's aims had a predominant influence on LEAs' policies in developing special needs provision. The impact of the report and the subsequent 1981 Act were much greater than might have been anticipated, given that the legislation was almost unique in promoting integration without allocating resources to achieve this aim. The research which my colleagues and I carried out on the implementation of the 1981 Act (Goacher *et al.*, 1988) showed that the majority of local education authorities (LEAs) actually allocated an increased proportion of their funds to the development of provision. However, the lack of resources was of the main problems to which the Commons Select Committee on Education pointed, when it reviewed the implementation of the 1981 Act (House of Commons, 1987). When it became apparent in the later 1980s that proposals were impending for new education policy and legislation, the status of special needs provision was still vulnerable. The proposed new national education legislation relegated the influence of the 1981 Act on local provision and practice. It is interesting to note that this change was not due to a change of government. The Warnock Committee was set up, and the 1981 Act was enacted, by a Conservative Government.

My own involvement with legislation derived originally from my being asked to carry out research to evaluate the 1981 Act and its implementation. My concern initially was that the developments in special needs education marked by the Warnock Report should be supported by secondary legislation consequent on the 1981 Act, and not smothered in procedural irrelevance. Although our research on the 1981 Act showed that the principles of the Warnock Report were not fully realized by the Act or by its implementation, in retrospect the years following the Act were a golden era for the development of special needs provision. There was a general feeling of commitment on the part of LEAs to extending support for pupils with special needs throughout the range of education. The later HMI/Audit Commission report (HMI/Audit Commission, 1992) on the implementation of the Act may have shown that these developments were not administered everywhere in the most efficient or effective way but there can be no denying the considerable commitment shown by the majority of LEAs. One of the main conclusions of the Commons Education Select Committee's report (House of Commons, 1987) was that:

> A policy for special education is something in which LEAs have a particularly important role to play. The difficulties which arise are too wide ranging to be soluble by schools alone and too localised to be capable of close direction by central government. . . . A successful implementation of the 1981 Act is very much dependent on the development by an LEA of a clear and coherent policy.

Many of the criticisms made later by the government of LEAs' administration of special needs provision were ones which had already been acknowledged (Housden, 1993). The solutions were, however, to be sought in finding ways to improve LEAs' administration and means of funding, rather than in doing away with their co-ordinating role.

THE 1988 ACT

The introduction of the Bill (which became the 1988 Act) in November 1987 was heralded by the publication of a consultation paper (Department of Education and Science, 1987) on the proposed National Curriculum and its assessment. This caused alarm amongst those concerned with education in general in the UK, because it appeared to represent a distorted view of curriculum content, and a simplistic notion of assessment. The limited ideas about curriculum were illustrated by the following quotation from paragraph 18 of the consultation document. Referring to the ten subjects of the proposed curriculum, the paragraph states: 'in addition there are a number of subjects or themes such as health education and the use of information technology, which can be taught through other subjects *without crowding out the essential subjects* [my italics]'. Not surprisingly, this view of the curriculum was regarded by those involved in meeting pupils' special educational needs (SENs) as jeopardizing the achievement of the broad aims of education stated in the Warnock Report (and later even of the 1988 Act itself). Similarly, the proposals for assessment promoted a single method for collecting information to serve the three very different purposes of assessment identified by the consultative paper. This approach to assessment was seen to be not only inappropriate, but also wasteful of effort and resources. The inadequacy of the assessment approaches applied even more seriously to pupils with SENs, particularly to those whose achievement would remain below Level 1 of the National Curriculum for some or all of their schooling. All in all, the curriculum and assessment proposals in the consultation paper appeared to ignore the basic assumption in the Warnock Report that 'the aims of education are the same for all pupils', and the 1981 Act's affirmation that SENs represented a continuum which included pupils in ordinary schools.

It was very apparent to those involved in the education of pupils with SENs that efforts had to be made to change the proposed legislation. Since the consultation paper was issued shortly before the end of the Summer school term, and responses were required by early Autumn, it was also difficult for many organizations to prepare an agreed response within the time limit. In my own case, concern was triggered by the consultation paper but not being versed in the art of lobbying my action was limited to responding to the invitation to send in views.

When the Bill was presented in Parliament, its content was unchanged with respect to the points of criticism which had been made regarding special needs education – as well as many other considerations. I was soon to learn that any other expectation was unrealistically optimistic. Mr Baker, the then Secretary of State for Education, intro-duced the Bill as the 'Great Educational Reform Bill', and so it promptly became known as the Gerbil.

The Department of Education and Science press release reported Mr Baker as saying in the House of Commons:

> The Bill's fundamental and unifying purpose is to lever up educational standards ...
> The Bill will galvanise parental involvement in schools. They will have a greater variety of schools to choose from ...
> The Bill will also release and focus the energies of headteachers, their staff and school governors ... control of school budgets will be pushed down to the level of individual schools ...
> The Bill will introduce competition into the public provision of education ... which will stimulate better standards all round.

In addition to introducing the National Curriculum, the Bill also promoted the opting out of schools from LEA education systems, and brought in requirements that the major proportion of education funds should be delegated to schools on the basis of pupil numbers. As indicated in Mr Baker's speech, the underlying premise was that the only way to improve education was through the competitive dynamics of the market economy.

Both the 1987 and the 1992 Bills were promoted with arguments which, at a superficial level, sounded quite reasonable. It was therefore important for those opposing the legislation not to fall into the trap of appearing to go against seemingly 'reasonable' aims. The criticisms had to show that the proposed provisions were likely, in practice, to defeat the realization of 'reasonable' aims. For example, it could be argued that a move towards greater consistency of curriculum content throughout the UK was likely to be beneficial, but not if the curriculum was over-prescriptive and narrow, and likely to exclude pupils with SENs. Giving schools greater say over their budgets could be regarded as a good way to make sure that they used their finances in a targeted and flexible way. However, when the Bill made schools' main source of funding depend on competition for pupil numbers, admitting pupils with SENs was not likely to prove attractive. Promoting parental choice of schools would seem a good idea. However, if it is not attractive for schools to admit pupils with SENs, it is in practice likely to be difficult for parents to have a choice of integrating their children into ordinary schools. Making LEAs give up their centrally funded services, and forcing the services to 'sell themselves in the market place' might appear a good way of ensuring that the services met the needs they were meant to serve. However, specialist services for pupils with SENs are inevitably expensive, and only required by those schools which actually had pupils with the relevant needs. Services are unlikely to survive under those circumstances, and once abandoned, the specialized personnel are unlikely to be recoverable.

It was quite a complex task to bring out these contradictions in the legislative proposals. Seen from 1995, it is sad to note how many of the anticipated negative consequences of the legislation did in fact occur. Some of the legislative provisions have subsequently been overturned, but in the meantime there has been a great cost to the education system and to the pupils it was meant to serve.

Lobbying about the provisions which affected special needs education in the 1988 Bill was not carried out in a co-ordinated way. The National Children's Bureau brought together some of the bodies at a conference in September 1987. The Children's Legal Centre played a co-ordinating role between the various bodies, and was able in May 1988 to refer in a letter to the Minister that the points raised were supported by an alliance of 70 bodies. The Association of Metropolitan Authorities (AMA) played a central role in lobbying about educational issues in general, and with their expertise were able to supply the opposition parties with proposals for amendments.

For my part, I encouraged a group of those involved in special needs education to issue a joint statement. The group included the deputy chairman of the Warnock Committee, a former inspector for special education, local authority special needs advisers, those concerned with teacher training and research in special education and others with significant responsibilities for children with SENs. The aim was that the membership of the group should cover a wide spectrum of those involved in special needs education. I had still to learn that, from the government's point of view, those professionally involved would be accused of promoting their personal interests in the proposals they put forward. However, we also found that there were many parliamentarians across the political spectrum who did not hold such a view.

The group issued a statement to all the members of the Commons Standing Committee, and to certain peers. A press release was also put out:

> The 20% of children in the country's schools who have special educational needs at some time are destined to get a raw deal from Mr Bakers' National Curriculum proposals, according to a statement issued this week by a group of prominent educationists.
>
> Within the Bill, reference to pupils with SENs is made only in terms of pupils with Statements and those in special schools, and yet it is evident that very many of the clauses would affect the education of pupils with SENs but without statements in ordinary schools.
>
> The Bill does not acknowledge the full breadth of curriculum objectives in terms of personal and social accomplishments which employers and parents alike expect their children to acquire.
>
> The Bill fails to distinguish the two main purposes which assessment may serve:
>
> - for all pupils, whether or not they have SENs, there is a next step in the progression of their learning, the achievement of which requires continuous rather than periodic assessment.
> - age-related norms are of use for monitoring the outcomes of education in groups of pupils, schools or whole LEAs. To be cost-effective, such monitoring can of course be limited to representative samples of pupils and schools within LEAs.
> - the choice of ordinary schools which can provide effective education for pupils with SENs is likely to be reduced because:
> - it is uncertain whether schools which opt out will give due attention to their responsibility to make appropriate provision for pupils with SENs,

- unless schools' resources are ensured, pressures will inevitably arise for a much higher proportion of pupils to receive additional support through the maintenance of statements,
- the arrangements for LEA-wide plans for support may be disrupted if schools opt out and colleges become independent.

In summary, the advances towards integration and improved resources within schools and colleges for children and young people with SENs may well be jeopardised by the implementation of some of the Bill's provisions.

There was some reference to the statement in the *Times Educational Supplement* but silence from the rest of the press. This was not only a strong lesson in presenting a case, but also a revelation that 'prominent educationists' concerned with special needs education were not the stuff of news.

The group subsequently worked closely with the AMA lobbying group. Amongst the issues on which amendments were proposed, one amendment to the very first clause of the Bill was suggested. In view of the points we had made about the Bill, we wanted the wording of the first clause to stress that the aims referred to *all* pupils in a school. We therefore proposed that the clause should read: 'the curriculum ... satisfies the requirements ... if it ... promotes ... the spiritual, moral, cultural, mental and physical development of *all* pupils at the school'.

By this time, the Bill had gone on to the Lords. *Hansard* records the following exchange between a peer and the government spokesperson:

Lord Carter: The amendment is designed to ensure that the objective applies to all children, particularly those with special educational needs.

Lady Hooper (for government): ... Although the phrase 'all pupils' is not stated explicitly in Clause 1, it is there implicitly, and the clause would be interpreted as if it were included.

At the end of the debate on this amendment, Lord Carter said:

I think that those Members who voted the amendment down can now start to see the kind of problems which will arise because of the very narrow prescriptive nature of the National Curriculum. The problems of the National Curriculum for children with special educational needs are only an exaggeration of the problems which will face all children ... The minister said that [the] amendment had no effect on the meaning of the Bill ... I simply ask, why not include it? ... Throughout we are required to take the Secretary of State on trust.

The government refused to accept the amendment. However, in the booklet *From Policy to Practice* which was issued by the Department of Education and Science after the Act came into force (Department of Education and Science, 1989a), the word 'all' not only appeared in the paragraph which referred to this point (paragraph 2.2), but it was also stressed with italics. However, the opportunity to give the point legal force had been turned down.

After the 1988 Act came into force, it was still necessary to monitor the many subsequent Circulars of Guidance. A number of bodies still continued to respond – particularly, of course, the AMA. However, important as this monitoring was, it was difficult for those who had daily jobs to carry out to maintain the additional load which was involved in this lobbying. Circular 22/89 (Department of Education and Science, 1989b) was of concern to me, although it arose out of a different context.

The Circular was issued in the wake of the Select Committee's report on the implementation of the 1981 Act (House of Commons, 1987), and of the research which others in addition to my colleagues and I had carried out. The draft did not explicitly require those contributing to the advice for a statement to set out the pupil's SENs *regardless* of the provision which was actually available. This was a point which had been included in Circular 1/83 (Department of Education and Science, 1983) on the operation of the 1981 Act procedures. It had allowed for the fact that those giving advice should not commit the LEA to any particular provision (Wedell, 1991). Our research and other findings had shown that statements had none the less often been written in a 'resource-led' way, and Circular 22/89 would have provided a good opportunity to reassert the point from Circular 1/83. However – one might cynically say, not surprisingly – the point was omitted from the final version of the Circular.

Another rather significant piece of legislation appeared in the period following the 1988 Act. The government was concerned to extend local management of schools (LMS) to special schools. In order to obtain ideas about how this might be done, it invited tenders from major firms of management consultants. Touche Ross obtained this contract, and had asked me to be its special educational consultant. I agreed to work with them, on condition that the inquiry was carried out with an open mind as to whether or not LMS could be extended in an educationally meaningful way. The inquiry concluded that LMS could be applied to special schools, so long as it did not link funding directly to pupil numbers. Clearly, it would be ludicrous to have a system which encouraged special schools to recruit or retain pupils for the purpose of increasing or even maintaining their income. Consequently, the Circular (7/91) (Department of Education and Science, 1991), based on the Touche Ross report (Touche Ross, 1990), set out ways in which LMS would be extended to special schools, but on the basis of planned *places* rather than actual pupil numbers. This formulation was in striking contrast to the competitive ethos inherent in the LMS provisions for ordinary schools, and illustrated the points of criticism made about the effect of the 1988 Act provisions on special needs education.

The report had also placed great emphasis on the need to plan places in special schools in relation to the LEA's overall plan for special needs provision. Consequently, paragraph 63 of the Circular states: '... the effective delivery of special education throughout an LEA depends upon a clear and coherent authority-wide policy'. This pronouncement seems somewhat nostalgic when it is considered that, only about twelve months later, we found it impossible to preserve the same principle within the 1992 Bill.

THE 1992 BILL

By the time that the next major Education Bill loomed on the horizon, we were resolved to learn the lessons from our previous experience. As before, the White Paper (*Choice and Diversity: A New Framework for Schools*, Department for Education, 1992a) was issued in late Summer for response by early Autumn. In addition, a paper was also issued – *Special Educational Needs: Access to the System* (Department for

Education, 1992b). In July of 1992, Paul Ennals, the chair of the Council for Disabled Children (CDC) and also director of education for the Royal National Institute for the Blind (RNIB) and I met to discuss the impending White Paper and legislation, and the need to be more effective in lobbying for the preservation of special needs services and provision. Paul, in his role as CDC chair, and with his parliamentary knowledge, saw that what was needed was a consortium of voluntary bodies concerned with special educational needs. The consortium would combine the power of all the bodies, without depriving them of their individual freedom to lobby on their own particular concerns. I was certainly clear that pronouncements from the 'educational establishment', as the government termed all those concerned in education, would be useless. The voluntary bodies represented 'customers', and perhaps even more relevantly, a substantial constituency of voters.

The main points of concern about the government's proposals from the point of view of special needs education were the further extension of market forces to the provision of education. The government proposed to increase the incentives for schools to opt out of their LEAs. It planned to set up a quango, the Funding Agency for Schools (FAS), to control the funding of these grant-maintained (GM) schools. When more than 10 per cent of either the primary or the secondary pupils (or both) were served by GM schools, the FAS would share responsibility for planning places within the LEA area, and beyond the 75 per cent level, the LEA would only be left with responsibility for pupils with statements of special need. This clearly left the meeting of the broad range of special needs to individual schools' commitment, and the 1988 Act had already shown how vulnerable schools were. The Bill also proposed that a higher proportion of LEAs' funds should be delegated to schools. This would have the effect of forcing LEAs to give up centrally funded support services and leave them to operate on market demand.

At the initiative of the CDC and its director, Philippa Russell, a meeting was called of the representatives of relevant voluntary bodies, to discuss the concerns about the impending legislation, and the advantages of collaboration in lobbying. Paul Ennals chaired the meeting and outlined an overall organizational pattern for the proposed consortium. A policy group would be formed of representatives of the participating bodies, which would identify those issues on which all were agreed that the consortium should campaign. This would meet at regular intervals. A small steering group would meet weekly to co-ordinate the lobbying. At longer intervals, the consortium would hold a consultative forum, where the consortium would provide updates on the lobbying to all who were interested.

Those present at the meeting supported these plans, and agreed that they would recommend their bodies to make contributions to the cost of the lobbying. A timely contribution from the RNIB made immediate funding possible. Paul Ennals was very appropriately elected as chair of the consortium. By 8 September, the newly formed Special Educational Consortium (SEC) was able to send out a press release: 'The Special Educational Consortium comprising major disability and educational organisations has been formed to secure improved provision for children with special educational needs. The Consortium believes that changes in the White Paper may pose a threat to these children ... '.

From that point on, there was continuous activity. Two part-time staff were appointed – a project officer and a special needs expert, Philippa Stobbs, who would take a major role in drafting briefing papers and amendments. The parliamentary officers of the voluntary bodies were also involved. As a member of the steering group, I was amazed by the encyclopaedic knowledge of the parliamentary officers. They knew when what would happen, and what would be initiated by whom within the parliamentary process. They knew such details of the Westminster parliamentary rituals as whether an MP could ask supplementary questions or not in which kind of debate. In the light of all this knowledge, the plans for amendments and briefings were built up once the Bill was published. Although the SEC operated at a non-political level, inevitably the large proportion of amendments were put up through the offices of the Opposition parties. Briefings about our concerns were, of course, issued to relevant MPs in all parties.

The policy group meetings were invaluable for enabling the consortium to ensure that it promoted only those issues on which there was consensus amongst member bodies. Correspondingly, member bodies then knew whether they needed to pursue certain issues on their own. One example of this was the issue of integration. One member body was concerned that the legislation should set a date for the right to virtually total integration. Discussion of this concern showed that there were differing opinions about this position, and the group then set about formulating a consensus view about integration. This did not lead to acrimony, since all respected the fact that the SEC could only function if it promoted a common view amongst its member organizations.

The weekly steering group meetings developed strategies for operating within the consensual areas. Once the Bill came into the Commons and later into the Lords' Committee Stages, amendments needed to be drafted and briefing papers written to support them. As mentioned above, although the SEC operated on a non-political basis, none of the amendments were accepted for promotion by the Government side. At the Commons Committee Stage, the number of MPs who were taking part was obviously limited. Conservative members did not inevitably disagree with some of the points of concern which we put forward, but when it came to a vote, the Government's built-in majority prevailed. Amendments were thus often aimed more at extracting commitments from the Government side in their attempts to defend their position. For example, many of our detailed demands for safeguarding the effectiveness of special needs provision were countered from the Government's side by claims that they would be better covered within the *Code of Practice* proposed in the Bill, than on the face of the Bill itself. Finally even Mr Forth, the Minister taking the Bill through the Committee Stage, found himself saying (as reported in *Hansard*), 'I am aware that I have raised expectations about the Code of Practice to an almost hysterical level.'

It seems fair to claim that the SEC did make a major contribution to extending the *Code of Practice* to require support for those pupils with special needs who did not have statements. Some of these provisions, and also the requirement that all schools should have whole-school policies for special needs, were in fact announced by Mr Forth at one of the meetings with representatives from the SEC.

From my own point of view, one of the most interesting challenges was the writing of briefing papers. In the course of work within one's own discipline, there is rarely a challenge to go back to basics in defending one's arguments. Furthermore, there is rarely a need to abandon entirely the dependence on the terminology used. However, if a briefing paper is to be of use, it has to enable a tired and probably harassed MP to get the main point of the argument quickly. Above all, the briefing should enable the MP to produce forceful counter-arguments from those opposing him or her. I found this a daunting challenge, but one which had a powerful effect in clarifying one's own thinking. It also taught one to be opportunistic about the use of the Opposition's arguments. The following example of a briefing used during the Lords' Committee Stage illustrates some of these points.

The particular amendment was concerned to support our view that it was essential for LEAs to be able to continue their co-ordinating role in the provision of special needs support within their areas. I happened to notice that the Minister taking the Bill through the Lords (Lady Blatch) had herself made the very arguments we proposed in relation to another amendment (not one of ours) that hospital schools should be allowed to apply for grant-maintained status. She had used the arguments to point out the inappropriateness of the provisions of this amendment. The SEC was therefore able to use her own points in support of our amendment:

> The SEC notes that these are the very criteria used by the Minister in arguing *against* the amendment to extend grant-maintained status to hospital schools. She said 'the kind of regime which the noble Lord has in mind would reduce the amounts available to authorities for the provision of education otherwise, and significantly lessen their scope to do so in cost-effective ways which took account of opportunities for financial planning and economies of scale'.
>
> Although the Minister made these points with respect to a parallel form of provision, it is significant that she enunciated the very points which also argue for the need for achieving a plan for special needs provision for all pupils within the LEA area. Without such a plan the LEA is left to cobble together provision across the interstices of a collection of school policies.

Credit for the 'interstices' bit has to go to Philippa Stobbs. The steering group members came to capitalize on each others' tactical phrasing! We were to press for the co-ordinating role throughout the parliamentary stages.

The argument was finally even put to the Minister by some members of his own party. The Conservative chair of the Commons Select Committee on Education (Sir Malcolm Thornton) had already commented on the government's proposals for allocating responsibility (*Times Educational Supplement*, 11 December 1992): 'If we really believe that SENs are going to be given a better deal under the new legislation than under the old system, then this is the biggest triumph of hope over experience that I have ever encountered.'

The only outcome of lobbying on this particular point was a very weak amendment, sponsored by the government, which exhorted all parties to co-operate. However, in Circular 6/94 (Department for Education, 1994a) which followed the enactment of the Bill, strong arguments were put for schools and LEAs to work together to provide co-ordinated services, in order to achieve efficiency and economies of scale.

Another task for the steering group was to keep Department for Education officials briefed about the amendments which were put forward. In the last analysis, our concern was to obtain concessions from the Government's side. Since we naturally assumed that our views represented logic and sense about special education policy, we were concerned to put our case also to those whose job it was to advise ministers. Furthermore, these were people with whom many of us had worked in the course of our normal activities in advising on special needs policy and, in my own case, in the course of my research. These meetings were held in a very positive way. However, we were fully aware that officials were obliged to base their reasoning on the underlying dogmas (in our view) of the government's policies. In a number of instances, these meetings then led to agreements that the SEC should put its case directly in a meeting with ministers.

The SEC's main focus was on the preparation of amendments, and on briefing members of the Commons and the Lords. The actual tactics of voting were, of course, matters for the parties. We also had to remember that ours was only one of many aspects of education which were being covered. None the less, it was remarkable what a substantial proportion of debating time was taken up by special needs issues. In view of the Government's majority in the House of Commons, there was little hope of winning a vote on amendments during that period, either during the Committee Stage or during the main debates. Whilst the Bill was going through the Lords, the prospect was not so bleak. The government was actually defeated on an amendment which required that the FAS should include someone with knowledge and experience of special needs education. The government's objection had been that it could not commit itself to allowing a 'minority group' to claim representation on the quango. This argument again illustrates how difficult it was for us to conceive of the level of thinking amongst those we were trying to persuade.

A more spectacular but less effective victory over the government's policies was achieved by non-government peers during one night's Committee Stage in the Lords. It involved a planned ambush of the government. During the later part of the evening, these members drifted out of the debating chamber, and appeared to leave for home. Before midnight even the SEC's special needs expert left the visitor's gallery, and departed for home in blissful ignorance. At this (as the SEC members like to believe), government members also began to leave, with only a small number remaining to support Lady Blatch the Minister of State. On the stroke of midnight, non-government members miraculously reappeared in their seats, leaving the government hopelessly outnumbered, and without a prospect of marshalling reinforcements. An orgy of retribution ensued, during which the hapless Minister accepted a raft of amendments wiping out large swathes of her policies without even pushing them to a vote. The success of the ambush probably was balm to the frustrated non-government noble lords, but alas the amendments were all overturned when the government wreaked its revenge in the final debate on the Bill.

In a number of ways, the government had, during the passage of the Bill, made minor but not insignificant modifications to the Bill regarding special needs issues. For example, it amended the proscription of LEAs' roles in supplying services to allow them to continue certain special needs ones. However, the main areas of concessions emerged within the proposals for the *Code of Practice*. Mr Forth had, as reported in *Hansard*, already mentioned in January 1993 during the Commons Committee Stage that, in drawing up the terms of the *Code of Practice*,

> We have also created an informal advisory group, which consists of experts in special needs from Local Authorities, a senior member of OFSTED and some senior and equally respected officials from my department ... We wished to include people of standing, expertise and impartiality from outside the Department to work on it.

This group became known as the Special Needs Advisory Group (SNAG). Although it operated separately from the SEC, the views of SEC were no doubt brought to the attention of members. In the light of the fact that LEAs would no longer have a co-ordinating role in ensuring provision for the broad range of pupils' SENs, the *Code* came to place a major emphasis on schools themselves recognizing their responsibilities in this regard. However, as has since become acutely apparent, this downward delegation of responsibility is a standard way of passing on the blame for inadequate provision resulting from insufficient funding.

The 1993 Act was followed by a spate of draft Circulars, and by the publication of the draft *Code of Practice* (Department for Education, 1994b). It was gratifying to note that considerable portions of the special needs aspects of these documents reflected points which we had put forward during the debates on the Bill. However, all Circulars contain an initial reminder that they do not have the force of law, and their provisions consequently have to be established in the courts. The status of the *Code* is still unclear. When this was raised during the debate in the House of Lords, the Minister stated that all those concerned 'would be required to have regard to its provisions'. One peer apparently commented that he had regard to many documents before throwing them into his waste-paper basket.

CONCLUSION

At the end of this phase of lobbying, the SEC was wound down. The aim in setting it up had just been to deal with the 1992 Bill and the legislation which followed when it became an Act. One inevitably asks oneself whether the immense amount of time and energy expended were worth while. There is little doubt that the activities of the SEC during the 1992 Bill were regarded as significant – even the ministers concerned were generous enough to acknowledge this during the parliamentary debates.

Few changes to the face of the Bills were achieved. However, the main impact of the lobbying was apparent only in the Circulars, the Regulations and the *Code of Practice*. The government was certainly prodded into remembering that pupils' SENs occurred across a continuum of degree, and that provision had to be assured for the needs of pupils who did not have statements. This had been one of the main concerns of the SEC from the start. The extension of the scope of the *Code of Practice* to the support of pupils with special needs in the ordinary school, and the focus on whole-school policies, has clearly been a major development. Paradoxically, it could be argued that it was only the potentially catastrophic dereliction of collective responsibility promoted by the 1993 Act which produced the demand that the *Code* should require the full range of pupils' SENs to be met. Whether the *Code* and the Circulars will provide a sufficient safeguard to maintain a realistic and effective level of support for the broad range of children and young people's SENs remains to be seen.

REFERENCES

Department for Education. 1992a. *Choice and Diversity: A New Framework for Schools*. London: HMSO

Department for Education. 1992b. *Special Educational Needs: Access to the System*. London: HMSO

Department for Education. 1994a. *The Organisation of Special Educational Provision*. London: DFE

Department for Education. 1994b. *Code of Practice on the Identification and Assessment of Special Educational Needs*. London: DFE

Department of Education and Science. 1978. *Special Educational Needs: Report of the Committee of Enquiry into the Education of Handicapped Children and Young People* (the Warnock Report). London: HMSO

Department of Education and Science. 1983. *Assessments and Statements of Special Educational Needs* (Circular 1/83). London: HMSO

Department of Education and Science. 1987. *The National Curriculum 5–16*, London: DES

Department of Education and Science. 1989a. *From Policy to Practice*. London: DES

Department of Education and Science. 1989b. *Assessments and Statements of Special Educational Needs: Procedures Within the Education, Health and Social Services* (Circular 22/89). London: HMSO

Department of Education and Science. 1991. *Local Management of Schools: Further Guidance* (Circular 7/91). London: DES

Goacher, B., Evans, J., Welton, J., and Wedell K. 1988. *Policy and Provision for Special Educational Needs: Implementing the 1981 Act*. London: Cassell

Her Majesty's Inspectors and the Audit Commission. 1992. *Getting in on the Act: Provision for Pupils with Special Educational Needs: The National Picture*, London: HMSO

Housden, P. 1993. Bucking the Market: LEAs and Special Needs in Special Educational Needs Policy Options Group. *Policy Options for Special Needs in the 1990s*. Stafford: National Association for Special Educational Needs Publications

House of Commons. 1987. *Special Educational Needs: Implementation of the Education Act 1981. Third Report of the Education, Science and Arts Committee*. London: HMSO

Touche Ross. 1990. *Extending Local Management to Special Schools*. Touche Ross Management Consultants

Wedell, K. 1991. Special Educational Provision in the Context of Legislative Changes. In S. Segal. and V. Varma (eds), *Prospects for People with Learning Difficulties*. London: Fulton

Chapter 7

Parents' Voices: Developing New Approaches to Family Support and Community Development

Philippa Russell

Truly a handicapped child is a handicapped family. Like all children, those with handicaps need first and foremost to be accepted and loved by their own families. But they also urgently require the appropriate treatment, therapy and education which will mitigate their disabilities and help them towards adult maturity and independence. In this sense, this is no more than we ask for our normal children and therefore we as parents would expect it to be possible for handicapped children to have basically the same place in family life as their more fortunate brothers and sisters.

After the initial shock of the diagnosis, the first hurdle to overcome was understanding and accepting our situation. Perhaps the greatest help we had at this stage was to talk to other parents with a child with a handicap like ours. The other parents either shut their minds to us or felt very sorry. We did not want to feel objects of pity. We had our lives to live and so did our child. Our paediatrician said we, the parents, had the power to do something to make things better. I hope we have done so. But the road is very long ...

'Living with Handicap', report of the Dame Eileen Younghusband Committee,
National Children's Bureau, 1974.

INTRODUCTION

In 1968, the National Bureau for Co-operation in Child Care (now the National Children's Bureau) initiated a major study of families with children with disabilities. The *Living with Handicap* working party was established because of a growing recognition that children with disabilities were often marginalized; that services were often fragmented; and that *parents* of children with disabilities were becoming increasingly articulate about their needs and their views of the services to meet them. As part of the study, Anne Allen wrote an article in a Sunday newspaper asking parents to tell her of their experiences. The letter was duplicated across the local and national press and nearly a thousand families and professionals supporting them responded. In general they wrote about the lack of understanding and sensitivity; the lack of respect and value placed on their children; the injustices, hardships and inadequacies in services offered. Not all the messages were discouraging. Some families had experienced outstanding professional support and advocacy, though – as one parent succinctly put it – 'If we had moved ten miles away, it would have been a very different story!' Other parents had discovered the solidarity of parent groups. One mother wrote:

I honestly think I would not have been able to cope in the first two years of 'Jeremy's' life without the help and support I received from other parents and the people running our local centre. I found out more in one day about what was going on than I did in weeks going to the local hospital. Most importantly, I met people who knew how it really is … it's wonderful not to have to pretend any more. Another parent wrote: '*So far as the education and support of our handicapped child is concerned, the law of chance prevails … we parents need to work together. We are like the lost tribes of Israel!*'

The Younghusband Report, taking into account the testimony of the parents, concluded that 'parents represent the future, but their ability to help their children will be directly affected by *how* they are supported and *how we* value the voice of parents in developing services'. Younghusband in effect endorsed the work of the 'new order' of parent organizations such as MENCAP and the then Spastics Society (now SCOPE) and laid the way for the Court Report (1976) and the Warnock Report (1978), with their new concepts of 'partnership with parents' and new vision of positive working relationships between families and professionals.

Just over twenty years on, the language of disability has changed. Services now, within a charter culture, attempt to address the views and needs of both parents *and* their children. The United Nations Convention on the Rights of the Child not only stresses the rights of disabled children to a full and positive life, but also underlines the rights of families to bring their children up in accordance with their own cultures and beliefs. The Children Act 1989 has underwritten the principle of partnership, but the 'parent power' forecast by Younghusband still has many battles to fight.

But the history of the parent movement is none the less positive. Parents have influenced the shape of legislation and increasingly families with disabled children or adult members can expect to see themselves as 'citizens' rather than 'patients'. Equal opportunity policies tend to be minimalist on disability equality issues. But the framework is there for a more equal society. When Younghusband reported, disability was seen as stigmatizing. The long-stay hospitals still admitted children and mainstream schools and other services rejected most comers. The concept of special educational needs, a curriculum for all and the possibility of educational achievement for children with learning disabilities, was seldom recognized. Access to services was determined largely by 'need', in effect by the threat of imminent (and costly) family breakdown. Few parents belonged to a family support or disability group because they simply did not know they existed. We have moved on and at a time of major economic and social change, it is interesting to look back to the 1960s, the Younghusband Committee and the first attempt to identify the weaknesses and the strengths of families caring for a disabled child by actually asking the consumers first.

FAMILY SUPPORT IN CONTEXT: CHANGES IN POLICY AND PRACTICE

Twenty or so years on since the publication of the Younghusband Report, there have been major developments in terms of policy and practice for families with children with disabilities or special needs. Both the Children Act 1989 and the community care arrangements emphasize the importance of *family*-based services and the need for services to be comprehensive, flexible and accessible.

However, recently we have seen the emergence of complex assessment systems and changes in the management of child health, education and social services. There is growing emphasis on quality in the *commissioning* of services, but *purchasing* arrangements in a contract culture may be variable and difficult for consumers of services to understand. Major changes in the social security system have improved the financial situation of some families, but there is growing evidence that many families are living in poor housing, with low incomes and may be in double jeopardy if a child has a disability. However, in a charter culture and in response to an increasingly strong parental voice, such changes will be profoundly influenced by consumer views and by a 'parent lobby' which has moved from aspirations to partnership to empowerment (and with an increasing will to pursue policy not only through negotiation but, if necessary, through the courts). In effect, the parent movement has become a force to be reckoned with.

It is estimated that there are around 360,000 children in the UK aged 16 or under with disabilities (about 3 per cent of the child population) (Office of Population and Census Surveys (OPCS), 1989). Of these children, all but 5,500 live in a family home. Of those living away from home, 33 per cent of families had felt the child's health or behaviour was too difficult to cope with. Forty-five per cent of all families with a disabled child felt their health was adversely affected by the pressures of caring. Thirty-three per cent of other families who could not continue to care had difficulties at home and presumably *could* have cared with adequate financial and practical support.

Disability can affect any section of the community and any age group. It is estimated by the OPCS that there may be six million adults with a disability in the UK. With an ageing population and major changes in mortality and morbidity amongst older people, local and health authorities face significant challenges for the 1990s. Additionally we are seeing the impact of the 'independent living movement', with new families emerging as disabled people themselves increasingly express their own desire for autonomy and establish their own families.

There have been changing patterns in provision for children with more complex needs. (In addition, with improved medical care – particularly in the neonatal period – there has been an increase in the numbers of children with very severe disabilities who are surviving much longer in childhood.) There are 16,500 children with special educational needs currently attending residential schools, with the largest proportion of 8,000 children being in schools for children with emotional and behavioural difficulties. The demand for residential education in some instances reflects an unmet need for respite care. It has been estimated that only about 4 per cent of parents of disabled children receive respite care – but the need for such a service is universally expressed in surveys of families' perceptions of need. Respite or short-term care is not only a priority for parents caring for children. A National Carers Association survey in 1993 found that over 91 per cent of *all* carers felt they needed and should have a legal right to respite or short-term care.

It is also important to put the above figures (OPCS, 1989) in the wider context of a period of major social change. The welcome shift from institutional care (often in NHS provision) to community care for children with severe disability has not always been matched by the development of good-quality community-based services. The principle of inclusion or integration still raises the question about *how* to meet some very specialist needs within a mainstream setting and how to train staff with generic children's services experience but with no knowledge of the often problematic and invariably inter-agency services which a disabled child requires. Equally there has been growing awareness that an emphasis on family support should not conceal the fact that disabled children are especially vulnerable to abuse and their welfare may therefore require special vigilance.

The UK is becoming an increasingly multicultural society, which creates challenges in providing and accessing services which are sensitive to different family needs. If ascertaining the views of families from a range of social and cultural backgrounds is problematic, the new duty under the Children Act to ascertain the wishes and feelings of the *child* is even more challenging. The potential for conflicts of interest between children with a disability and parents or carers has been little explored. The potential clash of interests between carer and cared-for extends into other families caring for a disabled person. The National Carers Association, in its survey in 1993 mentioned above, found that 51 per cent of carers felt that *their* needs were insufficiently addressed. Only 13 per cent of carers had had a separate assessment and the majority of carers felt that their competence and needs should be more fully recognized.

Towards a policy of family support

A number of studies carried out over the last twenty years about the everyday experiences of families with a disabled child, show a striking similarity. Wilkin (1979) and Glendinning (1983) reach very similar conclusions to OPCS (1989) and Hubert (1991). Caroline Glendinning's description of the 'daily grind' in *Unshared Care* (1983) and in *The Costs of Informal Care* (1992) is reinforced by the OPCS national survey (1989) which found that families with a disabled child were substantially worse off than their able-bodied peers. OPCS found that only 73 per cent of fathers of disabled children were in full-time employment, as compared to 88 per cent of the general population. Bradshaw (1980), using Family Fund data, had already noted that families were substantially affected by the inability of *mothers* to work. Sally Baldwin (1985), also using Family Fund data, noted that mothers of a disabled child were less likely to work (33 per cent as compared to 59 per cent of the general population), and that even if they worked, the hours and pay were below average. Sally Baldwin and Jane Carlisle (1994), in a review of the literature on social support for disabled children and their families, concluded that:

> It is extremely well documented that disability in a child both creates a need for additional expenditure and at the same time reduces the income available to pay for this by restricting the labour force participation of both mother and father ... It is quite clear that some families suffer from financial difficulties which they would not otherwise have encountered. Some very severely disabled children are living in conditions of *extreme* hardship which are partly related to their condition – and which must reduce their quality of life.

As one parent at a Council for Disabled Children workshop (personal communication) observed:

Motherhood is generally regarded as successful when it results in unemployment, that is to say when the children leave the family home. But carers don't have any unemployment. It's a job for life. It's not a bad job and most of us do believe in community care. But some of us would like to work, not necessarily full time, but we would like to use our professional skills, to enjoy the friendships and status that work brings. Why are there no services at times which enable us to do so? Crossroads Schemes are wonderful, but they don't exist everywhere. I've met disabled people in the same position. They could work too if only their personal care was reliable and it was accepted that they had important regular day-time commitments too.

Many families with children with learning disabilities have been disadvantaged by a wide range of social and economic factors in their particular local environment. The financial infrastructure of services is, however, only part of a wider range of issues relating to supporting and empowering families in the 1990s. Notwithstanding some major progress over the past decade, it is very clear that many families still encounter major difficulties in everyday life. Parker (1990), reviewing the research literature on informal (i.e. family) care, concluded that whilst a range of external factors (such as unemployment, poor housing etc.) did contribute to some of the high stress levels observed in many studies amongst parents of disabled children, none the less it was much less clear why some parents *did* cope. Parker also concluded that it would be timely to move away from research which tries and largely fails to look at stress in terms of structural differences between families and instead to 'emphasise the fact that many families *do* cope with and adapt to the stresses they experience and to seek to discover how they do it'.

Access to support will take different routes for different families. Equally, definitions of 'coping' will vary according to who is judging the ability of a family to survive well. Duckworth and Philp in a review of studies of families with disabled children in 1982 had concluded that:

Many families are not *really* coping even though they are not breaking down. Rather they experience and meet their problems to the best of their abilities and often face secondary problems as a result. It is often the accumulation of these problems that disturbs relationships within the family and between family and society ... in brief research is now beginning to demonstrate that the real problem is not so much one of family pathology as one of how to give practical assistance to families while, at the same time, keeping in mind that the tasks they face are so difficult that only a few exceptional families can be expected to be fully equipped to undertake them without help from the outside.

The reality of life with a disabled child will present many challenges to families. Notwithstanding many changes and developments over the past decade, the reality of life for some families has changed little. Baldwin and Carlisle (1994) note the connection between stress and inadequate support at periods of transition:

The need for information and advice or counselling is ongoing but becomes more crucial at critical *transition* periods. These may be transitions and changes in the *condition* or commonly accepted developmental milestones often accompanied by changes in *statutory* provision ... information needs to encompass the condition itself, its prognosis and practical management, the remit of and help available from statutory and voluntary sector sources, the benefit system and so on.

Developing a Policy of Family Support: The Parents' Perspective

'Parents need a help-line – it's no good having benefits, respite care, all those services if parents don't know they exist.'

'Professionals should get *their* act together before they talk to parents. What are parents to believe if the *professionals* fall out amongst themselves?'

'Parents are partners in the care of their child – they deserve respect, sensitivity. No one chooses to have a disabled child ... you shouldn't have to break down in order to get services.'

'Everyone is affected by disability in the family. Siblings and parents have needs too. *Everyone* in the family should be asked what they think and want.'

'My child is seen as a problem, too difficult, too expensive, too demanding ... but to me she isn't a syndrome, she isn't a burden, she is my child – if you see her as a child first, then it's easier to think of the services we need to stay together as a family.'

(Quotations from parents' workshops, Russell (1994))

But access to the system may not be easy. The parent movement of the 1980s and 1990s has increasingly had to demonstrate the complexity and lack of 'user-friendliness' of many services. Sloper and Turner (1992) found that respondents to a survey had been in contact with an average of ten professionals in the preceding year. Such fragmentation was costly and disruptive, not least because of the changing lives of many parents – in particular, the expectations of working women. Byrne and Cunningham (1985) noted the wish of parents to feel *in control* and not be passive recipients of services, and paid tribute to the impact of local and national consultations with parents. Consultations with parent organizations in a number of local authorities as part of planning for the Children Act identified a similar range of needs, namely:

- information and advice and counselling (including advice on financial support);
- effective medical and educational provision;
- friendship and a social life;
- access to services and resources which are child-centred, local, available at times compatible with family life and which do not require protracted and complex assessment systems; and
- protection from abuse.

Effective care in the family and local community is now increasingly seen as a matter of *negotiation* with parents and service users. Such consultation is, however, a process and not a state. Changes in legislation and public policy only produce positive changes if they take account of the reality of family life when a child has a disability or special need and the impact that the child has on the everyday lives of those in the family.

Growing awareness of the wish for (and possibility of) much greater community integration for children with disabilities has sometimes clouded the wider debate about *how* children with more complex needs will have specialist care within more dispersed service settings. Parents have higher expectations of being involved in a creative and ongoing dialogue about their child's needs and how best to meet them. Assessment under the Children Act 1989 and under the 1993 Education Act place great emphasis on ascertaining the wishes and views of parents *and* children and in ensuring that assessment is speedy, relevant, linked to clear outcomes and comprehensible to all participants. Though the reality may be rather different to the aspiration, the real voice of parents is increasingly seen as an integral element in service design, implementation and evaluation. Parents will always be lobbyists and agents for change. But the greatest opportunities and challenges for the parent movement increasingly lie in being part of the complex network of planning, resource allocation and prioritization at a local level and influencing the outcomes of the multiple dilemmas (and competition between client groups) which form part of 'community care'.

Growing interest in early intervention has shown that *early* support (with counselling and advice to meet parents' emotional as well as practical needs) will have major impact on subsequent coping strategies. With the increasing complexity of services (and the growing expectations of families), the Children Act offers new opportunities for developing a coherent approach to providing support services for children with disabilities and their carers. It is also a reminder of the complex interaction of the three statutory services (health, education and social services) in meeting the needs of children and families – and of the real challenges in developing sensitive and comprehensive assessment systems which acknowledge the complementary but not always compatible needs of all the family members, but which equally builds on *parents'* strengths whilst listening to the *children's* wishes and feelings.

PARENT EMPOWERMENT: CHANGING THE SYSTEM

> *The observation that handicapped children generally make handicapped parents is almost a cliché today.*
>
> *(Macdonald, quoted in Gartner, Lipsky and Turnbull (1990))*

> *The most important thing that happens when a child is born with disabilities is that a child is born. The most important thing that happens when a couple becomes parents of a child with disabilities is that a couple becomes parents.*
>
> *(Ferguson and Ferguson (1989))*

In many practical respects, parents with children with learning disabilities are still being challenged by the system. Disability is still too frequently associated with multiple problems relating to poorly co-ordinated services and financial disadvantage. But the world has moved on from the individual parents who responded so passionately to Anne Allen and the Eileen Younghusband Committee. The 1980s saw the rapid growth of parent support organizations. MENCAP had local branches in very region. Some new organizations like Contact a Family emerged, which focused on a wider range of families and which did not differentiate between specific disabilities. Additionally a wider range of voluntary organizations – ranging from Save the Children, the Children's Society to the Pre-School Playgroups Association and the Children's Legal

Centre – began to address issues relating to disability and children in the context of wider work in providing practical support or developing policy at local and national level.

In the 1950s, parents had begun increasingly to demand better community-based services for their children. Families rejected what they saw as custodial and hostile institutions which 'removed' their children. By the 1960s the voluntary sector was moving beyond demanding more individualized and home-based services (with the emergence of home-based learning programmes such as Portage) and promoting the concept of parents not only as partners but as co-professionals with skills and expertise of their own to share. Many voluntary organizations, dissatisfied with the quality of 'traditional' provision for children with learning disabilities, began to run their own community programmes. Parents began to demand inclusion within local authority (and health service) planning systems and by the late 1970s parents were beginning to participate in training programmes for professionals.

Although the disability equality movement came later to the UK than to the USA, the 1970s saw the emergence of a strong belief that people with learning disabilities should be seen as 'people first' and that inclusion or integration within society was a real possibility. Although now little discussed, the 1970 Education of Handicapped Children Act marked a watershed in acknowledging that *all* children were educable. The Act represented the climax of a passionate campaign led by Professor Stanley Segal and MENCAP to ensure that children with learning disabilities had access to education. Although that education was largely to be in *special* schools and little was known about the curriculum needs of children with severe learning disabilities, the Act led to a sea change amongst both parents and the education system. The writer – one of those parents who fought with MENCAP for her son's right to go to school – can recall the jubilation of parents at the Café Royal where Alice Bacon, Minister of Education at the time, acknowledged that it was 'a tribute to parents' commitment and belief in their children's future' that England and Wales would at last have a universal education system for *all* children.

Influencing legislation and policy and practice at national level carries its own price. Some of those parents who lived through the stigma, fear and sometimes rejection of those decades acknowledge the personal cost of campaigning. Today's parents see it very properly as their right to be *ordinary*. The concept of integration and inclusion extends beyond the debate about where and how children should be educated to the right of parents to live their lives as *they* choose and to have individualized services to suit *their* needs. The 1981 and 1993 Education Acts had profound impacts on social policy as well as on the educational systems open to children with learning disabilities. The right to access to information encapsulated within the 1981 Act opened new doors to the parent movement, which expected partnership to involve real and open negotiation and honesty between and with professionals. The education debate also provided a focal point for the sometimes parallel, sometimes shared (but sometimes very distinct) agendas of disabled people themselves. The emergence of People First and the British Council of Organisations for Disabled People acknowledged a further major cultural change in acknowledging that disabled people could and should speak for *themselves* – and that even children with complex disabilities could express views and should be heard. This principle for children with learning disabilities was reinforced by the UN Convention on the Rights of the Child and most importantly by the Children Act 1989.

The Children Act 1989 was been widely welcomed for bringing together most public and private law relating to children and for establishing a new and unified approach to local authority services for children and families in England and Wales. Many of the changes (and challenges) of the Children Act will be most apparent in services for children with disabilities and their parents. Historically, such services have been provided through health as well as local authorities, with confusing variations in local management and many conspicuous gaps in service. The Children Act restored the leadership to social services departments and importantly requires that 'every local authority shall have services designed: to minimise the effect on disabled children within their area of disability, and to give such children the opportunity to lead lives which are as normal as possible' (schedule 2, paragraph 6.).

The Children Act 1989 had been preceded by a Child Care Law Review Working Party and that working party received mixed messages initially about the possibility of including children with disabilities within the forthcoming Act. Given the significance of the Children Act, which was likely to set the scene for services to all children until the end of the century, the voluntary sector and parent organizations were quick to raise their concerns that the Children Act should not be a missed opportunity yet again for children often seen as 'too difficult or too different' to include within mainstream legislation. Many children with learning disabilities will require health *and* social care, both at home and in educational contexts, if they are to achieve their full potential. However, a 'single door' approach to services could only happen if definitions of 'need' and assessment arrangements dovetail and inter-agency support systems for individuals were complementary, well organized, of good quality and convenient to user families, with no waste of resources.

Several years into implementation of the Children Act, it is clear that the majority of local authorities are seriously addressing new models of services for children and young people with a range of disabilities. The Audit Commission (1994), in *Seen But Not Heard*, found that only 25 per cent of parents of disabled children felt that services were adequately co-ordinated. But the majority of local authorities are developing new (and sometimes creative) ways of working with parents in developing and improving local strategies. Some parent-led voluntary organizations have conversely found themselves acting as providers within the new internal market with all the internal stresses of running cost-effective services which are innovative, consumer-sensitive and account-able to purchasers and parent-led management committees. Although the parent lobby organizations have always run innovative 'model' services over several decades, few had previously attempted to run universal services. It remains to be seen whether parents' responsibilities as providers will in the future create uncomfortable conflicts of interest.

A key theme in the Children Act is that of *partnership* with parents, and the Act has been widely welcomed in providing a new legal framework for the provision of services for children with a range of disabilities, and in particular for including children with disabilities within a wider framework of legal powers, duties and protections which relate to the welfare of *all* children and in that context see that all children are literally children first.

As Baldwin and Carlisle (1994) state, any support system for families with disabled children *must* be based on four key criteria:

- The availability of sufficient information for informed choice.
- Recognizing the emotional and social context of assessment and the feelings of parents during assessment and in using special provision.
- Recognizing the degree of stress which some parents live under.
- Involving those parents whose personal circumstances make it difficult for them to use parent networks and other community support systems for information, advice and practical help without additional support.

In all these situations, access to the system is unlikely to be assured without *personal* support and information on all services and ongoing individual advice, befriending, support and advocacy – often provided through the voluntary sector. Perhaps the marked change in such provision at the end of the century will be the growing demands from parent organizations for access to local authority resources (for example, in implementing the befriending and advice roles of the named person in the 1993 Education Act) or in running the independent advice and advocacy schemes which are crucial for the active participation of many families (and increasingly young people with learning disabilities) in assessment and decision-making. The new focus on civil rights has resource implications both in terms of actual financial costs but – perhaps more importantly – in terms of the need for highly skilled, competent and readily available lay volunteers (who, in turn, may increasingly be 'gamekeepers turned poachers' in the form of early retired professionals moving to join the parents in the pursuit of better services!).

LOBBYING ISSUES AND THE FAMILY IN THE NEXT CENTURY?

Where will the parent movement go next? In examining family life and disability with a forward perspective, it is perhaps helpful to look at the wider family context of Europe and the consequences for all of us of major social and economic changes over the coming decade. The Children Act 1989 encapsulates the principle of a 'home life' for *all* children and appropriate support for parents (or other carers) in order to achieve this end. But in practice the achievement of the goal of a 'home life' for everybody with the family as primary carers will not be easy to achieve. Looking towards the twenty-first century, we need to remind ourselves of the major policy challenges which will face the whole of the European Union and which warn against too simplistic (or nostalgic) visions of what family life could and should mean.

To coincide with the Maastricht Treaty, the European Commission published a *Green Paper on Social Policy in Europe*. The Commission believed that there was a high risk of creating a 'dual society' of wealth creators and a growing number of non-economically-active people in receipt of transferred income (i.e. social security). The Commission argued for an *alternative* vision of a European society that is an active society invoking the active contribution of all individuals and that has an explicit social welfare policy for those who need support. The Green Paper has some relevant (and warning) messages for those of us seeking to address issues relating to the support of families living with disability. It indicates in particular a number of key areas for discussion in supporting the European family (particularly when that family has a caring role), namely:

- The growing power and influence of consumers as forces for change – the model of the passive recipient of welfare services is disappearing. The European dimension of 'parental power' has yet to be exploited, but the multinational parents' organization as a force for change within the European Union is likely to emerge during the next couple of decades.
- The changing role of women and the need to look wider in society in defining carer roles. In effect, lobbying for *parents' rights* needs to take account of the different roles and responsibilities allocated to women within current care arrangements.
- Recognition of the changing nature of family life (in particular, the increase in single parents and the impact of increases in the longevity (and hence increased morbidity) of European populations (and the competition for resources).
- The need to acknowledge the contribution of (and the importance of monitoring) the private and independent sectors (with parents and carers increasingly needing to influence the purchasers of very diverse services).
- The importance of debating openly and honestly how one defines 'need'. We have all developed policies on the basis of notions of absolute need which, once identified, will be met. But decline in resources and escalation in demand may necessitate a more *relative* definition of need and some rethinking about the personal responsibilities of families. At a time of major world recession, the concept of absolute need and what one parent described as 'pure needs' may not be tenable. Hence, parent organizations' lobbying will include working with statutory services to determine how services may most equitably be allocated.
- The significance of consortia and shared agendas. The Council for Disabled Children was the outcome of the Younghusband Report's prescience about the need for future alliances of parent organizations and the importance of lobbying through *corporate action* on some key issues. The unity of the disability and parent sectors around the need to implement enforceable anti-discrimination legislation is an illustration of a current consortium, as was the Special Educational Consortium during the passage of the 1993 Education Act. New alliances are beginning to be a characteristic of lobbying by both parent and disabled people's policy groups. But many of the constituent members of these minority groups still have little voice and are able to make only minimal contributions to local or national policy development. As Micheline Mason, a disabled parent with a disabled child, has commented: 'We reject the inhumanity and "medical" model of thinking involved in labelling and identifying people simply by their impairing conditions ... the social model of disability identifies prejudice and discrimination across institutions, policies, structures and the environment of society as the principal reason for our exclusion ... we must *all* reject the legacy of the past that has excluded us' (Mason and Rieser, 1994).

  Micheline Mason talks of the 'relentless oppression' still to be tackled and the role for *all* disabled people, parents and society as a whole in continuing to lobby for disabled people to be seen as 'real people leading real lives'. In effect, the battle moves on from the campaign for particular specialist services to a wider and more positive definition of citizenship and the recognition that the next decades will see parents *and* disabled people increasingly working in new partnerships to promote their own vision of citizenship in a hopefully more co-operative (but potentially competitive) Europe and beyond.

- Understanding and celebrating the diversity of family life – but recognizing that care within the family for people with increasingly complex disabilities and medical needs will require regular support, specialist services and financial recognition of the implications of caring. Any neglect of family support could mean a return to expensive and inappropriate institutional care.

In effect, families caring for a member with a learning disability must be seen as part of a wider community with hopes, aspirations, capacities and needs. Equally, disabled people may not always choose the family as their primary carer. We need to avoid nostalgia and also to recognize that the independent living movement is part of a civil rights thrust towards disabled people having the right to their *own* families and homes. The past decade has seen major changes in the role and recognition of carers. But parents and carers want their own competence to be recognized, with a greater investment in opportunities so that they may extend their knowledge and expertise to improve their own caring abilities – and also to respond more effectively to the raised expectations of those they care for. Community care is about the needs of all the family. Bernard Williams (*Times*, 24 October 1994) observes that:

> The post-war welfare state provided insurance against the reasonably predictable life-cycle risks of the industrial worker and his family – ill health and disability, unemployment and old age. But the risks are changing and an 'intelligent welfare state' is needed to enable men and women to negotiate almost constant change within the family, the work-place and society.

The greatest challenge for the next decade will be the acknowledgement of mutual and reciprocal rights for all family members and acceptance that within an increasingly multicultural and changing society, the definition of 'family' will need constant revision and exploration. Bernard Williams's concept of an *intelligent welfare state* will challenge us all. In terms of children with learning disabilities – and the adults they will become – within the context of family and community, the parent movement will continue to play a major role. However, the greatest challenge to *parents* over the coming decades may well be the balancing of their interests with those of *service users*.

REFERENCES

Audit Commission. 1992. *Community Care: Managing the Cascade of Change*, London: Audit Commission

Audit Commission. 1994. *Seen But Not Heard: Co-ordinating Community Child Health and Social Services for Children in Need*. London: Audit Commission

Baldwin, S. 1985. *The Costs of Caring: Families with Disabled Children*. London: Routledge & Kegan Paul

Baldwin, S. and Carlisle, J. 1994. *Social Support for Disabled Children and their Families: A Review of the Literature*. (Social Work Services Inspectorate). Edinburgh: HMSO

Bradshaw, J. 1980. *The Family Fund: An Initiative in Social Policy*. London: Routledge & Kegan Paul

Bradshaw, J. 1985. 75,000 Severely Disabled Children. *Development Medicine and Child Neurology*, **27**, 25–32

Byrne, E., Cunningham, C. and Sloper, P. 1985. *Families and their Children with Down's Syndrome: One Feature in Common*. London: Routledge & Kegan Paul

Cameron, R. 1986. *Portage: Ten Years of Achievement*. Windsor: NFER-Nelson

Cunningham, C. and Davis, H. 1985. *Working with Parents: a Framework for Collaboration*. Milton Keynes: Open University Press

Davis, H. 1991. Counselling and supporting parents of children with development delay: a research evaluation. *Journal of Mental Deficiency Research*, **34**, 3, 341–412

Department of Health. 1992. *The Children Act 1989 Guidance and Regulations. Volume 6, Children with Disabilities*. London: HMSO

Duckworth, D. and Philp, M. 1982. *Children with Disabilities and their Families: A Review of the Literature*. Windsor: NFER-Nelson

Family Policy Studies Centre. 1994. *A Crisis in Care? The Future of Family and State Care for Older People in the European Union*, London: Family Policy Study Centre

Family Policy Studies Centre. 1994. *Families in the European Union*, London: Family Policy Studies Centre

Ferguson, P.M. and Ferguson, D. 1989. What we want for our children: Perspectives of parents and children with disabilities. In D. Biklen, *Schooling and Disability*. Chicago: University of Chicago Press

Gartner, A., Lipsky, D. and Turnbull, T. 1990. *Supporting Families with a Child with a Disability: An International Outlook*. Baltimore: Paul H. Brookes Publishing.

Glendinning, C. 1983. *Unshared Care: Parents and their Disabled Children*. London: Routledge & Kegan Paul

Glendinning, C. 1992. *The Costs of Informal Care: Looking Inside the Household*. (SPRU Papers). London: HMSO

Hubert, J. 1991. *Home-bound: Crisis in the Care of Young People with Severe Learning Difficulties: A Story of 20 Families*. London: Kings Fund Centre

Kiernan, C. 1994. *Survey of Portage Provision 1992–3*. Winchester: National Portage Association.

Mason, M. and Rieser, R. 1994. *Altogether Better*. London: Comic Relief

Office of Population and Census Surveys (OPCS). 1989. *OPCS Surveys of Disability in Great Britain. Report 3: Prevalence of Disability Among Children. Report 5: Financial Circumstances of Families*. London: HMSO

Parker, G. 1990. *With Due Care and Attention*. London: Family Policy Studies Centre

Russell, P. 1994. *Developing a Policy of Family Support: New Ways of Working with Parents of Disabled Children*. London: Council for Disabled Children

Shah, R. 1992. *The Silent Minority: Children with Disabilities in Asian Families*. London: National Children's Bureau

Sloper, P. and Turner, S. 1992. Service needs of families of children with severe physical disability. *Child: Care, Health and Development*, **18**, 250–282

Social Services Inspectorate. 1994. *Services to Disabled Children and their Families: Report of the National Inspection of Services to Disabled Children and their Families*. London: HMSO

Wilkin, D. 1979. *Caring for the Mentally Handicapped Child*. London: Croom Helm

Chapter 8

The Fight for Self-Advocacy

Andrea Whittaker

This chapter looks back over twenty years of self-advocacy in the UK. It covers a period when there have been major changes in services for people with learning difficulties, not the least of which is a change in terminology from 'the mentally handicapped' to the current label of 'people with learning disabilities/difficulties'. It covers a period at the beginning of which it was considered progress to upgrade a hospital ward so that people had individually coloured bedspreads and their own bedside locker to the present day when people with learning difficulties run their own organizations and play an influential part in the development of services. The chapter attempts to draw out some of the lessons of these twenty years – what influences have had an effect, what have been the struggles and what have been the achievements.

THE BEGINNINGS

The 1970s saw tremendous changes in attitudes and in services to people with learning difficulties, spurred on by influences at home and from overseas. The 1971 Government White Paper, *Better Services for the Mentally Handicapped*, had set out a new vision of services for people with learning difficulties; some highly publicized scandals had focused not only the services' but also the public's attention on the disadvantages of institutional living. More thinking about people as individuals deserving dignity and respect and about their rights as human beings was being reflected in thinking about services. These changes were not only taking place in health and social services but also in education where, for example, the phrase 'no child is ineducable' – the title of one of Stan Segal's most important books – became a part of the language. Overseas, moves towards self-advocacy began in Sweden in the 1960s when courses were provided to teach people the skills of decision-making, committee work and voting, particularly to enable them to run their own social and leisure clubs. In 1970, a three-day conference was attended by 50 representatives from Sweden and Denmark. News of this spread to other countries including Canada, the USA and the UK. A similar conference was held in British Columbia in 1973. Three delegates from Oregon decided to set up their own organization for people with learning difficulties. This was the beginning of the People First movement in the USA.

In the UK, the first conference for people with learning difficulties, entitled 'Our Life', was held in 1972. From that time onwards, participation events and conferences organized by VIA (then the Campaign for People with Mental Handicap), MENCAP and others, continued and many training centres set up their own user committees.

In July 1984, 18 people from the London area (nine of them self-advocates) attended the first People First International Self-Advocacy Leadership Conference in Tacoma, Washington, USA, and as a result People First began in the UK.

ORGANIZATIONAL INFLUENCES

In 1971, the King's Fund appointed James Elliott to set up the Mental Handicap Project which, when it started, was about improving the lives of people in hospital. James Elliott had been so moved by dreadful conditions in his local mental handicap hospitals that he had written to the King's Fund expressing his concerns. He was subsequently invited to come and try and do something about it. He began linking up with other concerned professionals and thus began a period of intense activity which pushed services for people with learning difficulties higher up the health and social services agenda and provided many new opportunities for change.

Also in 1971, the Campaign for Mentally Handicapped People (now Values Into Action) was formed by a small group of people committed to empowering people with learning difficulties. As early as 1972, they organized participation weekends where people with learning difficulties met together as equals with staff and other supporters. Operating outside the service structure as an independent group, they have campaigned successfully for better services and promoted values of equality, dignity and respect in relation to people with learning difficulties.

In 1973 the Association of Professions for Mentally Handicapped People (APMH) (now called BRIDGES) was formed to help break down professional barriers and enable different professions to work together. If people with learning difficulties were to live ordinary lives, services needed to consider each person's life as a whole – housing, leisure, work, education – and this would not happen if services did not learn to work across the departmental barriers. APMH was the first national organization to involve people with learning difficulties as speakers at its annual conference in 1983.

Later in the 1970s, stories from Canada and the USA of people moving out of institutions and living in their local community began to filter back to the UK. People were fired with enthusiasm to try and develop similar services in the UK and this led to the publication in 1980 of the King's Fund's *An Ordinary Life* (King's Fund, 1980). This set out a vision of life in the community based on ordinary housing '. . . to see mentally handicapped people in the mainstream of life, living in ordinary houses, in ordinary streets, with the same range of choices as any citizen and mixing as equals with the other and mostly not handicapped, members of their own community'. It was followed by *An Ordinary Working Life* in 1984 and then *Ties and Connections* in 1988.

Very early on, the King's Fund started to include people with learning difficulties in conferences and held workshops which had teams of users and professionals working together. Training departments began to recognize the value of this by agreeing to pay for users to attend conferences as well as staff.

Slowly but surely, isolated examples of good practice became more generalized. Stories of people's lives being dramatically changed helped to convince the unconvinced. Service systems gradually began to change. The concept of 'an ordinary life' changed from being thought of as an unrealistic, trendy dream to being an essential principle underlying any worthwhile service development. However, though major change has been achieved, services still struggle with the challenge of overcoming the barriers which systems, by their very nature, seem to create, and which prevent the people they serve leading really ordinary lives.

SPEAKING UP FOR THEMSELVES

Alongside these organizational changes, attitudes and ways of working with individuals began to change. Enlightened staff in day centres and residential establishments started helping people to speak up for themselves. This in itself was something of a breakthrough. Historically, people with learning difficulties had not been thought capable of having opinions of their own, so first of all they had to learn that they had a right to speak up and make choices. This was often a very slow process. If someone has always made decisions for you, you have never been expected to speak up for yourself or to make any choices yourself and so it can take a very long time to build up these skills. Even something as simple as choosing between tea or coffee was a major achievement.

The introduction of personal programme plans was a real step forward in helping services think in terms of the needs of individuals rather than groups. Personal programme plans have gone through a number of variations, with different names (PPPs, PAPs, IPPs) and different emphases, but in spite of varying degrees of success in terms of how they are used, the degree of staff commitment and the outcomes for people, they have continued to be a way of focusing on individual wishes and needs and helping people to take some control of their lives. They have been a means of people gaining the sort of confidence that has led to joining or forming a centre committee or user group.

FACING NEW CHALLENGES

These new ways of thinking and working were strengthened by staff who were prepared to stand up for and support people's right to speak up. In those early days, this could be very difficult as it was often an isolated staff member in an otherwise hostile environment. Much training was needed to enlighten, persuade and challenge professionals to create and support new opportunities for people. There was a need to change the culture from one of 'they can't' to one of 'they can'. Many staff felt threatened by the new thinking.

There was a fear of losing their jobs, of losing control over people. The growth of a user voice asking for change to the old ways was seen as disruption, disobedience and in any case unrealistic. In many cases, services resorted to a tokenistic belief in self-advocacy – giving lip-service to the concept but not really taking people's requests seriously.

It was a difficult time, too, for many parents. Since services had been telling them for years that their sons and daughters could not cope in the ordinary world, they saw the new moves as threatening their son's or daughter's security. As people began to speak up for themselves and become more independent, parents also felt a sense of guilt – 'Why didn't I do this before?' – and also loss of self-esteem – 'I know my son/daughter best – how come that professional can do better?'

But also there were parents who welcomed the new moves with open arms as something they had always wished for their sons and daughters. They were prepared to take the necessary risks and 'let go'.

THE DEVELOPMENT OF SELF-ADVOCACY GROUPS

Most of the early activity in the UK relating to self-advocacy took place in day centres. In 1980, 22 per cent of centres had a group. By 1986 this had risen to 60 per cent (Crawley, 1988). In the early stages, group activities focused on specific local objectives like getting a vending machine for drinks, organizing social events, or improving relationships between staff and users (Whittaker, 1990).

Labelling

Gradually they began to take up broader issues. For many groups, the first issue was labelling, particularly getting rid of the words 'mentally handicapped', and many groups advocated successfully on their own behalf about different aspects of labelling. Members of a self-advocacy group in south London went to a meeting of their social services committee and asked for the term to be changed to 'people with learning difficulties'. As a result, the new term was adopted by the whole borough. At some day centres, people advocated for a change in how they were described (trainee/client/ student). Elsewhere, people campaigned to get devaluing labelling taken off minibuses.

Having service users themselves come and ask for changes was a revelation for many senior managers and others in influential positions and had a powerful effect on their decision-making.

People had learnt not only to say what they did not like but also to ask for it to be changed. They proved that they had opinions which should be valued and that they were capable of learning how to get things changed. They met together in conferences and workshops. This strengthened the self-advocacy movement and increased the influence they were having on the world around them. Services began to take their views seriously. People began to think more about working with users to develop services.

Rocking the boat

But with the increase in self-awareness and independence came new tensions and conflicts, sometimes between different groups of staff, sometimes between families and staff. For example, people were developing confidence and assertiveness at their day centre but this might not be allowed at home. Residential staff would find that their relationship with residents was changing and they were being challenged more. Parents were sometimes alarmed rather than pleased at the changes they noticed in their son or daughter. Some parents and staff reacted very defensively and negatively; others reacted more positively, saw this as a transition and moved through it to a more positive and open relationship.

In the desire to promote people's rights – and people's understanding of those rights – the need to understand responsibilities was often left out. This could lead to unrealistic expectations and demands being made by individuals and groups. It also meant new challenges for staff interpreting their relationship with service users. For example, if someone said they did not want to get up, had they the right to stay in bed all day? How was one to interpret a person's rights when it came to personal hygiene or social interaction?

Groups began to encounter battles with services. One of the earliest examples of this was the Southend ATC (Adult Training Centre) group who wanted to change their name from client to student (Williams and Schoultz, 1982). Groups in day centres were allowed to suggest minor changes but anything that involved real change was blocked. These days conflicts are more likely to centre around who controls the group and, in particular, who controls the funding for the group.

Becoming independent

As long as groups remained within the service structure and remained dependent on services, it was going to be extremely difficult for them to achieve major change. If people and structures which were supporting them were within the service system, there would always be a conflict of interest. Therefore, groups needed to be as independent as possible and their supporters also needed to be independent. Groups started to find places to meet away from day centres or other service venues and also to find supporters and advisers who would be independent of services. This need was recognized early on by Hillingdon Social Services who were one of the first to provide funds for their local People First group to meet in an ordinary community setting – a local church hall. Other areas soon followed suit and now most groups aim to start from the very beginning as an independent group with an independent adviser outside services.

People First

People First, now eleven years old, was fortunate in that it was independent right from the start. Being based at the King's Fund Centre, it had the advantage – unique in those early days – of meeting in an independent venue (away from services) and having independent advisers. The founding members came from various London boroughs and a supporters' group was formed to help the group develop. Now there is a network of People First groups around the UK working in various ways to promote the rights of people with learning difficulties and the development of better services.

Many groups concentrate on campaigning about local issues such as changes in their day centre. Others, like People First Northampton, work closely with the local authorities to improve services countywide. In Wales, early commitment to self-advocacy by the Welsh Office through its All Wales Strategy has been influential in enabling the development of People First Wales and its involvement in service change.

People First London Boroughs, partly because of its unique position as the founding group and its national profile, has had particular opportunities for growth during its ten-year history. It is run by a management committee made up entirely of people with learning difficulties and its office is staffed by people with learning difficulties as well as supporters. It undertakes a wide range of service development and has led successful campaigns such as getting rid of MENCAP's 'sad little Stephen' logo and changing the Charity Commission rulings relating to membership of management committees. It is also well known for its easy-to-read publications.

WORKING WITH SERVICES

It is undoubtedly true that the growth of self-advocacy, not only amongst people with learning difficulties, but also amongst other service users, has resulted in fundamental changes in service culture. Current community care legislation demonstrates this with its emphasis on the importance of users being involved, the importance of individual needs and the requirement on authorities to take this on board. Whilst it is still true that many more of the right words are said and written than action taken as a result, there is much more evidence of services and service users working together on many aspects of running and developing services.

Getting information

A basic need for anyone who wants to advocate for themselves or on behalf of others is good information. The written word is the most usual form of giving information about services, often in language which is full of jargon. In recognition of the need to make information accessible to people with learning difficulties, much work has been going on using tapes, video, signs, symbols, pictures and photographs. Most authorities began by making their information leaflets more accessible and have moved on to documents like complaints procedures. The Phoenix Trust in Bristol was the first authority to set up a department, Connect, specifically to produce material which service users would find easy to use (Whittaker, 1991).

Consultation

This is still the most common method of involving users to date, with widely varying degrees of effectiveness. Many workshops and conferences have been organized to give users the chance to say what they want from services. Every district should now consult users about their Community Care Plan. But although much has been written about how to consult effectively, good practice is still the exception rather than the rule.

Authorities that have been successful are those which have built in adequate time for the consultation; provided information in an easy-to-use format (simple written versions or on tape or pictorially); and made sure that users had their own supporters to assist with the whole process (Whittaker, 1993).

Participation

Some areas have moved on to working alongside people in the operation of services. Many users are involved as representatives on various committees and subcommittees within the service structure. In Clwyd, users are members of the County Planning Group; in Suffolk, subgroups within the local authority committee structure are now made up of equal numbers of users, parents and staff, thus going some way towards overcoming the problem of the one token user. In Surrey, a structure was developed which enabled users to collect the views and wishes of their peers and meet with managers on a regular basis to get things changed. The first issue tackled was having more control over their weekly personal money. This was achieved and the first users who learnt to look after their own money then helped others learn too. Quality Action Groups are another way of enabling people with learning difficulties to have an ongoing influence on how services are run (Milner, 1991).

Many self-advocacy groups and organizations are represented on local, regional and national committees which are influential in producing service change. More often than not, participation in this instance means attending meetings and the quality of the involvement will depend on how well the meeting involves service users. Are members prepared to stop using jargon? Are they willing to try different formats? What if the pace of the meeting slows down? What support will be available: taped minutes, summaries of background papers, an independent support person to help prepare for the meetings? Is the venue accessible, local and at times when users can attend?

User-led monitoring and evaluation

For some years now, researchers involved in evaluating services have recognized the importance of including the views of people with learning difficulties in their work, but it is only comparatively recently that users themselves have had the opportunity to design and carry out their own evaluations.

People First London Boroughs led the way with their evaluation of residential services in the London Borough of Hillingdon in 1990 (Whittaker *et al.*, 1990). Since then they have undertaken a much larger evaluation of two London boroughs (People First, 1994) and several smaller projects. Now it is possible to point to a small but growing number of other examples where people with learning difficulties have taken the lead in such work or have been involved as equal partners. In Plymouth, two users undertook interviewing and observation in local group homes, as part of an evaluation of catering and nutrition standards. In Dundee, day centre users undertook a survey of their local neighbourhood. In Bristol, people with learning difficulties have been involved in various research projects at the Norah Fry Centre.

Appointing staff

It is becoming increasingly common for people with learning difficulties to be involved in appointing staff. Usually their involvement is still on an informal basis – clients show prospective candidates around the day centre or group home, they interview the candidates informally and pass their opinions on to management. However, in some places a more structured system has been developed which enables people with learning difficulties to take part in the whole process in a more formal way, including influencing the final decision. As one person living in a group home said, 'It is important that we choose the staff we work with because we live at Claremont and it is our home. The staff finish their shift and go home. It is also us who pay their wages!' (Whittaker, 1991).

As might be expected, most examples of users being in control of appointing staff are from self-advocacy groups (appointing their own advisers) and self-advocacy organizations. Barriers to people being more widely involved in appointing staff are the attitudes of some local unions, the way equal opportunities policies are interpreted and the amount of training users would be expected to undertake.

Users bring a unique insight and perspective to the selection process. Because of their own life experience, they see and judge candidates in a way which is not possible for professional or other interviewers. They can also shed light on the way a candidate relates to and works with users. 'The person with learning difficulties had some speech difficulty and it was not always easy to understand him. This was an important factor in judging reactions/interaction between him and the candidate. Although he was not able to express himself in language very clearly, his gut reaction about the candidates was important' (Whittaker, 1991).

Staff training

Another important area of participation is staff training. This is most effective when staff and users are training together and has been developed considerably by organizations like Advocacy in Action (Nottingham), Skills for People (Newcastle) and People First. Training in this way can have a profound effect on staff. The following comments from some People First training are typical:

It was good that both users and carers worked together and also separately and could also freely speak in their ways.

All aspects were useful, especially learning alongside users and learning from users.

Self-advocacy training without having users involved would be a mockery.

Particularly enjoyed/recognize the importance of trainers who are also users.

The most useful part of the course was users and staff coming back together on the first day. The atmosphere was completely different. Equality was evident.

INCLUDING EVERYONE

Many supporters of self-advocacy are rightly concerned that everyone's voice is heard, in spite of how difficult this might be for some people. Much effort is being put into devising new ways of making it possible for even the most disabled people to take part. This ranges from enabling people to make very basic choices about everyday living through to enabling people to take part in the most sophisticated aspects of service planning and delivery. It includes releasing people's ability to communicate through methods such as Facilitated Communication, having people create their own 'language' of signs, symbols and pictures linked with training programmes for staff and carers which is being developed in Somerset and the picture dictionary of jargon service words being created by People First London Boroughs.

The positive side of all this activity is that without the influence of self-advocacy on service culture, it might never have happened. But it raises a number of questions. Are we concentrating too much on the 'tools' of communication? Tools on their own will not solve people's communication problems. Are they being used as an 'easy substitute' for the much more demanding challenge of spending enough time on a regular basis with individuals to get to know how each person communicates?

There is also a potential problem because so many different 'languages' are being developed. No currently available system seems adequately to meet the needs of self-advocacy and user involvement. Some current material which could be useful is not in an easily-transferable form for new users, for example computer programs. As a result, people are devising their own local resources using material from many different sources and adding their own. More often than not, they have to resort to drawing, photocopying and cut-and-paste methods to use this material – which is very time-consuming.

Are we defining a person's involvement too much by our usual criteria? We need to think more creatively about how people contribute. At a People First staff workshop for staff and users, users were having a session on their own. One young man did not like sitting for long periods in the room listening, and spent most of his time outside. But every so often he came to the door, looked around, smiled and went off again. Occasionally he stayed a bit longer watching. Was this just an unthinking mechanical behaviour pattern, or was it this person's way of saying 'I like this. I feel part of what's going on. I support what you are doing'?

There is a great need for more co-operation in this area, more thinking as to what is the right way forward – most importantly for the sake of people with learning difficulties themselves, but also to minimize the waste of resources, time and energy from so much overlap of effort.

WHY THE FIGHT NEEDS TO CONTINUE

In spite of all the progress during the last twenty years, it is by no means sure that self-advocacy is built on secure foundations. There are still many areas where it is relatively undeveloped. It is also a fact that in some areas, self-advocacy started strongly, apparently became well-established but has since declined. Why is this?

Relying on individuals

There is still too much reliance on the enthusiasm and commitment of individual supporters: groups can collapse if that person leaves. Self-advocacy is still often thought of as an optional extra, rather than as an essential part of people's lives. There is still a need to understand that self-advocacy is a way of life, not just a subject on a curriculum to be 'learnt' for an hour a week. Services need to have the strategies for enabling and supporting self-advocacy and user involvement so firmly embedded in their systems from top to bottom that they will survive changes in personnel or organization.

Taking enough time

Another reason is a lack of understanding of the time it takes and the support that is needed to lay firm foundations. For example, it has been common practice for a social work student on a six-month placement to be asked to establish a self-advocacy group. This is an impossible task in such a short time. Groups need consistent support over a long period in order to develop in a way that will enable members to be in control and in order that a long-lasting future for the group is ensured.

In areas where self-advocacy is undeveloped, speaking up is likely to be a new experience for people with learning difficulties. This is particularly true of people who are just about to leave hospital or who have recently moved out. Often these people have had less opportunity to speak up than their peers who have grown up in the community. Much time needs to be spent helping people understand that they have the right to speak up and the right to be critical and in helping them to learn to make decisions and to get the feel of what it means to be part of and running a group that could actually take steps to change things.

Groups that have survived, grown and developed have done so because they 'grew at a pace where the members understood the process and had power. The members were clear from the beginning that this was their group' (Worrell, 1988).

The pressures of development

In the early stages everything is new and exciting, there is a great feeling of solidarity, with everyone united in the same struggle. People experience the power of speaking out collectively. There is a strong sense of 'we are right and you are wrong'. The outside world looks on in amazement and applauds. However, as groups progress, they attract both greater expectation and greater criticism.

Leaders, in particular, can come under great pressure. For people with learning difficulties this is likely to be caused by being constantly in the spotlight, receiving many plaudits. However, as time goes on, one receives more critical judgement both from one's peers and the outside world. For supporters pressure is likely to come from the constant, delicate balancing act of providing the right amount of support but still enabling members of the group or organization to be in control. Where a group is not independent, conflict of interest becomes a problem for the supporter: should she or he be loyal to the group or loyal to the boss or the organization through which funding is being channelled to the group?

When the group develops to the point where they form their own organization, the challenges for supporters increase. Along with greater demands and expectations come greater responsibilities. A more sophisticated level of skills is required of members to carry out the work effectively. The supporter can find herself or himself caught between the expectations of the outside world and the desire to foster development of a genuinely user-controlled organization. As members learn new tasks and take more control, their relationship with supporters also changes. This can be very positive and rewarding. But it can also create new tensions – between individuals and between groups.

There is a danger of expecting too much too soon. People should not be pushed into the pace of the rest of the world: they need to progress at their own pace. On the other hand, they need to know how to work within a wider context if they are to be treated on an equal basis with other stakeholders who also have a valid voice. The self-advocacy movement needs to develop partnerships – both within the movement and with the outside world – which will consolidate the many achievements to date and ensure future progress. This means partnerships that allow for constructive criticism on both sides, that can include different points of view and that can share power. This will not always be easy, but it is necessary if people with learning difficulties are to be vital partners in the overall effort to improve their life choices and opportunities.

CONCLUSION

The development of self-advocacy in the UK is a story of amazing and exciting successes for many people with learning difficulties and the organizations they have founded. It is a story of much pioneering effort by many supporters who persevered with the struggle because they believed passionately in the right of people with learning difficulties to have more control over their lives. It is now difficult to imagine the field of learning difficulties without self-advocacy. Everyone agrees it is a good thing. But there is no room for complacency. The attitudinal and theoretical battle has been won, but the battle to turn theory into consistent good practice is still being fought.

In 1986, Gary Bourlet, a founder member of People First and one of the early leaders of the movement, said at a conference on working together:

It's very important that they take notice of what we have to say. In the past we were never given this opportunity, and it's great to have this opportunity for people to speak up for themselves for the very first time. I hope people from all organisations consider planning new services for our people, and bring self-advocacy into their new schemes. We also want people to be together again, not to be separated. It's this that people need to consider, to improve society, our livelihoods and the way we live.

Nearly ten years on, these goals are still relevant.

ACKNOWLEDGEMENT

I would like to acknowledge the valuable help of John Hersov in planning this chapter and commenting on drafts. John has been involved with the self-advocacy movement from the beginning and was adviser to one of the first groups, the Participation Forum based at London MENCAP. John now works freelance as a consultant and trainer in self-advocacy and related areas.

REFERENCES AND FURTHER READING

Crawley, B. *et al.* 1988. *Learning about Self-advocacy (LASA)*. London: Campaign for People with Mental Handicacp.
Crawley, B. 1988. *The Growing Voice: A Survey of Self-advocacy Groups in Adult Training Centres and Hospitals in Great Britain*. London: Campaign for People with Mental Handicap
Dowson, S. 1991. *Keeping it Safe: Values Into Action*, London,
Dowson, S. and Whittaker A. 1993. *On One Side*. London: King's Fund Project

King's Fund. 1980. *An Ordinary Life*. King's Fund Project Paper No. 24. London: King's Fund Centre.

King's Fund. 1984. *An Ordinary Working Life*. Project Paper No. 50. London: King's Fund Centre

King's Fund. 1988. *Ties and Connections: An Ordinary Community Life for People with Learning Difficulties*. London: King's Fund Centre

Milner, L. 1991. Collective Action. *LLAIS*, Autumn, 13–14, London.

People First. 1994. *Outside but not Inside... Yet! Leaving Hospital and Living in the Community: An Evaluation by People with Learning Difficulties*. London: People First.

Whittaker, A. 1990. *How Are Self-advocacy Groups Developing?* London: King's Fund Centre

Whittaker, A. 1990. Involving people with learning difficulties in meetings. In L. Winn, (ed.), *Power to the People*. London: King's Fund Centre

Whittaker, A. (ed.). 1991. *Supporting Self-Advocacy*. London: King's Fund Centre

Whittaker, A. (ed.). 1991, 1993. *Information Exchange on Self-Advocacy and User Participation*. Nos. 1, 5. London: King's Fund Centre

Whittaker, A., Gardner, S. and Kershaw, J. 1991. *Evaluation by People with Learning Difficulties*. London: King's Fund Centre.

Whittaker, A., Wright, J. and Bourlet, G. 1990. Setting Up for Self-advocacy. In T. Booth,(ed.), *Better Lives: Changing Services for People with Learning Difficulties*. Social Services Monographs. Sheffield: Joint Unit Social Services Research, University of Sheffield.

Williams, P. and Schoultz, B. 1982. *We Can Speak for Ourselves*. London: Souvenir Press

Worrell, B. 1988. *People First: Advice for Advisers*. Toronto: National People First Project

Chapter 9

Disability and the European Community: Sources of Initiative

Patrick Daunt

INTRODUCTION

In this chapter I shall give an account of the ways in which positive initiatives to promote a better quality of life for people with disabilities have taken place in the European Union, and of the contribution which lobbying on the part of organizations of or for disabled people has made to these. The account will be confined to what has happened at the European level and will not address the very different task of summarizing action of this kind within the various present or future Member States.

There are four principal characters in this story. These are the three chief institutions of the European Union – the Parliament, the Commission and the Council – and the non-governmental organizations (NGOs) active in this field on the European or international scene.

As for the European institutions, some knowledge of their powers, responsibilities and relationships is by now fairly widespread, even in the UK. There is a summary of their functions in my account of the origins and development of the Community's disability action programmes (Daunt, 1991).

Among of the NGOs, it is as important at the European level as it is within each country to distinguish those which are organized largely if not entirely *by* disabled people from those whose membership and management include professionals or parents who may be the predominant partners: whilst the latter organizations *for* disabled people represent the interests of disabled people, the former organizations 'of' disabled people represent, or claim to represent, disabled people themselves. Whilst both kinds of organization have been active in lobbying, those managed entirely by disabled people are generally associated with a more militant style; at the risk of over-simplification, we may say that they are particularly associated with the promotion of advocacy, independent living and equality of opportunity, and less associated with prevention, basic education or (more generally) the needs of children or older people. The relationship between the two kinds has not always been a happy one; the creation of Disabled People's International (DPI) by means of a breakaway from Rehabilitation International, which took place at the latter's world conference in Winnipeg in 1981, is an example of how this tension can become manifest. The approach of the European Commission has consciously been to encourage co-operation between the European examples of the two sorts of association by bringing them together in a common forum and by not showing favour to either.

As to the level of operations of the NGOs, activity at international level has generally preceded specifically European programmes. Increasingly, however, since the early 1980s, the larger organizations at least have established committees to co-ordinate co-operation between their members in countries of the European Union and to ensure their liaison with the European Commission; a number, as we shall see, have set up offices in Brussels for this purpose.

Evidently, the ways in which the relationship between these NGOs and the institutions of the Union has developed will form an important part of our story. They provide an interesting contrast with the experience and approach of the governmental international organizations. Of these, the United Nations in Vienna, in its follow-up to the 1981 International Year of Disabled People, and the International Labour Organization (ILO), notably at the time of the adoption of the Convention on Vocational Rehabilitation and Employment (ILO, 1983), have been more closely associated with the fostering of militancy than have, for example, the Organization for Economic Co-operation and Development (OECD) or the Council of Europe. The approach of the European institutions has been, predictably more complex – reconciliatory on the part of the Commission, haphazardly supportive on that of the Parliament and generally dismissive on that of the Council.

THE INTERNATIONAL YEAR: THE LEAD-UP AND THE EFFECTS

The 1970s

Selwyn Goldsmith, in an unpublished paper delivered at a Rehabilitation International seminar on housing and the environment held at Bois Larris in France in 1984, proposed an explanation of why the militant lobby of disabled people in the USA has been more effective than the one in Europe has been. In the USA, he argued, the traditional stress on self-reliance has motivated the formation of dynamic and assertive groupings of independent people determined not to become isolated, whilst in Europe a more collective social economy has tended to result in the isolation of disabled people as the individual clients of services. Certainly, at the European level, lobbying initiatives on the part of disabled people themselves played little or no part in the establishment of the Community's activities in the field of disability, were slow to emerge into any prominence in the 1970s and 1980s and have only recently applied anything approaching political pressure.

This does not mean that there was no lobbying of any kind in the wake of the adoption of the Commission's Social Action Programme (OJEC, 1974a). There was, but the agents were professionals. Before the International Year, the two significant actions of the Commission relevant to the needs of disabled people were the operations of the European Social Fund (ESF) and the co-ordination of a European Network of Rehabilitation Centres (OJEC, 1974b).

Whilst the objectives of the Network were confined to professional co-operation in the exchange of ideas and information, the Fund, through the operation of reciprocal study visit programmes and low-budget joint training sessions, was able to offer substantial financial support to vocational training programmes. From its earliest days until its so-called reform in 1983, disabled people were well served by the Fund in terms of both the number of beneficiaries and the range and quality of innovative endeavours supported (Mulhouse, 1982). Moreover, people with mental handicaps (as they were then invariably called) benefited both from the Fund and the Network quite as much as those with physical impairments did. (The benefits may not have been immediate, but they occurred very soon after the inception of these endeavours.)

Between the Fund and the Network there was an important operational relationship: the close contact with the Commission, and understanding of its not totally transparent ways of working, gave to member centres of the Network a particularly good opportunity to bring forward well-prepared and well-presented applications for financial grants from the Fund. Not untypically, this was never understood by what was then the Manpower Services Commission in Sheffield, which preferred to regard the Network with contempt. Very different was the approach of the Director of the National Rehabilitation Board in Dublin, John Furey, the effectiveness of whose perfectly lawful and correct lobbying activity in Brussels could be seen in the very substantial benefits afforded to the Irish Network members, the Rehabilitation Institute and the COPE Foundation in Cork. Equally productive was the work of Francesco Calmerini, of the independent organization ENAIP, in winning the support of the Fund to the implementation of the national policy of deinstitutionalizing 'democratic psychiatry', by means of the establishment of sometimes highly innovatory training centres and employment co-operatives throughout Italy. These benefits extended to other Italian members of the Network, such as the Don Calabria Centre in Verona, the Capodarco Community in Rome and the Centro di Addestramento in Bologna. In all these contexts, in both countries, people (including young people) with intellectual or psychological disabilities were the most prominent beneficiaries.

Certainly, the Irish and the Italians had the underlying advantage of the Fund's general priority in favour of regions of the Community assessed as being economically unfavoured. Yet the experience of Greece in the 1980s proved that without good management, of which effective lobbying is a part, such an advantage can fail to produce good results. Success obviously depends on the ability to deliver results in one's own country, but it also depends on a certain attitude towards the Community, its institutions and its officers. One cannot lobby an organization which one feels superior to or which one finds distasteful.

The International Year

The effect of the United Nations International Year of Disabled People in 1981 was to set off a concerted but what we might call 'unlobbied' series of initiatives undertaken by the European institutions, leading to the adoption at the very end of the Year of the First Action Programme to promote the social and vocational integration of disabled people. The process had two interesting characteristics.

The first is the quite astonishingly preponderant role of British people in bringing it about; it has all the appearance of an insular conspiracy. The MEP who started the whole initiative, the rapporteur who drew up the response of the Economic and Social

Committee, the desk officer who designed the Commission's programme proposal, the director in the Commission's service who backed it, the member of the responsible Commissioner's cabinet who put the finishing political touches on it, the Commissioner himself (Ivor Richard) who formally put it to the Council, the chairman of the Social Questions Group of the Council who drafted the enabling instrument, the chairman of the Committee of Permanent Representatives of the Member States, and finally the chairman (Norman Tebbit, no less) of the Social Council which formally adopted the programme – all these were subjects of Her Britannic Majesty.

The second remarkable feature was the copy-book behaviour of the three institutions, each performing its prescribed role to perfection, enhanced by the positive spirit in which they conducted themselves (OJEC, 1981a; 1981b; 1981c; 1981d). Looking at these two phenomena together, particularly as they manifested themselves in the context of the Council and its committees, we can see what a very different political world it was then compared the one in which we in the UK now find ourselves, as far as the Community is concerned. In the Social Questions Group of the Council, the diplomats were accompanied by national 'experts' competent in the field of disability and genuinely concerned to see effective action on the part of the Community; a whole new policy area, that of education, omitted for legal reasons from the Commission's proposal, was added at the demand of national representatives; and the British civil servant chairing the group formulated the draft Resolution in close consultation with the Commission and without any dilutions. At the next level in the process, the British deputy ambassador demolished the objections to the whole programme voiced by his Danish colleague by means of a volley of sublime invective.

Whilst the parliamentary rapporteur no doubt consulted as widely as time permitted, and the Commission evidently drew on its knowledge of professional preoccupations acquired in the operation of the Fund and the Network, there was throughout this whole process no example of active lobbying on the part of professionals, parents or disabled people. Yet, simply as a political process, what happened has intrinsic interest; and one of its chief consequences was to open up opportunities for lobbying which had never existed before.

The early 1980s: a lobby begins to emerge

One of the principal objectives of the First Action Programme launched in 1982 was to initiate a series of Community policy instruments intended over time – a period of about ten years was envisaged – to establish a comprehensive Community policy for the social, vocational and educational integration of disabled people.

It must be said at once that this endeavour has failed. Very likely it was too ambitious: the Commission's service has never overcome an initial lack of the resources of personnel needed to make such a difficult goal attainable. Moreover, during the later 1980s the political climate, in spite of the Social Charter, and in spite of the Maastricht Treaty, became steadily more hostile to progress at policy level in the field of disability, this deterioration of political will culminating in the recent fashion for the concept of subsidiarity which at the least imperils further advance at policy level if it does not actually exclude it.

The failure is all the more disappointing in view of the fact that the Commission's unique freedom to organize studies and meetings made it possible to have established, by the end of the First Action Programme in 1987, the technical basis for such policy instruments in all the fields of employment, transport and public access, and to be well on the way on the topic of housing too.

This technical progress, by which is meant a reasonably systematic knowledge of the needs and of the known effective measures for meeting them, was very largely due to the means of consultation which the Commission's freedom of initiative enabled it to set up. What happened was that the Commission, finding that there was no disability lobby, invented one.

By implication at least, this was the intention at the top level of the Commission: the small unit created with responsibility for managing the Action Programme was, exceptionally, called a 'Bureau'. Now, there were only two bureaux already existing in the Commission's headquarters services in Brussels, one for liaison with the 'social partners' (that is, the two sides of industry), and the other concerned with equality of opportunity for women. The term 'bureau' was therefore intended to designate a unit with a mandate to be more open to dialogue with its target population than would be normal practice in Brussels.

Powerful European lobbies of the two social partners existed already of course, but as for women so for disabled people: the lobbies had to be created by the Commission itself. Apart from anything else, disability NGOs have very limited funds to enable them to travel across frontiers in order to meet each other, let alone to pay for the expense of translation and interpretation which multicultural encounters in Europe generally require. (It is particularly hard for anglophones to have to learn the apparent paradox that you can organize an effective international meeting in one language (English) but that if you try to run a European encounter on that basis you will end up with a badly distorted participation.)

The Commission's plan consisted of three components. First, an annual programme of grants was established to enable disability NGOs to operate and to develop their activities and membership at European level. This encouraged the larger international NGOs to give higher priority to European work, and enabled entirely new European NGOs, for example, Autism Europe, to be created. The process of discussing programmes and managing grants brought the NGOs into close and generally friendly relations with the Commission's bureau, and enabled them to acquire a good understanding of the way the Community institutions work.

Amongst the most active of those taking part in this programme were the World Federation of the Deaf and the European Blind Union. A deaf representative of the UK Breakthrough Trust was the first individual disabled person to penetrate to the bureau's offices and demand what was on offer – the moment of the first conception of the lobby, one might say. This visit led to the first meeting in Brussels of deaf people from seven or so different Member States. It was a chaotic but seminal affair, the deaf representatives crowded together in a small room with an irrational assortment of spoken and sign language interpreters. The bureau invented a rule that, as a fair compensation for communication difficulties, the representatives of blind and deaf people should be allowed (against the regulations) to avail themselves, without charge, of the Commission's own rooms and spoken interpretation service for their main annual meetings. Over time progress was made, from reimbursement by the Commission of the travel costs of sign interpreters, to payment of their subsistence and finally to provision of a fee for their services. Meanwhile the European deaf community formalized their organization and set about establishing a means of electronic communication amongst their membership.

The second element in the plan for creating the lobby was the establishment of a Dialogue Group, which brought together once a year all the principal European disability NGOs for the exchange of information and ideas between each other and with the Commission's officials and experts. Within a few years, there were some thirty members of the group; each was allowed to send two representatives at Commission's expense, at least one of whom was encouraged (but not required) to be disabled. The group included the European level representatives of the International League of Societies for Persons with Mental Handicap (ILSMH), the World Federation for Mental Health (WFMH), Rehabilitation International, DPI, the Federation Internationale des Mutiles, des Invalides de Travail et Invalides Civiles (FIMITIC) and Mobility International, as well as the European Blind Union (EBU) and the European Community Regional Secretariat of the World Federation of the Deaf (WFD/ECRS). NGOs with other remits but with a close concern for disability were also represented, such a Eurolink Age and the Confederation of Family Organizations in the European Community (COFACE).

The third strategy for the development of the lobby was the organization by the Commission of multisectoral operational workshops as a regular element in the process of policy development. During the First Action Programme there were three of these – one was concerned with employment, another with mobility and transport and another with public accessibility. They were timed to take place after the Commission had completed its programme of policy studies on each theme and before the drafting of the policy instrument had begun. In these workshops, the NGO representatives worked with representatives of the Community's Network of Rehabilitation Centres and local integration projects, together with the Commission's experts. The understanding of Community possibilities and procedures which the NGOs had acquired ensured that their contribution had a direct influence on the development of policy; this qualitative element would not have been available without the co-operative programmes which had enabled them to develop a European perspective and European know-how.

Meanwhile the Parliament had also played a positive part, again one not so much of responding to a lobby as helping to create one. An informal All-Party Disablement Group, founded and run throughout this period by the MEP for Hertfordshire, Derek Prag, met regularly during plenary sessions of the Parliament in Strasbourg. Lack of a secretariat created difficulties, and too few other than British MEPs generally attended, but this was the one serious effort of the Parliament to give continuity to its concern for disabled people, and to develop contacts with, amongst others, disability NGOs. There were valuable initiatives on the part of individual MEPs too. The interest of an Irish member in the deaf community led to the holding of a hearing before the Parliament's Social Affairs Committee of representatives of deaf organizations and later to the adoption of a Resolution on the Official Recognition of Sign Languages within the European Community (OJEC, 1988b). Similarly, a Parliament hearing on mobility, followed by a Resolution on the Transport of Elderly and Handicapped Persons (OJEC, 1987), resulted from the personal initiative of a Spanish parliamentarian; this offered the opportunity, too, for close collaboration with the Commission, the hearing being organized in association with the Commission's workshop on the same theme.

Throughout this decade, then, the organizations of disabled people were playing an important and growing part in the development of European policy, but they were doing this largely in response to invitations from the Commission or the Parliament rather than on their own initiative. Even where there was effective political as well as technical activity within Member States, this did not translate itself into assertive European action. It is surprising, for example, that the Groupement pour les Personnes Handicapées Physiques (GIHP) in France, which could claim to be one of the oldest and most effective organizations in the world run entirely for disabled people by disabled people, did not endeavour to influence European programmes and policies through parliamentarians or by other means; this may reflect a general French failure to grasp the potential of the Community outside the purely economic domain.

Indeed, France was prominent in the initiation of what were probably the most impressive actions of European militancy during this period, but significantly this was outside the Community context. Two congresses organized by Les Paralyses de France in Strasbourg were the only large-scale European encounters of disabled people during these years; from them has come the still active European Network for Independent Living. A very different European network also originated from France: a parent of a son with learning difficulties, Francois Vittecoq, set up 'Euramis', a collaborative network of parents and professionals concerned with mental disability. Here, however, exchange of experience rather than lobbying was the primary objective.

Inexperience with working with a number of cultures has pitfalls. At the first full conference of the Commission's network of local projects, a group of disabled people from Lambeth brought forward, without warning, a resolution demanding that in future at least half the members of all delegations to such conferences should be disabled people. This proposal was put forward 'on behalf of the disabled people at the conference'. However, the two project leaders who were disabled had not been involved in the initiative, which thereupon collapsed in such a way as to rule out what it intended to promote for the rest of the programme.

One problem for disabled people, which came out most clearly in the behaviour towards the Community's programme of DPI, reflected an ambiguity if not a hostility towards the Community itself. For several years DPI, still at this time weak in a number of Community countries, was represented at meetings of the Dialogue Group by young Scandinavians from outside the then Community, not all of whom were likely to be lovers of what has been seen as a 'rich man's club'. Moreover the Commission's strategy of developing relations with NGOs by means of grant aid as well as consultation was not necessarily welcome to militant disabled people inclined to associate subvention with an outmoded and unacceptable tradition of charity.

In substance, this default was compensated by the solid contribution of other principal NGOs. The European secretaries of Rehabilitation International regularly adapted their seminar programme to Community priorities; the International League held in Hamburg a major European conference in which important progress was made in the active participation of people with learning difficulties; and Mobility International undertook highly innovatory annual programmes for disabled people and professionals, a number of these extending to the geographical margins of the Community or involving severe disabilities, such as deaf-blindness and autism; and so on. However, there may have been a real danger that good relations with the Commission, and so the emerging European disability lobby, would be monopolized by what might be perceived as an 'establishment' of parents and professionals, if the organizations of blind people and even more prominently the European deaf community had not set about participating in all aspects of the programme with such gusto and creativity.

THE SECOND DECADE (1985–1995)

The downside: a deteriorating political climate

The last ten years have seen two countervailing developments in the endeavour to promote a better quality of life for disabled people by means of action at the level of the European Community, now known as the European Union.

The first has been a marked deterioration in the political context and climate in which this endeavour is set. Whilst the financial interventions of the European Social Fund have been reinforced and extended by means of the Horizon programme, all attempts on the part of the Commission to make progress in the development of disability policy have proved more or less abortive.

The decline in the political will of the Member States was made only too clear by the response of the Council to the Commission's draft Recommendation on the Employment of Disabled People in the European Community (OJEC, 1986). No 'experts' with an actual understanding of the field of disability were now included in the national delegations on the key Council committee. In addition, powerful countries such as France and Germany that should have supported the Commission's proposal did nothing of the kind, no doubt by arrangement with others, notably the UK, which was determined to prevent an outcome with any force in it. And so the weak document eventually adopted achieved the remarkable result of having no effect at all. By way of epitaph, this reality was elegantly expressed by the Council itself three years later: 'The Recommendation has offered a Community reference framework for measures which were being prepared when it was adopted' (OJEC, 1989).

As planned, the next policy initiative of the Commission concerned mobility and transport (OJEC, 1991a). This time it took the form of a draft Directive (i.e. once adopted, a constraining legal instrument). In order for it to be eligible for adoption by majority rather than unanimous vote of the Member States, the Commission brought it forward under Article 118A of the Treaty (*Bulletin of EC*, 1986), which deals with the living and working conditions of workers. Whatever the detailed merits and demerits of the proposal, it constituted a courageous first endeavour to legislate in favour of disabled people at the level of the Community, and as such was doomed to fall victim to the scourge of the subsidiarity principle. There was hope that as the UK government took over the presidency of the European Community it might offer a counter-proposal of a more specific but equally constructive character, but by then (late in 1991) the advance of the subsidiarity plague had gone too far for that to be possible. It appears that the Commission is still intending to 'press for the adoption of the proposal for a directive on transport for workers with reduced mobility' (Helios, 1994), but the chances of success cannot be good.

Not everything that has happened in the realm of policy is as bleakly negative as that. Whilst intervention on the part of the Parliament was the principal cause of delay in the adoption of the second Helios programme to promote integration, and it was a Dutch member who played the leading part in this (OJEC, 1991b; 1993), it was also a Dutch minister who initiated through the Council (OJEC, 1992) a second proposal for action on mobility, involving a more flexible approach than the Commission's draft directive. Champions of subsidiarity succeeded in delaying any practical follow-up to this, but not in the end in preventing it: the Commission has presented an Action Programme on mobility (European Commission, 1993), a somewhat opaque document perhaps but containing the only promise of policy proposals related to disability which can be said to be currently in serious contention.

Meanwhile the most dramatic of all the failures to make progress with important policy implications has concerned the Union's own personnel. The Commission's modest proposal that a mere 25 posts in its services should be reserved for disabled people (a self-imposed quota of about 0.25 per cent, compared with a 6 per cent mandatory quota for both public and private sectors in Germany), was rejected by the Council on financial grounds. This is shocking certainly, but not in the least surprising; anyone with direct experience of the Budget Committee of the Council would know that it would be incapable of any other decision.

To understand these impediments to progress, we need to set them in a wider context of social policy. The principle of subsidiarity has enabled the German government to do what it has for years longed to do, which is to obliterate the Union's Anti-Poverty Programme. At the Council of Ministers of Social Affairs under the German presidency, the Commission's proposal for a new programme to combat exclusion and promote solidarity was not on the agenda.

Even the Commission itself, it must be admitted, has proved capable of taking a restrictive rather than an inclusive approach to policy development. What was first conceived as a fundamental charter of social rights for all citizens ended up as a Social Charter for Workers, the word 'social' here approximating to its narrowest French use, meaning little more than 'industrial'. In the badly drafted Article 118A of the Treaty (*Bulletin of EC, op. cit.*), the expression 'improvements, especially in the work place' has been generally interpreted as if it meant 'exclusively in the work place', and the parts of the Action Programme of the Social Charter which concern 'living and working conditions', important as they are in their own right, do not reach beyond the normal preoccupations of labour law. And there is the threat (at least) of worse to come: the senior British Commissioner, Leon Brittan, has proposed a rationalization of the Union's corpus of policy into a reduced number of portfolios, one of which would be 'competition, including education, social affairs and research'. It would be hard to go much further, in a certain direction, than this, and hard to imagine a direction less favourable to the aspirations of people with physical or mental disabilities.

The upside: the lobby grows in strength

In spite of, or perhaps because of, this worsening of the political context, the last decade has seen a compensating growth in the range of operations, representativity and effectiveness of the disability lobby.

The most dramatic manifestation of this enhancement occurred during the early days of the first Helios programme. A campaign was initiated and co-ordinated by the European Community Regional Secretariat of the World Federation of the Deaf (ECRS-WFD) aimed at bringing about a significant increase in the budget available to the Commission's bureau for the implementation of the programme, and in particular that element of it which supported the activities of NGOs. The deaf community won the support of all the principal European or international disability NGOs, with the exception (I do not know why) of DPI. Experience of the European scene acquired during the First Action Programme enabled the campaigners to lobby the Social Affairs and Budget Committees of the Parliament so effectively that the extra credits were conclusively voted; the effort was a total success. It is extremely difficult for voluntary organizations even to keep track of what decisions are being made, and when and where they are being made, during the complex process of establishing the Union's annual budget. To have actually influenced the process so exactly according to plan was a triumph of energetic and precisely targeted lobbying.

A lesson that has been well learnt is the importance of keeping in touch with what is going on by actively seeking out information – those who think that what they need to know is going to drop from the sky are left with nothing. Not so long ago, the International League and COFACE were the only NGOs with a major concern for disability having their own offices in Brussels. Now they have been joined by ECRS-WFD, Rehabilitation International, Eurolink Age and Mobility International. Recent dramatic improvements in the newsletters of the League, DPI and Rehabilitation International reflect a complementary awareness of the importance of quality in dissemination of information as well as in its acquisition.

When the first Helios programme was being designed in 1987, the Commission proposed that there should be one advisory committee to assist the Commission in the implementation of it, on which the governmental delegations of the Member States and the representatives of the organizations of and for disabled people should sit as equal members. That proposal was blocked, the UK being the first country to come out in opposition to it. The inequality still persists: the governments and the NGOs meet together with the Commission in an informal liaison group, whilst the governments retain their formal discussions with the Commission on their own (OJEC, 1988a). In contrast, for years now in the Social Fund committee (for example) and the advisory committee for vocational training, governmental representatives have had to sit as equals with those of the social partners, just as they do in the ILO. Disabled people, it must be clearly understood, are officially still assigned to the margin.

In spite of this setback, there has been, thanks to the Commission, the Parliament and the NGOs themselves, some progress in the instruments of consultation available to disabled people in Europe. Still during the first Helios programme, the NGOs in 1990 extended the opportunity offered by the annual meetings with the Commission for the disability forum to set up its own independent body, 'NGOs in Consultation'. This gave it 'a reinforced facility for exploring common positions in advance of formal meetings with the Commission, and for planning other initiatives in relation to the European Institutions' (Daunt, *op. cit.*).

The delayed adoption of the second Helios programme in February 1993 brought to the process of consultation progress of a different kind. For the first time the disability forum comprised, as well as 12 European NGOs, representatives of national 'umbrella' organizations in each of the then 12 Member States. It must be said at once that the character of this national representation is not altogether satisfactory. Whilst it may or may not be a good thing that in some countries, such as France and the UK, new groupings for this specific purpose have had to be created since none suitable existed already, there can be no question that there are in the forum previously existing national organizations from other countries which do not represent all disabled people. This is particularly evident in the case of Germany and the Netherlands, whose national member organizations on the forum do not represent people, or the interests of people, with learning difficulties, still less those of users of mental health services. It is indeed doubtful to what extent the interests of mental health service users are represented amongst the national members of the forum at all. In the case of Germany, the present arrangement is so obviously unacceptable as to put the process of selection into question.

None the less, the addition to the forum of national members as well as European ones is a step forward and potentially an extremely important one. The reason for this is that all final decision-making power in the Union rests with the Council of Ministers, the one of the three institutions (as we have seen) with by far the worst record in the disability field. Now, the Council consists of the appropriate ministers of national governments, advised by their civil servants operating either in the national capital or on secondment to their embassies in Brussels. These are people most of whom neither know nor care what European disability NGOs exist, let alone what their opinions may be on any issue. They can only be influenced back at home, and, as far as the voluntary sector goes, it is only national NGOs that can do that. As members of the European forum NGOs will now for the first time have the information and motivation which will enable them to play that part. The introduction within the second Helios programme of a Union-funded series of national information days in all the Member States should further help to foster national lobbying on European issues.

Meanwhile there has been substantial and significant progress in the active involvement of militant people with motor disabilities in the promotion of good European policy and practice. The second meeting, in 1989, of people with severe disabilities in Strasbourg was followed by another in the Netherlands in 1990. This established an effective pressure group, the European Network on Independent Living (ENIL), closely linked to DPI. As well as 'Disabled People's International Europe', there is now a European Communities Committee of DPI, and in Maastricht in 1993 DPI organized an event under the title 'EURABLE – the first European Conference of People with a Disability' (EURABLE, 1993). The idea of funding support from the European Commission now seems to be accepted.

Also in 1993, the establishment of 3 December each year as the European Day of Disabled People gave to DPI the opportunity it had been looking for both for manifestation of its priorities and for leadership of European militancy. A critical breakthrough occurred when the disabled people who came together in Brussels on that occasion were permitted, after an initial refusal, to use the hemicycle of the European Parliament there. On the same date the following year further progress was made when the report on 'human rights' emerging from the EURABLE conference was presented in the Parliament building to an audience which included 30 members of Parliament. As well as stressing the duty of governments to remove the social, economic and environmental barriers which face disabled people, the report attacks the notion that disabled people's lives are tragic, with its implication that prenatal diagnosis offers the final solution to disability.

In parallel with these initiatives, developments of equal importance have taken place within the International League of Societies for Persons with a Mental Handicap

(ILSMH). In 1991 a young Canadian woman with this disability, Barb Goode, started a President's Committee on Self-Advocacy, and in 1992 she became the first self-advocate elected to the Council of the International League. By 1993 it was possible to organize in the Netherlands a meeting of self-advocates from eight countries, including four Member States of the Union (the UK, the Netherlands, Germany and Sweden). The members of the meeting were accompanied by their support people, the clear definition of whose role has been one of the most seminal of the early achievements of the group.

As to the Parliament, it is reasonable to hope that the new membership will achieve a more positive and consistent record in the matter of disability than their predecessors. In 1986 the Parliament made many brave threats and promises concerning the employment of disabled people – yet nearly a decade later, there was nothing perceptible to show for them. Now, the signs so far are encouraging: the All-party Disablement Group is not only to continue, under the new chairmanship of the German MEP Ms Barbara Schmidbauer, but has also established a secretariat in Brussels. There is a very good chance that long-standing and intransigent problems of communication and continuity will at last be overcome.

THE FUTURE OF THE LOBBY

Significant commitment on the part of the European Commission and Parliament to the promotion of a better quality of life for disabled people derives, as we have seen, from an initiative of the United Nations, in the designation of 1981 as the International Year of Disabled People. Now that the United Nations is under such heavy attack from trendy illiberals and neo-nationalists, it is gratifying as well as appropriate to see that it is now another UN initiative which is offering the framework for a second critical development in the vision which the European institutions have of their role and of the potential of their contribution. I am referring to the *Standard Rules on the Equalization of Opportunities for Persons with Disabilities* (United Nations, 1994). It is highly encouraging that the Commission's responsible service has already declared its intention to 'prepare an appropriate instrument endorsing the UN Standard Rules' (Helios, 1994).

Recent interchange between government and a widely based disability lobby in the UK demonstrates how progress can be made, even against the most obdurate opposition. In the years leading up to and into the next century, we can look forward with some confidence to the emergence at European level as well of the same quality of campaigning for disabled people's rights. Certainly unless there is to be some big political change – something more fundamental than the new Nordic Council members (Sweden and Finland) will be able to bring about on their own – there will be no diminution of the need for campaigning skill and determination of high quality. The most likely future is one of a heightening of the democratic combat between an increasingly effective lobby and entrenched, budget-cutting governments.

This is not a pessimistic prediction; solid headway is a real possibility. Yet there is a hidden danger which threatens the interest of people with learning difficulties, as well as users of mental health services and all older people and children with disabilities, and which needs to be brought out into the open.

In an important and obvious way, it is correct and enlightened of the Commission to specify the priority it gives in the second Helios programme (OJEC, 1991b) to organizations 'of' rather than 'for' disabled people. It is not, however, at all certain that associations which only include disabled people as members will in the foreseeable future be the best vehicles for representing the interest of people with learning difficulties, users of mental health services or people with multihandicaps, or indeed for that matter the generality of children or old people with disabilities. To take the last point first: by far the majority, some 70 per cent or more, of disabled people are elderly. I do not see that they are, as a general rule, directly represented in the active groups of militant disabled people, let alone forming a majority amongst them. Since their juniors do not have experience of ageing, their claim to speak on behalf of those who do have that experience does not appear to constitute more than the kind of indirect representation which the more militant lobby does not typically regard as authentic. Besides, as well as 'long-term' disabled people who encounter ageing ('the elderly disabled'), there are quite as many who encounter disability for the first time in association with advancing age ('the disabled elderly') and who may have very different life experiences and expectations (Daunt, 1990).

We have seen the progress that the ILSMH is making in facilitating self-advocacy amongst those of its members who have the disability, and there can be no doubt that further progress in this direction will take place in the years ahead. None the less – or even for that very reason – it is at least arguable that for the foreseeable future the League will be the better vehicle for the international promotion of the interest of people with learning difficulties than any existing or imaginable organization with a purely disabled membership. If this is right, a policy which excludes from its highest priority any organization with a mixed membership of professionals, family members and disabled people would render a disservice to people with learning difficulties amongst others.

The problem would not appear to be simply one of principle. The degree of prominence which is given by physically disabled adults in the prime of life to the promotion of independent living as a prime objective, if not the prime objective, of policy may not be altogether appropriate to the needs of those with learning difficulties or histories of mental illness. There are dangers in over-protective or merely selfish paternalism, of course – equally, there is plenty of evidence of what happens if too much independence is forced on people who cannot manage it and may not want it. Independence may be an important component of a good quality of life for most adult people, but its relative importance compared to other components will vary both from one person to another and at various times in the life of any individual. It is one thing to agree that children and young people with disabilities need to be educated and trained for a future of more or less independent living but adults must also recognize that the quality of life of children needs to be made up of components which reflect their actual needs and desires during childhood itself and that independence may figure as one of the less prominent amongst them.

All this is relevant to the future development of the disability lobby in Europe, and to what might be done to optimize it. It would be good to see a disability forum actively lobbying the European Parliament as well as advising the Commission on the development of policy. Its capacity to do these things successfully would only be increased if organizations 'for' disabled people such as ILSMH had a guaranteed future of equal representation and equal accreditation with those associations having a purely disabled membership. This equality could be both validated and manifested if all member associations of the forum were required to be represented by a person with the disability, who could be accompanied by one other. This other person might be a disabled colleague, a friend (who might or might not be a partner, parent or other family member) or a professional (for example, a sign interpreter or a personal assistant).

A forum composed in this way would have the technical knowledge, the political clout and the moral standing to bring to bear the democratic pressure that will be needed if the European Union is to follow the path that the United Nations has laid out. Anything less firmly constructed will not do.

CONCLUSIONS

If we have in mind again the four 'characters in the story' which we identified at the beginning of this chapter, the three institutions of the Union and the NGOs, we can identify five lessons emerging clearly from the experience of the last two decades:

1. The 'empowerment' of disabled people on the European scene will depend to a large extent on the technical and moral strength of the *forum of disability NGOs*.

   The first conclusion is therefore that any weakness in the representativity of the forum must be put right. At the level of the European organizations, this will involve giving equal status to the representatives of the users of mental health services. The Commission will need to resist the tendency of national officials, notably from Germany, to behave as if such people do not exist, or, if they do, at least should not be talked about. It will be important also to maintain the influence of the 'transverse' associations, such as EASE and COFACE on behalf of children with special needs and Eurolink Age for older people with disabilities. Even more important will be the need to ensure that the national representatives on the forum are authentic 'umbrellas' which can speak for those with 'mental' as well as physical impairments, for older disabled people and for the interests of disabled children. It would be good to see the Commission taking a strong line here, establishing rigorous criteria and refusing a place at the table for any national representative failing to meet them.

2. The *European Commission* has been a consistently good friend to disabled people. The strength of its role has been based in the official unit (sadly, no longer called a bureau) responsible both for the design and operation of the Action Programmes and the preparation of policy instruments. The latter task is much harder than the former, however. A weakness in the quality of the few draft policy instruments which the Commission's service has presented is palpable and had better be admitted. The reason for this is that the unit has always been critically under-manned, owing to the relatively low priority afforded to its work within the Social Action Programme as a whole. Traditionally and understandably, the Commission resists any attempt on the part of the Parliament to influence its personnel arrangements. The only means for putting this right therefore is a direct approach to the Commissioner, currently Padraig Flynn.

Consequently, the second conclusion is that the disability lobby, once strengthened in the way I have described, should bring pressure to bear on the Commissioner to afford to the disability unit in the Commission's services the resources of personnel essential to enable it to perform its political task.

3. We have seen that the underlying, occasionally 'outcropping', goodwill of the *European Parliament* has suffered from a lack both of continuity of concern and of understanding of the issues.

   The third conclusion is the simple one that the Parliament should give official recognition to the disability forum of NGOs as its regular interlocutor on disability questions in general, and in particular in relationship to the now reinforced All-Party Disablement Group of MEPs. This will have the double effect of increasing the status, understanding and influence of the forum and enhancing the regularity, relevance and knowledge base of the work of the parliamentary Group.

4. The greatest weakness of the disability lobby, as with many other lobbies, is at the point of greatest importance, that is in relation to the *Council of Ministers*. In the more favourable political climate of the mid-1970s to the mid-1980s this hardly mattered. During the last decade its critical character has become increasingly apparent, and in the future failure to correct it might well entail the futility of all other effort. Its recent refusal to honour its own commitments in the matter of the secrecy of its proceedings makes it all too clear that the Council will defend its exemption from the normal processes of democracy with the utmost vigour and skill.

   Our fourth conclusion then is that, provided its national representation is reformed on the lines suggested, the forum should devise something entirely new, that is a strategy for the systematic and effective lobbying of the Council. The plan will need to operate at two levels, of which the national is most important: this will involve carefully planned lobbying by each national forum representative of individual national parliamentarians, and even more importantly of relevant national parliamentary committees and responsible national ministers, whenever a European Union initiative of relevance to disabled people is under discussion, and above all before a proposal is about to come before the Council of Ministers for decision. To this it would be useful to add a second line of attack, at the European level itself, by means of a forum lobby and press conference in Brussels organized whenever Ministers, such as those of Social Affairs, Employment or Transport, were meeting in Council with an item of concern to disabled people on their agenda.

5. So much for the development of the lobby and the processes of lobbying. What about the *objectives and the agenda*? The vision formed within the Commission's bureau in 1982 of the gradual accumulation, item by item, of a global European policy for the disabled citizens of Europe has not been realized. The arrival on the scene of the United Nations *Standard Rules* offers, however, the opportunity for a new and quite different approach.

   The fifth conclusion is evidently that the declared intention of the Commission's disability unit to 'endorse' the *Standard Rules* by means of an 'appropriate instrument' affords the hope that we may see, within the duration of the second Helios programme, the adoption of a Council Resolution or Decision setting out the framework – the legal basis, scope and objectives – of a comprehensive Union policy aimed at promoting and ensuring the best possible quality of life for disabled people. Such an instrument could mandate the Commission to bring forward proposals for Directives and Decisions on specific topics according to an agreed work programme.

If this could be achieved, the Union would be found taking a lead in the inevitably continuing competition for resources and the battle for men's minds. Clearly, however, without success in reaching the goals described above in the first four conclusions, there is very little chance of any progress at all in the direction of the fifth.

REFERENCES

Bulletin of EC. 1986. Supplement 2/86: Single European Act. Luxembourg: European Commission

Centre de Readaption. 1982. Seminaire sur l'aide du Fonds Social Europeen en faveur des personnes handicapées. Mulhouse: Centre de Readaptation

Daunt, P. 1990. *Age and Disability: A Challenge for Europe.* Report of a European seminar organized by Eurolink Age in Florence, 15–17 March 1990. London: Eurolink Age

Daunt, P. 1991. *Meeting Disability: A European Response.* London: Cassell

EURABLE. 1993. *'Pride in Ourselves'.* First European Conference of People with a Disability. Maastricht: Stichting Eurable

European Commission. 1993. Report from the Commission to the Council concerning the actions to be taken in the Community regarding the accessibility of transport to persons with reduced mobility. COM (93) 433 of 26 November 1993

Helios. 1994. *Helios Flash 6.* Brussels: European Commission

ILO (International Labour Organization). 1983. Convention No. 159 on the vocational rehabilitation and employment of disabled people. Geneva: ILO

OJEC (*Official Journal of the European Communities*). 1974a. Resolution of the Council of 21 January 1974 concerning a social action programme. OJ No. C13/1 of 12 February 1974. Luxembourg: European Commission

OJEC. 1974b. Resolution of the Council of 27 June 1974 establishing the initial Community action programme for the vocational rehabilitation of handicapped persons. OJ No. C80/30 of 9 July 1974

OJEC. 1981a. Resolution of the Parliament of 11 March 1981 concerning the economic, social and vocational integration of disabled people in the European Community. OJ No. C77/27 of 6 April 1981

OJEC. 1981b. Opinion of the Economic and Social Committee of 18 April 1981 on the situation and problems of the handicapped. OJ No. C230/38 of 10 September 1981

OJEC. 1981c. Communication of the Commission to the Council of 14 November 1981: The social integration of disabled people – A framework for the development of Community action. OJ No. C347/14 of 31 December 1981

OJEC. 1981d. Resolution of the Council and of the governments of the Member States of 21 December 1981 on the social integration of disabled people. OJ No. C347/1 of 31 December 1981

OJEC. 1986. Recommendation of the Council of 24 July 1986 on the employment of disabled people in the Community. OJ No. C225/43 of 12 August 1986

OJEC. 1987. Resolution of the Parliament of 16 September 1987 on the transport of elderly and handicapped persons. OJ No. C281/87 of 12 October 1987

OJEC. 1988a. Decision of the Council of 18 April 1988 establishing a second Community action programme for disabled people (Helios). OJ No. L104/38 of 23 April 1988

OJEC. 1988b. Resolution of the Parliament of 17 June 1988 on the official recognition of sign languages within the European Community. OJ No. 187/1 of 18 July 1988

OJEC. 1989. Conclusions of the Council of 12 June 1989 on the employment of disabled people in the European Community. OJ No. C173/1 of 8 July 1989

OJEC. 1991a. Proposal for a Council Directive on minimum requirements to improve the mobility and safe transport of workers with reduced mobility. OJ No. C68/7 of 16 March 1991

OJEC. 1991b. Proposal for a Council Decision establishing a third Community action programme to assist disabled people, Helios II (1992–1996). OJ No. C293/2 of 12 November 1991

OJEC. 1992. Resolution of the Council and of the representatives of the governments of the Member States meeting within the Council of 16 December 1991 concerning a Community action programme on the accessibility of transport to persons with reduced mobility. OJ No. C18/1 of 21 January 1992

OJEC. 1993. Decision of the Council of 25 February 1993 on the establishment of a third Community action programme in favour of disabled people (Helios II 1993–1996). OJ No. L56/30 of 9 March 1993

United Nations. 1994. *Standard Rules on the Equalization of Opportunities for Persons with Disabilities*. New York: United Nations

Part II

Changing Practice

Chapter 10

Changing Classroom Practice

Jean Garnett

BACKGROUND

Legislation during the last two decades has brought about unprecedented change in education. Through the years of turbulence and political hype, a 'quiet revolution' has been taking place in the way schools in general recognize and address the special educational needs which emerge in them. This has had a profound effect on many schools' approaches to the whole curriculum and general classroom practice.

Towards the end of the 1960s, as the integration movement was gaining momentum, Oxfordshire was one of the first LEAs to provide special education attached to ordinary schools. When I joined Bicester School in 1969 to set up the Progress (ESN) Unit, the county educational psychologist said kindly, 'You just look after them, my dear. You won't teach them to read; just make them happy.' But I was a teacher and I expected to teach! This small incident gives some indication of the kind of attitude towards children ascertained as 'educationally subnormal' that was prevailing at that time. If such was the message from the powers that be, where did the practitioners stand?

Across the service it seemed to be accepted that for children with special educational needs, whether in remedial departments or special schools, there existed a kind of ability barrier (the 'glass ceiling') which was unsurpassable and that therefore the curriculum for them must be different from that available to pupils in the mainstream. This meant in effect that the longer a child remained in the special environment the slimmer were his chances of getting out of it.

During a visit to a well-regarded special school one girl asked me, 'Miss, do you teach people like us?' Jane's question sparked off a thoughtful discussion with this small group of 15-year-olds who did not see themselves as being essentially different from others in ordinary schools but were made to feel so. Later in the staffroom I observed, 'Jane's an interesting girl, isn't she?' The ensuing silence was broken by the remark, 'She's not as intelligent as she seems, you know.' The 'glass ceiling' was firmly in place for Jane.

The saddening aspect of this was the teacher's complete lack of awareness of the implications of such judgements for youngsters like Jane: that they would only serve to restrict intellectual growth and the pupils' capacity to explore their own thinking power and learning potential.

This phenomenon was not uncommon at that time in special schools and remedial departments and I believe it had a profound effect on both the self-esteem of many children and the quality of teaching, in that it encouraged a kind of hopelessness in the pupils and a damping down of optimism in their teachers.

Teaching in the special needs field often tended to be narrow, restrictive and unstimulating because a substantial number of teachers took posts in remedial departments and special schools not because they had a particular vocation or training but because they had failed to make the grade in the mainstream or thought it was easier or less traumatic. Frequently teachers who had problems in ordinary schools were offered positions in the peripatetic remedial services. The result was a strangely mixed bag, with highly competent, committed practitioners at one end of a wide spectrum and teachers coping as much with their own problems as with their pupils' at the other. (This was particularly true in schools for educationally subnormal and maladjusted pupils.) It was not surprising, therefore, that in many establishments, the backcloth of educational expectation for these children was low and the curriculum dull and unchallenging.

To compound the situation, the world of special and remedial education created its own professional mystique and this encouraged teachers in the mainstream to consider themselves unqualified and unskilled to deal with such children. Because special children were thought to need a special (different) curriculum delivered by specially trained experts, teachers in ordinary classrooms tended to give up the unequal struggle of coping with the hard to teach. The 'experts' had the answers. The emphasis was on what a child could NOT do, rather than on the positive characteristics and capacities he/ she might bring to bear on a situation. Thus special needs could actually be exacerbated and even created by the learning environment in which the child was placed.

In fact the number of specially trained teachers was sparse, except in the physical and sensory fields, for which some excellent courses were available. Courses for learning and behaviour difficulties were slower to get off the ground and it took some time for them to gain credibility and therefore status in the universities and training colleges.

The Warnock Committee (Department of Education and Science, 1978), in recommending that children with special educational needs should be educated as far as practicable in ordinary schools, brought the issue of integration to the top of the agenda. I believe that the intention was not that integration should replace special school provision, but rather that from the start, if possible children with special needs should be able to attend ordinary schools with their contemporaries for as long as feasible and with appropriate support according to their individual needs. In other words, non-segregation as distinct from universal movement of children from special to mainstream, the consequences of which would have been disastrous for unprepared teachers, parents and, above all, children.

The Committee's recommendation to replace the categories of handicap with the more generic term 'special educational need' confirmed the idea of a continuum of need which had already begun to take root as the categories became less acceptable.

During the run-up to Warnock, many in the field had begun to question seriously what was essentially different between the curricular aims for children with special educational needs and those for others. The report dispensed with the great divide which had separated 'special' from 'normal'. The realization that every teacher was likely to meet (in fact was already meeting) up to five children with significant difficulties in every class of 30 pupils they taught gradually led the profession to wake up to the fact that all teachers have a responsibility to take account of this as they develop their classroom practices; that is to say, all teachers are, in a very real sense, special educators in some degree. Classroom practices were going to have to change to accommodate these recommendations as they became incorporated into the 1981 Education Act.

As financial cuts began to bite in the early 1980s, remedial provision was usually the first to lose staff. This led departments to redefine their roles in terms of becoming the schools' support agents and facilitators, working more alongside class and subject teachers instead of relieving them of their difficult pupils. The same need to redefine their role applied to the external support services (see Bines, 1986).

It began to be recognized that the real commonality between children in school is that they are all different, especially in the ways they acquire learning; that intelligence is not fixed; that learning can be achieved through methods other than the written word and reading ability is not necessarily intelligence-related; that interest is a powerful motivator and speed of achievement does not necessarily indicate depth of learning or indeed thought; that, above all, teachers' attitudes to their pupils and confidence in their ability to learn, whatever their difficulties, matters; and that synthesizing learning skills is as important in the process as delivery of curriculum content. These ideas are still delicate seedlings and need to be carefully nurtured if they are to grow lasting roots.

IMPROVING PRACTICE

Changes in classroom practice have taken place as a result of:

- perceived needs by teachers as they expand their roles to meet special educational needs (SEN);
- changes in the role of support services both in and outside the schools;
- recognition that the closer in-service training is to the classroom, the more effective it is likely to be; and
- some of the more positive influences of recent legislation and now the new *Code of Practice*

Here we will focus on some actual situations where changes in practice have been observed, on factors that have influenced their progress, and on some of the principles that have emerged.

The Coventry City Special Needs Support Team

In 1982, as a result of severe cuts in staffing, the Remedial Service for Coventry City changed its role from providing a traditional peripatetic withdrawal service to one of advising and enabling class teachers to identify and meet more effectively the SEN which emerged in their schools. The service altered its name to the Special Needs Support Team (SNST) to reflect this change.

For some time the team had realized that the practice of removing children with learning difficulties from the classroom to be taught by an outsider for major areas of the curriculum – literacy and numeracy – did not achieve the expected 'remedial' effect on the majority of affected pupils. Neither did it assist the class teachers in providing for their special needs during the rest of the school week. The class teachers saw themselves as not having the qualifications or experience to meet the SENs of these youngsters and this led to some abdication of responsibility for their learning in general. As mentioned earlier, this was the experts' responsibility: such was the mystique developed by remedial services. Class teachers had therefore not been encouraged to increase their own skills in addressing the variety of educational needs that came before them. They were, though, able to identify the things that the pupils could NOT do but were not practised in identifying what they COULD do or how to set about planning appropriate learning for them.

The LEA, including the SNST, embarked on developing the Special Needs Action Programme (SNAP), a major city-wide in-service training initiative, first for the primary schools and later for the secondaries. SNAP is described in some detail in Gross and Gipps (1987) at pages 76–110.

The primary aim of SNAP was to encourage the headteachers of all the primary schools in the city to identify a member of their staff to act as the school's special needs co-ordinator and then to set about providing them with skills and approaches to meet special needs which could be incorporated into the curriculum and managed by class teachers. Dissemination of the programme worked on the cascade model. Cascades have a nasty habit of disappearing into the ground and it was essential that the SNST and educational psychologists, all of whom helped to develop the materials and therefore were the first course tutors, should make sure that subsequent INSET initiatives met the training needs identified by the practitioners themselves. This led the team to explore the most effective ways of ensuring that training made a difference.

Effective in-service training

'When teachers participate in the determination, initiation and organisation of their own in-service programmes, the incentive to achieve is greatly strengthened'. (Jensen *et al.*, 1973)

There is much evidence to show that INSET in the past has made a limited impact in terms of lasting changes in classroom practice. Meaningful INSET effects positive change in knowledge (which is easy), skills (which is harder) and attitudes (the hardest of all). Attitude change is, though, the most important factor if INSET is to be taken on board and reflected by the teachers in the classroom.

Back in 1983 Powers sought literature-based guidelines on effective INSET. In summary his conclusions were that:

Teachers learn from teachers and should have the opportunity to:

- construct new ideas
- share them with others
- help each other in development and revision of ideas.

The more practical the INSET and the closer to the classroom, the better it is.

The most effective chain of events in providing INSET is:

- Assessment of needs – taking account of the kind of audience, kind of content, backgrounds, skills, attitudes, etc.
- Planning that should involve the participants – appropriate setting, mode and means of delivery, aims and objectives.
- Implementation – timing, who does what, when and how.
- Future directions – what should happen next? Where do we go now?

The team and colleagues in the schools found that developing the INSET programme in this way not only facilitated improvement in skills and knowledge but also affected the attitudes of teachers towards their responsibilities to meet the special needs in their schools. During the next few years, when teachers sought help from the SNST, the emphasis changed from 'What are you going to do about this pupil?' to 'How can we solve this problem or address this issue?' Changes were also observed in the way teachers assessed their pupils, looking for what a pupil could do and finding a starting point rather than listing all the problems. In schools where the senior management saw special needs as a whole-school issue they began to develop what is now commonly accepted as the 'whole-school approach'. The concept gained currency when the 1988 Education Reform Act legislated for educational entitlement for all to a broad and balanced curriculum.

Similar developments were taking place across the country in many other authorities and cross-authority sharing of ideas and expertise grew. And as the education cuts began to bite deeper and staffing in school tightened, schools woke up to the real necessity for all teachers to be more able to assess and meet their own pupils' special needs within the context of the classroom and curriculum. The notion that all teachers are special educators was gaining ground.

What of the special schools?

If the response to the 1988 Education Reform Act by the special schools in Coventry was reflected in the rest of the country (and there is some evidence that it was), they grasped the nettle of entitlement to the National Curriculum immediately and enthusiastically. They did not wait to take advantage of the extra year's grace offered them, but set about finding ways of making the curriculum accessible to their pupils.

As with many other authorities, Coventry LEA recognized that the best special schools had important areas of expertise to share with their mainstream colleagues (and in our view, vice versa). An 'Outreach' project was already under way to bring about sharing of knowledge and expertise on SEN between special and mainstream schools. Each found that they had much to offer the other. Certain special schools brought their experience in task analysis and step-by-step planning to bear on the National Curriculum and this not only helped them to make it more accessible to their own pupils but also gave guidance to mainstream colleagues trying to achieve differentiated teaching in their classes. Some of the first attempts at relating the Attainment Targets to cross-curricular themes were made in special schools.

How teachers plan their lessons to accommodate the different learning abilities of their students and at the same time keep up with the demands of the curriculum is the great challenge. In an English lesson I recently observed, the theme was to do with holidays abroad and the assignment for the students was to write a letter of complaint to the tour operator about the poor hotel facilities and then write a reply. Many of the students seemed to settle easily to the task but some found it hard. The problem was that the teacher wanted the same thing from everyone. With help from the support teacher involved, she could have offered a range of simple to complex tasks to match the differing abilities of the students; for example, something like this:

1. Make a list of the things that were wrong in the hotel.
2. Put them in order, the worst at the top and the least bad at the bottom.
3. Write a letter to Mr Blank giving him the list of things that were wrong. Remember to put your address at the top right-hand corner. Date your letter.
4. Write a letter to Mr Blank listing your complaints. Remember to put your address at the top right-hand corner and his name and address at the top left. Date your letter.
5. Write Mr Blank's reply.

All the students could have completed the first task and almost all the second, whilst most would achieve the third. The two pupils with special needs could have managed the first, probably the second and perhaps with help from the support teacher, gone on to complete the third. The quickest students would have chosen to go to tasks four and five and might also have gone on to write about what they would do next. All class members would have achieved a satisfactory outcome, each at their own pace and level. In this lesson, little was achieved by the two students with special needs who were confused by the size of the task and lost track. They had been given too much to assimilate at one go but, with a step-by-step approach, could have achieved much more than they did.

This is no reflection on the teacher; she had not had experience in these methods and was used to a traditional class teaching approach. It is merely an illustration of how analysis of the task in relation to the capacities of the students can improve learning, certainly for students with SEN, but also for the rest of the class including those at the other end of the spectrum. This is what the special schools helped their mainstream colleagues to master.

A subjective observation of changes in attitudes of special school teachers to the possible learning capacities of their pupils suggested that rubbing shoulders with their 'normal' school colleagues actually helped some to breach, and even dispense with, that so limiting 'glass ceiling' that had hitherto hampered the progress of so many children. At joint-in-service meetings it became not unusual to hear remarks like 'I didn't believe my pupils could achieve that!'

Current practice observed in two mainstream schools

A primary school situated on a large council estate

This estate, sited on the edge of a medium-sized town, is still in its infancy as regards developing its own community mores and traditions and the school receives a greater than usual number of pupils with emotional and behaviour difficulties with associated learning problems.

It comprises some 150 pupils with six classes – three infant and three junior set under one roof. An associated nursery school has recently opened on the campus. Staffing consists of a headteacher, deputy and 5.3 teachers including an identified SEN co-ordinator. An advisory teacher is bought in for 1.25 days a week to support the school's 'Pause, Prompt, Praise' reading project and advise the class teachers on managing SEN. The school employs 3 learning support assistants (LSAs) who give individual attention to certain pupils including two with statements, and offer general classroom support, sometimes carrying out extra activities with a class to free up the teacher to work with individual pupils. They also assist with some administration.

Organization The school works on the principle of non-segregation, supporting SENs as they emerge. The special needs co-ordinator's role (besides being a class teacher) is threefold:

1. co-ordination of policy and work to meet SEN across the school;
2. liaison with external agencies, especially the advisory teacher and educational psychologist;
3. monitoring of pupils' progress, keeping the special needs records up to date and organizing the termly reviews for children with SEN.

Her comment is that she has ' ... an emerging role which is changing according to people's perception of communication. But it has to be flexible.'

She supports her colleagues in maintaining their confidence in the development of individual learning materials and approaches and gives high priority to pinning down what has been achieved, then identifying further steps to be taken. This helps to focus attention on setting work at appropriate levels for all the pupils and identifying achievable learning outcomes. Coping with the delivery of the content can overpower the much more important matter of making sure that coherent learning is being achieved by everyone.

The class teachers still lack confidence in their own capacity to meet all the individual and special needs which face them and look for expert help whilst at the same time not letting go of their own responsibility.

Classroom support from the LSAs is seen as a critical factor (but not the only one) in the smooth running of the school and this includes:

- supporting individual programmes and small group work;
- preparing differentiated learning materials; and
- building up resources to meet particular needs (this is seen as the sharp end of the exploratory process).

The statutory teacher assessment procedures assist in the monitoring of progress but the school is still searching for effective ways to assess transfer of learning from the particular to the general.

Nobody in the school would claim that it is meeting effectively all needs but the staff are developing agreed principles of management that are becoming consistent throughout the school and which are especially crucial for those with behaviour problems. This is being achieved because:

- the whole-school approach philosophy is embedded in its ethos;
- all teachers see themselves as having primary responsibility for meeting SENs as they emerge;

- sound support mechanisms are in place which do not displace the class teacher's role;
- the layout of the school lends itself to natural interaction between the adults; and
- there is a sound policy of parental involvement which is not easy to achieve in the kind of community in which this school is placed.

An 11 to 16 mixed comprehensive set in a rural area

This school of 1,000 students receives fewer youngsters with SEN than many, owing to its mainly rural catchment area. Originally the school was provided by the LEA with a special unit for pupils with moderate learning difficulties. This facility was eventually redefined in line with the school's non-segregational policy. Now it maintains a learning support team which works to support subject teachers in meeting the individual and special needs of all students as they emerge. Currently some fifteen students with statements are supported within the context of the classroom. One room is wired for a student with profound hearing loss.

Identification of special needs comes first through information passed on by the primary schools with whom there is a confident and trusting relationship. An LEA-supported policy of 'clustering' has been practised for some time and the partnership between this school and its feeder primaries is strong. A screening process is carried out at entry. Students are taught in mixed-ability groups in Year 7 and setting is introduced in Year 8 in a number of subject areas.

Organization   The school's learning support team comprises a full-time co-ordinator, one full-time SEN teacher with two others offering 0.4 and 0.3 of their time supporting students with SEN. Ten part-time LSAs are also employed to support students and subject teachers within the classroom. It is thus possible to operate fairly flexible withdrawal procedures to meet specific learning needs as they arise. The main thrust, though, is through in-class support and the school is grappling with the challenges and opportunities that this throws up (see Garnett, 1988).

The role of the co-ordinator and staff   The co-ordinator's role is, briefly, to manage, co-ordinate, organize, support and enable. She manages the team and the LSAs, co-ordinates the team's work with that of the subject teachers and organizes the LSAs' classroom support attachments, in order to enable the subject teachers to meet most learning needs in their classes. Besides this she is responsible, with a deputy head, for liaising with external agencies and primary schools as well as developing an INSET programme on differentiation and responsiveness to individual needs throughout the school. It is a tall order and requires a level of expertise and quality rarely available in the days of 'remedial' departments.

The co-ordinator states:

For me the 'whole-school' approach means promoting excellent standards in all aspects of learning support work:

- raising the professionalism and profile of the support staff;
- talking to staff and students with commitment and faith in what you are asking of them;
- assuming each teacher's responsibility for all students;

- offering practical advice as well as listening;
- being positive with students about their achievements.

The support team works in different ways, sometimes supporting students in class, sometimes working in small groups and occasionally giving individual tuition, depending on the needs of the situation. The aim is 'to enable all students to learn in a supportive and enriching environment'. As their work develops, the standing of the team and interaction with the staff is growing. In the main, the teachers of the team have their role and standing well recognized across the school. The role of the LSAs is still at a developmental stage and for this reason I am going to dwell on that for a moment.

The role of the LSAs The LSAs are an important element in the school's support provision and the co-ordinator is vocal about the quality of this group: 'We are incredibly fortunate that all our LSAs are "on the ball", well informed and conscientious – not without a sense of humour!' She includes them in INSET initiatives, which assists in confirming their status in the eyes of other staff.

It is notable how often schools find that the quality of people who go into this kind of work in schools, on shamefully low pay, is so consistently high. Is it that parental experience can actually be a 'training' for those who have a particular bent? Is it also that this work attracts people with the kind of qualities needed? What must be recognized is that there is out there a market which needs to be tapped, trained and valued.

The LSAs at this school see their role very clearly and they have been able to express their views during INSET sessions. This has enabled the teachers to consider more carefully how they could use this support more effectively. The LSAs feel that they should be actively involved with the teachers as well as students, and be used to help interpret lessons for the students, building self-esteem and confidence. They therefore need to be informed of the lesson content, have access to materials and above all have status in the classroom. No student should find it easy to say 'You aren't a teacher; I don't have to do as you say!' And it is essential that strategies for maintaining classroom control are agreed by both teacher and LSA.

LSAs work best when the teacher shares what is to happen in each lesson, has a well-organized classroom, recognizes the LSA as a valued colleague and considers with the LSA the best mode of support in each circumstance. LSAs like it when they are involved, made to feel welcome and used to capacity. They don't like it when lessons are not properly planned and teachers don't acknowledge them.

All innovation takes a long time to consolidate and what is described above is a part of that process. The important thing is that the school, through the concerted efforts of the senior management team, certain key members of staff, and a carefully planned INSET programme which is exploring the principles, problems and practice of achieving a whole-school approach to the education of its students, is managing the process at a pace that is within the capacities of its members. That is crucial.

Because the policy is supported from governing body level through the senior management to the staff, it is slowly gaining ground as the teachers become more committed to and confident in their capacity to address all pupils' individual learning needs, whilst at the same time meeting the challenges presented by a curriculum overburdened by content.

It cannot be said that all the staff are yet totally committed to the policy or that the problem of achieving the most effective classroom support has been resolved. What is happening, though, is a concerted exploration of the true nature of differentiation, its meaning in the classrooms of this school, and the kinds of support measures that will work best for this school's teachers and students.

CONCLUSION

Whatever people feel about the political implications of the various aspects of the current reforms, schools are now embarked on a process that is encapsulated in the concept of 'the whole-school approach' and takes cognizance of each individual pupil's learning needs and capacities.

The principles emerging can be summarized thus:

- All teachers are responsible for addressing SENs and, in taking such responsibility, their teaching skills expand. This is what the 'whole-school approach' is about.
- Support services are there to support, not take away, and must aim to underpin the work in the classroom, providing that extra enabling facility which meets identified and individual needs.
- Support staff should develop flexibility, providing a variety of measures to meet needs as they arise: full classroom back-up, classroom help for individuals, 'tutorial' time for small groups and individuals, besides putting heads together with colleagues to solve difficulties.
- Sharing of knowledge, experience and expertise between teacher and teacher, teacher and support staff, and between school and school enables dissemination of good practice. 'Clustering' of schools adds an important dimension to the process.
- INSET should be responsive to the training needs identified by the practitioners and as close to the practicalities of the classroom as possible.
- Schools should agree consistent management principles which all staff can develop in the classroom.

This then is the 'quiet revolution' and it is not yet complete. Perhaps it never will be. Now the aim must be to achieve a proper balance between the mainstream teachers' recognized responsibility for their pupils' SENs, and the back-up they require from the support agencies, whether external or within the school, to enable them to carry out that responsibility effectively.

REFERENCES

Bines, H. 1986. *Redefining Remedial Education*, London: Croom Helm
Department of Education and Science. 1978. *Special Education Needs*. London: HMSO
Garnett, J. 1988. Support teaching: taking a closer look. *British Journal of Special Education*, **15**, 1, 15–18
Gross, H. and Gipps, C. 1987. *Supporting Warnock's Eighteen Percent*, London: Falmer
Jensen, D. Betz, L. and Zigarmy, P. 1978. If you are listening to teachers, here is how you will organise in-service. *NASSP Bulletin* 2, 9–14
Powers, D.A. 1983. Mainstreaming and the in-service training of teachers. *Exceptional Children*, **49**, 5, 432–9

Chapter 11

Changing Residential Services: From Institutions to Ordinary Living

David Felce

Institutions have cast a long shadow. About 17,000 people in England and Wales still live in mental handicap hospitals despite nearly three decades of reform. My personal involvement in the field only extends back to the beginning of their end, so, out of necessity, I start by passing on an account of the past which I learnt from those more closely involved. My first job was in Wessex where I joined a research team headed by Albert Kushlick engaged in evaluating the 'Wessex experiment'. This was one of the first attempts to provide small, domestic settings in the community for children, and latterly for adults, who had severe or profound learning disabilities. The developments in Wessex stemmed from the close involvement in service planning of not only Albert Kushlick but also Jack Tizard. Via this link, one can see how immediate post-war research experience was translated into evolving policy and practice.

Institutional reform is symbolic of the changing ideas in the post-war era about the place of people with disabilities in our society. The institutions had become purveyors of segregation as a deliberate act of social control. A specific rationale for the restriction of people with learning disabilities emerged about a century ago with fears of contamination of the national genotype if people with low intelligence were allowed to breed unhindered. Existing institutionalization for possibly more humane reasons was overtaken by a motivation which owed nothing to any concern for the welfare of the group affected: it was separation to prevent procreation. The institutional population expanded. Tredgold (1952) noted that the numbers under various forms of care and control of the Mental Deficiency Acts increased sevenfold from about 12,000 in 1920 to about 100,000 in 1950. As O'Connor stated (1965). 'The tendency to build large institutions for about 2,000 patients in isolated country areas was a definite policy'. The extent of the exclusion and the denial of opportunities and experience of everyday life achieved gives the subsequent process of institutional reform a special poignancy.

THE MOMENTUM BEHIND REFORM

The post-war movement towards reform derived from a variety of factors which were felt in various ways in much of the developed world. Social justice and equality promoted the right to live in the least restrictive environment possible and the right to developmental opportunity. The unacceptable standards of institutional care were exposed and normalization emerged as a new guiding principle. Research provided a more accurate understanding about the abilities and potential of people with learning disabilities and a rationale of scientific inquiry permitted the first tentative steps to be taken to providing alternative forms of care.

The fears of the eugenics period had moderated by the 1950s and earlier claims about the inevitable hereditability of low intelligence, the decline in the intellectual quality of the population and the link between low intelligence and criminality were overturned (Maxwell, 1961; Sutherland and Cressey, 1960). The enforced separation of people with mild or borderline learning disabilities on the grounds of preventing genetic pollution became redundant. At the same time, research on the prevalence of learning disabilities and on social definitions of disability and labelling underlined the gross restriction of civil liberties which had been imposed on a group of people who like so many of their peers not so labelled could have lived ordinary independent lives in the community had they not been institutionalized. Protection of people from institutionalization without receipt of treatment in their own best interests and the safeguarding of access to life in the community were established as rights issues. In the USA, protection was pursued in the courts and through amendments to the constitution, establishing the rights to habilitation and to treatment in the least restrictive environment (*Wyatt* v. *Stickney*, 1972; *O'Connor* v. *Donaldson*, 1975; *Haldeman* v. *Pennhurst State School and Hospital*, 1977; 1985). In Sweden and Denmark, normalization was enacted as the guiding principle for the development of services for people with learning disabilities.

In Britain, the ideology which informed the foundation of the welfare state set a new context for defining the function of institutions for those people who clearly required service support and help (Scull, 1977). Those settings, originally developed to incarcerate and segregate, were now to be defined in terms of the benefits they brought to their users. Pragmatic concern for the economic burden to society of the earlier rapid expansion of institutional places had already surfaced and led to the adoption of a model of self-sufficient, economic community. The productive use of land and associated craft activities which stemmed from this emphasis created an account of constructive purpose to institutional life and a genuine asylum based on the evocation of village life from a supposedly more benign and caring era. The incorporation of the local authority colonies into the National Health Service, with its association of treatment and cure, completed the metamorphosis of the institutions from places of restriction of individual liberty and rights in the interests of society to places of treatment, protection and care for the benefit of their inmates.

Such a change in the representation of the institutions was achieved against a backdrop which allowed their internal workings to be a closed arena. However, gradually their functions and the realities of their organization became open to detailed scrutiny. Scandalous events and conditions in the institutions came to public attention and prompted a series of official inquiries (e.g., DHSS, 1969; 1971b; 1978; House of Commons, 1974). These highlighted the significance of academic critique and journalistic coverage in developing an accurate description of institutional life (Blatt and Kaplan, 1966; Goffman, 1961: Morris, 1969; Oswin, 1971; Shearer, 1968). The attention of politicians, service providers, the research community and the public was brought to the fact that institutions were places of profound humiliation, which stripped individuals of human worth and dignity. This multiple exposure brought the basic issue of the duty of care owed to vulnerable members of society into the public domain, and established the lack of legitimacy of the institutions which, despite vested interests and natural conservatism, they could never regain.

Open to scrutiny, little was found to be defensible on therapeutic, habilitative or humanitarian grounds. The conditions for people with learning disabilities in institutional care were poor: the buildings were old, the settings impoverished, and the staffing insufficient and ill-qualified. Documented benefits for residents were few or non-existent. Despite being accorded the status of hospital after 1948, and the long-standing involvement of medical personnel, and the specific registration in mental handicap nursing, the claim to being an appropriate treatment environment could not be sustained and other occupational groupings emerged to make claims of professional competency (Scull, 1977). The frame of reference for defining the underlying problem was shifting from medical to educational and for defining the nature of ongoing care from nursing to social support. Even at a simple level, the ability to represent mental handicap hospitals as centres of treatment excellence was undermined by their unfavourable comparison to hospitals for other client groups. Expenditures per person were lower. Professional staff were fewer and generally viewed as being of lower calibre and of lesser status than their colleagues in other services.

In support of the evolving definition of the condition towards what is now seen primarily as a learning disability, educational research was producing a new view about what could positively be achieved. Early post-war work demonstrated that a large proportion of adolescents and adults living in institutions were capable of employment in the community (O'Connor and Tizard, 1951; 1956) and that people with more severe disabilities could learn functional skills (Clark and Hermelin, 1955). The application and dissemination of teaching expertise, stemming from the development of behavioural psychology in the USA, had a major impact in demonstrating the habilitation potential of people with severe or profound learning disabilities (Berkson and Landesman-Dwyer, 1977).

The new-found concern for maximizing the potential of people with severe learning disabilities, coupled with Bowlby's findings (1951) on the negative effects of institutional care on children, directed attention to whether the normal opportunities and conditions for development existed within institutions. Again, institutions were exposed for their barrenness, their lack of stimulation, their lack of a normal social milieu and their detrimental effect on development (Oswin, 1971; Lyle, 1959; 1960). Moreover, their deficiencies were seen as inherent in their size, remoteness and professionalized structures (Jones, 1953; Goffman, 1961; Rapoport, 1960). In the 'small is beautiful' climate emerging in the late 1960s (Schumacher, 1973), the more radical analysis suggested that improvement required a reinvestment of resources in a new pattern of services rather than reform of those which existed.

EARLY REFORMS: ALTERNATIVES TO INSTITUTIONS IN THE 1950s AND 1960s

The White Paper, *Better Services for the Mentally Handicapped* (DHSS, 1971a), showed that the institutional population was fairly constant throughout the 1950s and 1960s, at just under 60,000, a likely underestimate given the 64,000 recorded in the census of hospitals in England and Wales at the end of 1970 (DHSS, 1972). Local authority, private or voluntary provision was mainly in large hostels or even larger settings similar to the hospitals, despite the relative ability of the people served. The 1950s and 1960s are significant for two service developments associated with research which began to test the monopoly claims of the institutional system as the only feasible mode of service delivery.

Tizard (1960; 1964) responded to his own research on the educability of people with learning disabilities and to the growing criticisms of institutional care by moving a group of children from a hospital ward to a smaller, more homely setting, run on educational principles, and comparing their development to a similar group who remained in the hospital (see Figure 11.1 for a summary of the dimensions of the 'Brooklands

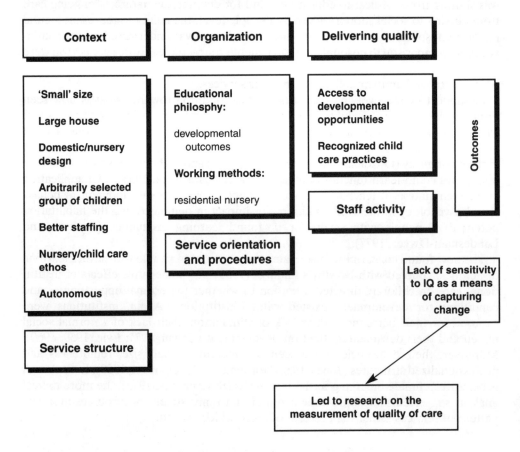

Figure 11.1   *Creating a developmental environment: the Brooklands Project*
Reported in J. Tizard, *Community Services for the Mentally Handicapped.* London: Oxford University Press, 1964.

experiment'). Although only marginal gains in IQ were found for the children at Brooklands, an alternative had been demonstrated. Moreover, the quality of the milieu established seemed so much better. A film of Brooklands had been made and it was this that had the greater impact. The fact that IQ measures had so signally failed to capture the effect of the quality of care differences which had stood out so clearly to the casual observer led Tizard to his collaboration with two sociologists, Roy King and Norma Raynes, in order to seek to develop a research means of encapsulating quality directly. The conceptual basis underpinning their resulting research (King *et al.*, 1971), Goffman's (1961) analysis of the negative characteristics of total institutions, provided the language for the next reforms in Wessex. Establishing homely, well furnished, family-style residences where the staff were seen as 'houseparents' was seen as the antidote to 'block treatment', 'rigidity of routine', 'social distance' and 'depersonalization'.

The Wessex initiative occurred for very tangible reasons. The Wessex Regional Hospital Board was created in 1959 to administer health services in Hampshire, Dorset, the Isle of Wight and part of Wiltshire, an area which had previously been part of the South West Metropolitan Hospital Board. The constraint of having in the future to place all people with learning disabilities within its new boundaries highlighted the deficiency of residential places within the region and caused the board to direct its attention towards the problems of overcrowding in its residential institutions and of a growing waiting list for placement. Following the publication of the *Hospital Plan for England and Wales* (Ministry of Health, 1962), the board proposed that an additional 450 places should be provided within Wessex in order to meet the specified norms.

Rather than simply providing a new 450-place institution (which was one of the options entertained), regional officers asked Tizard for guidance. He advised the conduct of a prevalence survey to identify all known people with learning disabilities within or from the region so as to base the proposed provision on assessed need. The data, taken together with the emerging framework for operationalizing quality provided by King *et al.* (1971), led to the recommendation to establish a number of dispersed 'experimental' services – at first for children and later for adults – in the community (Kushlick, 1967). The survey data was influential in two ways. Good information was provided on the balance of institutional and family home care which gave reassurance that the proposed community provision would prove feasible. Despite the emphasis on institutionalization in the first half of the century, the majority of children and a large proportion of adults lived in the community with their parents or other relatives (Kushlick, 1970; DHSS, 1971a). In relation to children, it could not even be said that institutional care was necessary for those with the greatest disabilities or with additional difficulties. Not all of such individuals were institutionalized; at least as many with similar characteristics remained in the family home. Community care would be feasible if a staffed service could match what many families were achieving, often with very little help.

Secondly, the practice in epidemiology of expressing the prevalence of a condition in terms of crude rates per standard population size, say in this case per 100,000 total population, led to a seemingly data-based rationale for the size of the settings to be provided. It was found that about 20 children per 100,000 total population were in institutional care in Wessex in 1963. A further coincidence was that the largest two cities in Wessex, Southampton and Portsmouth, both had populations of about 200,000. The initial experimental proposal was to provide a locally-based unit in each city with a remit to serve all children in need of residential care comprehensively from half of their respective populations. Children from the remaining halves were to stay in traditional institutional care and to serve as a control group. A setting with about 20 to 25 places would meet existing need and make some allowance for waiting lists. Thus, the notion of a 'correct' size was born. Although founded on a series of irrelevant coincidences, it became part of received wisdom. Even ten years later when we hosted visitors to the new housing developments in Andover, one of the most frequent queries was 'had not Kushlick shown that 20–25 places was the ideal size?'

Despite the rationales in support of the Wessex experiment, it did not receive the immediate go-ahead. The proposals challenged traditional orthodoxy in a number of ways. The settings were considered small and escalating costs were predicted. They were designed to serve all people from their designated local catchment areas comprehensively, no matter how severe their disabilities or additional difficulties and to do so in residential areas in the middle of town, whilst at the same time departing from the traditional reliance on hospital-based medical input or direct-care staff qualified in nursing. Placement breakdowns were predicted and it was anticipated in many quarters that such settings would not be feasible. Indeed, permission to proceed was probably linked to the Ely Hospital scandal. Once it was clear that what had passed at Ely would become public, the government responded by saying that it had anticipated the problem and was funding research in Wessex to investigate service alternatives. Figure 11.2 illustrates the evolving service design as it informed the Wessex developments.

Wessex was much visited through the early 1970s and mid-1970s, as I know from personal experience. It was influential in shaping thinking and had a tangible impact on a number of other schemes which were proposed to provide alternatives to institutions, notably in south-west Wales (Hemming *et al.*, 1981) and Sheffield (Heron, 1982). Subsequently, the Wessex research showed that the services were not only feasible and affordable but also brought benefits: in increased development, family contact and day-to-day activity (Felce *et al.*, 1980). Moreover, although soon to lose any significance in terms of the precise design of the services provided – they were an intermediate stage on the way to genuinely small homes – the Wessex reforms had an enduring importance in demonstrating that community care for people with the greatest disabilities and difficulties who were then in institutions was possible. By this time, support for the direction of reform was becoming established. For example, Barbara Castle gave the failure by field authorities to replicate the moves in Wessex as one reason for her decision to establish the National Development Group and the National Development Team. Service development and research from around the world showed that reinvestment of resources to provide a new pattern of community-based services was possible and desirable.

DEVELOPING IDEAS IN THE 1970s

The themes emerging in the post-war decades were further consolidated during the 1970s as a result of a continuing critique and reappraisal, at home and abroad, of the place of people with disabilities in society and the role and function of services. The principle of normalization had articulated the rights to equal opportunity for people with learning disabilities in Scandinavia. Originating in Denmark in the 1959 Mental Retardation Act, it expressed the aim of services as 'to create an existence for the mentally retarded as close to normal living conditions as possible' (Bank-Mikkelson,

1980, p. 56). Later, the definition was elaborated to include 'making normal, mentally retarded people's housing, education, working, and leisure conditions ... bringing them the legal and human rights of all other citizens' (Bank-Mikkelson, *op. cit.*, p. 56). In similar vein, Nirje (1980, p. 33) defined normalization with regard to services in Sweden as 'making available to all mentally retarded people patterns of life and conditions of everyday living which are as close as possible to the regular circumstances and ways of life'. In both countries, these statements highlighted access to normal patterns of living for all, irrespective of level of disability.

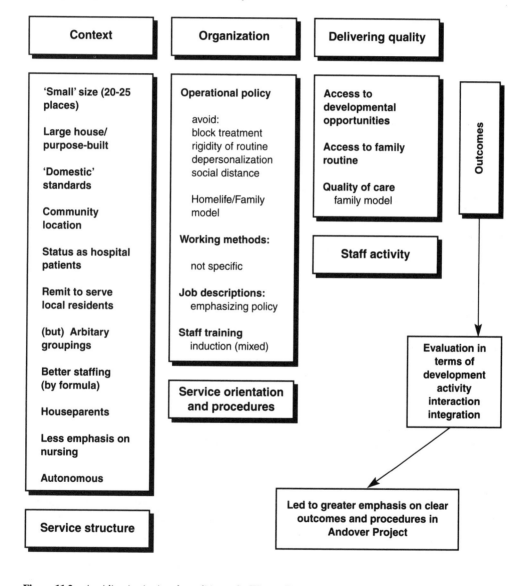

Figure 11.2 *Avoiding institutional conditions: the Wessex Project*
Reported in A. Kushlick, Residential care for the mentally subnormal. *Royal Society of Health Journal*, **90**, 255–61.

Although policy in Britain throughout the 1970s remained equivocal, couched in terms of maintaining 'as normal a life as . . . handicap or handicaps permit' (DHSS, 1971a, p. 10), developments in Scandinavia, particularly the use of ordinary housing for providing residential services, illustrated and added a further impetus to the extent of reform which would have to be undertaken if the large institutions were to be replaced. More radical reform messages were also coming from the USA. Wolfensberger (1972) had elaborated the normalization principle as a more general theory. Normative standards and equality on such issues as rights, individuality, development, social integration, culture-appropriateness, age-appropriateness, access to generic services and typical patterns of living were explicit benchmarks within his framework by which the impact of services on people's lives could be judged. The introduction to the UK and spread of training based on Wolfensberger's conceptualization of normalization (Wolfensberger, 1972; Wolfensberger and Glenn, 1975), and, later, social role valorization (Wolfensberger, 1983; Wolfensberger and Thomas, 1983) from the late 1970s onwards consolidated its influence on service reform in the UK (Brown and Smith, 1992).

Deinstitutionalization as a movement had gathered pace in the USA from the mid-1960s onwards (Lakin *et al.*, 1992). Wolfensberger's work on the implications of normalization for the design of services had a direct influence on the Eastern Nebraska Community Office of Retardation (ENCOR). The ENCOR service attracted particular attention in the UK in the late 1970s as a model which provided residential services in genuinely small settings in ordinary housing (Thomas *et al.*, 1978). As in Scandinavia, the separation of specialist services from the medical model allowed an alternative formulation of social care. The Wessex locally-based hospital units, proclaimed at the beginning of the decade as examples of domestic-style accommodation, were being criticized by the end of the decade as not going far enough (King's Fund, 1980). The expanded remit for social services departments in the White Paper (DHSS, 1971a), but one which still only established them as equal provision partners with health, was deemed insufficient. Adoption of a new model of care and the transfer of agency responsibilities for provision and for the training of staff was advocated (DHSS, 1979; King's Fund, 1980). The King's Fund Centre's *An Ordinary Life* initiative acted as a focus for the conceptualization, design and implementation of community services throughout the 1980s.

The positive perspective on developmental outcome gathering pace through the 1950s and 1960s was sustained through the 1970s. Whereas the earlier analysis of the negative effects of institutions had only provided a reactive prescription to guide an alternative service, the technology of behaviour analysis applied to the field of learning disabilities was demonstrating some very tangible positive achievements associated with equally tangible courses of action. The new optimism that development could be enhanced by more intense and well-targeted education saw expression in many areas: from early education through the development of individual educational plans within schools to adult life. In the UK, practical guidance for residential services was issued by the National Development Group (NDG, 1978), guidance which perhaps did not get the support and recognition it deserved as it was directed towards improving hospitals.

FOLLOW-ON RESEARCH DEVELOPMENTS – ORDINARY HOUSING AND POSITIVE PROGRAMMING

These evolving ideas were translated into practice in the next moves towards the adoption of ordinary housing as the basis of residential provision. Thomas (1985) established a number of houses in Northumberland in order to resettle children from the Northgate Hospital, and housing developments for adults with severe or profound learning disabilities, all associated with research, were pursued in Andover (Mansell *et al.*, 1983), Bristol (Ward, 1986) and Cardiff (Mathieson and Blunden, 1980). Two of these, Andover and Cardiff, represented explicit attempts to bring together the macro-analysis of the required context for ordinary living with the micro-analysis of positive programming procedures (see Figure 11.3). That there were similarities in the conceptualization of this next step was perhaps not surprising, given the links between the researchers involved. Both teams had had a personal involvement with the Wessex experiment, both had members who had worked in Todd Risley's behavioural research group in the USA and both had undertaken research on environmental organization, goal planning and individual programming (e.g. Revill and Blunden, 1979; Porterfield, Blunden and Blewitt, 1980; Felce, de Kock, Mansell and Jenkins, 1984; Mansell, Felce, de Kock and Jenkins, 1982), the lessons from which were incorporated within the design of the new housing services.

The Andover project was a direct successor to the Wessex experiment. Although, the earlier Wessex units had compared favourably to hospitals, we were left with more ideas for further improvement than satisfaction that good quality services had been provided. An important observation was that, although in keeping with emerging definitions of service aims we had evaluated the settings in terms of such indicators as developmental progress, social and family contact, and engagement in activity, there was nothing specific in the training of staff and working methods of the services evaluated which were directed at achieving such outcomes. So, in addition to moving towards smaller scale, ordinary housing and genuine domestic standards, we were concerned to introduce a set of working methods and to train staff accordingly so as to maximize the likelihood that defined outcomes such as community integration, engagement in activity, greater individual choice, continued progress and the fostering of alternatives to challenging behaviour would be achieved (see Mansell *et al.*, 1987; Felce, 1991). The Andover houses were designed to serve adults with the most severe or profound learning disabilities comprehensively, including people with severely challenging behaviour. The first was opened in 1981.

The Cardiff development – NIMROD or New Ideas for the care of Mentally Retarded people in Ordinary Dwellings – was significant not only for embracing ordinary housing but also for setting the residential component of services within a wider context. It was one of the first attempts to bring together a number of elements of a comprehensive local service under one administrative entity – intensively and minimally staffed residential accommodation, individual and family support services, professional services, a volunteer service and an administrative base which also housed an information and resource library – and to offer them to all people with learning disabilities in a defined geographical area. It was developed to serve a part of Cardiff, an area of about 60,000 total population. No one was considered to be too severely disabled or too behaviourally problematic to serve.

Services were opened in turn in each of four communities, each comprising a quarter of the total population of the area. Services became operational in the first community in 1981. Those in the remaining communities opened during 1982 and 1983. As in the

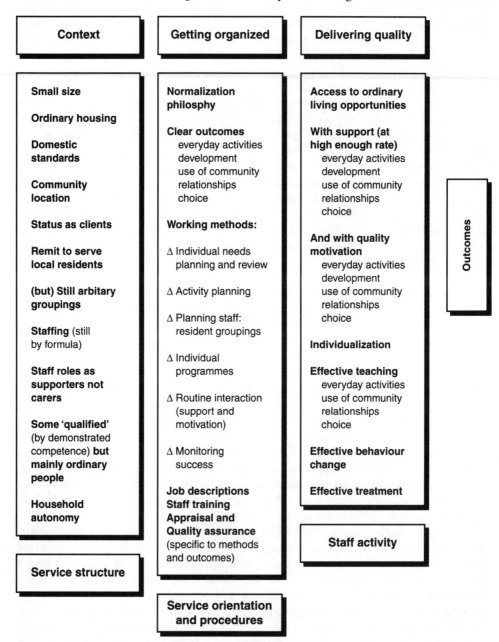

Figure 11.3 *Housing services and an ordinary life: the Andover Project and NIMROD (early 1980s)*
Adapted from D. Felce and K. Love, Supporting people with severe learning disabilities and challenging behaviours, in C. Kiernan (ed.) *Research to Practice: Implications of Research on the Challenging Behaviour of People with Learning Disabilities.* (British Institute of Learning Disabilities, 1993)

Andover project, ordinary housing was, in general, being advocated as possessing inherent opportunities for more normal development and quality of life but these were not seen as an inevitable outcome. Rather, a structured approach to working methods was taken to reinforce the natural advantages of the setting. Staff practices were developed in a series of procedural guides relating to, amongst other things, how to implement individual programming, teach new skills, organize activities, support resident involvement and monitor outcome (e.g., the success of programmes, the opportunities available for activity). Staff were given tailor-made induction and in-service training on the use of these methods.

Taken together, the Andover (Felce, 1989) and NIMROD (Lowe and de Paiva, 1991) research provide good evidence that (a) house residents made significantly better progress in skills than did comparison groups in hospital or family homes; (b) there were greater opportunities and support for participation in household, leisure and social activities than in hospital or larger community units; (c) staff–resident interaction was significantly greater; (d) family and friendship contact was significantly greater for those residents moving back to be near families from distant hospitals but there were no significant differences when comparison was made to other local but larger settings; and (e) use of community amenities by house residents was significantly greater than that by comparison groups in hospitals or larger community units, irrespective of the fact that some of the latter facilities were located within the community. However, the research gives no evidence of challenging behaviours reducing. None the less, the evaluations showed that staffed community housing for people with severe or profound learning disabilities, some with severely challenging behaviour, was feasible, brought beneficial outcomes and could be achieved without excessive revenue increases beyond what was required to rectify the most obvious deficiencies of institutional staffing levels.

The emphasis given to working methods in both services in order to make high-quality staff performance and, thus, beneficial outcome more likely has to be remembered in interpreting this research. Ordinary housing, decent furnishings, community location, reasonable staffing, a change away from institutional and nursing-oriented staff, and the general principles associated with the ordinary life model are only part of the story. Operational methods, staff roles and duties, staff procedures and training are also implicated. One cannot assume that similar outcomes for people with severe learning disabilities or ability to cope with people with severely challenging behaviour will be a feature of all community housing services unless equal care is taken to establish equally effective methods. Such caution in interpretation has led Bratt and Johnston (1988) to call for the continued evaluation of what they termed 'second generation' projects, those provided by routine service operation in the wake of the specially developed 'model' projects.

WIDESPREAD IMPLEMENTATION OF INSTITUTIONAL ALTERNATIVES – THE 1980s AND 1990s

The development of institutional alternatives became widespread following the announcement of the All Wales Mental Handicap Strategy and the adoption of the Care in the Community policy in England, just a few years after the Andover and NIMROD developments. Between 1980 and 1992, hospital populations fell to 44 per cent and 53 per cent of their 1980 size in England and Wales respectively (Emerson and Hatton, in press) – an exodus of about 29,250 people. The number of community homes trebled to 3,600 and the number of places in community homes doubled to 40,000, indicating an overall reduction in the average size of home (Mental Health Foundation, 1993). The independent sector has expanded its provision considerably, becoming of equal significance to local authorities, and likely only to increase its role in the future.

Beyer *et al.* (1991) described these trends in Wales. The hospital population in Wales in 1983 comprised about two-thirds of all people in any form of service accommodation. Few amongst the remaining third lived in ordinary housing and change in traditional social services hostel provision has also contributed to the net total reform undertaken in the last ten years. Between 1983 and 1988, local authorities and private bodies and voluntary bodies opened 45, 30 and 26 new settings respectively, representing a 75 per cent, 214 per cent and 433 per cent growth in provision for the three sectors. The number of residences other than hospitals increased from 80 to 181. Moreover, the new settings broadly conformed to the small-home model, although new private provision still tended towards larger than desirable size. For example, between 1987 and 1988, 13 new private homes opened with a median size of six places. In comparison, 19 voluntary sector homes opened that year with a mean size of four places. The median size of staffed local authority accommodation fell from 20 in 1983 to 6 by 1988. The number of people accommodated in the independent sector more than doubled in the same period, particularly accelerating from 1987 as the emerging partnerships between voluntary bodies and housing associations working in tandem with the statutory sector began to flourish. By 1990, provision of ordinary housing had increased to 986 places, a rate of development of 186 places per year over the previous two years compared to 116 per year between 1983 and 1988. In addition, individual placements outside the scope of official statistics contributed to a growing diversity which included individual tenancies supported by peripatetic staff, adult family placements and life-sharing arrangements, collectively providing about 400 places in the eight Welsh counties by 1988.

One cannot assume that all institutional alternatives have been based in ordinary housing, although certain regions, such as Wales, the North West and South East Thames, and districts, such as Cornwall, have committed themselves to ordinary housing. Even so, ordinary housing services have, on the whole, tended to follow the more general King's Fund, 'ordinary life,' prescription which gave little attention to defined working methods and associated practical training. A number of factors might account for this. Clearly, a relatively simple 'ordinary house, ordinary street, ordinary staff' model is easier to follow than one which demands operational expertise. In addition, the change in lead agency from Health to Social Services may have acted to diminish the significance of interpretation and analysis stemming from behavioural psychology and increased the expectation of the level of change which would naturally follow from deinstitutionalization and a departure from the medical model.

The lack of definition of specialist expertise matched the position of the new lead agency. Further, ideological or values-based training following the dissemination of normalization supplanted practical training. Indeed, any attempt to establish working methods or structure was widely interpreted as incompatible with the emphasis on individualization and choice conveyed within such training. In particular, the status of developmental progress as a goal and allied processes such as assessment, goal-setting and skill-teaching were subordinated to the wider conceptualization of the 'Five Accomplishments' (O'Brien, 1987) – even though the achievement of competence was one of their number. Behavioural analysis and technology was consigned to the dustbin of the previous decade, only to be allowed out grudgingly in the extremis of severely challenging behaviour.

THE QUALITY OF ORDINARY HOUSING PROVISION

Perhaps not surprisingly, the new services provided in the wake of deinstitutionalization have brought residents better material standards (Emerson and Hatton, in press). Two surveys in England (Raynes *et al.*, 1994) and Wales (Perry and Felce, in press) covering between them about 130 settings showed that scores on scales of physical quality and homeliness averaged about 67 per cent of their possible totals. Staffing levels have also increased over time. An appraisal published by the Office of Health Economics (Taylor and Taylor, 1986) showed the extent to which falling institutional populations through the late 1970s and early 1980s resulted in increases in staff per occupied hospital place. Knapp *et al.* (1992) later described community services which started with even higher staff:resident ratios as a planned development, or started at parity but revised them upwards on the basis of experience. Felce and Perry (in press) showed that recently provided housing services in Wales tended to have considerably increased staffing compared to, say, earlier Andover project levels.

 However, as Emerson and Hatton (in press) show, improved outcomes in terms of resident experience or development have not always accompanied the creation of this preferable environmental and resource context. Bratt and Johnston (1988) found that residents in one housing scheme were not being supported to gain the domestic skills required for greater independence. Fleming and Stenfert Kroese (1990) reported that residents' competence did not increase when they moved to community-based group homes unless structured staff procedures were implemented. Similarly, Beswick (1992) found that moving to community settings did not lead to increased skill acquisition. Overall, Emerson and Hatton (in press) report that no statistically significant improvement in resident skills was apparent in 33 per cent of the evaluations conducted in Britain on people moving from hospital to the community (including 42 per cent of comparisons between hospitals and staffed housing).

 Fleming and Stenfert Kroese (1990) also reported that residents had few meaningful relationships after their move and little real community integration. Jahoda *et al.* (1990) found that moving out led to more community-based activities but very few opportunities to meet people without learning disabilities. In keeping with this, Donegan and Potts (1988) commented that ' ... most ... live on the fringes of society ... although they live in their own homes independently within the community, the majority do not take part in many community activities'. Two-thirds of evaluative studies, in fact, do reveal that the range and frequency of community activities have increased on moving to the community (Emerson and Hatton, in press). However, limited social networks for people with learning disabilities also appear to be the norm (e.g., Firth and Short, 1987; de Kock *et al.*, 1988; Todd *et al.*, 1990).

Emerson and Hatton (in press) also show that, whilst increased resident engagement in activity generally followed moving to less restrictive settings, a quarter of the comparisons between hospitals and community housing services included in their review reported no significant change. Even where increased activity has been found, such a result may depend on the precise internal organization of the setting rather than being a general consequence of the change in environment. For example, the extent of assistance received by people who lack independent abilities is probably the key to their participation in activity. Felce and Perry (in press) found that more recent, better resourced houses in Wales did not support a similar level of constructive activity amongst residents compared to the earlier Andover and NIMROD services (Felce *et al.*, 1986; Felce *et al.*, 1991). The conclusion that this deficiency was due to the low proportion of staff contact given in the form of assistance is supported by a reanalysis of the data from the Andover research (Felce, in press) and by recent research on residential services provided for multiply disabled people (reported in Emerson and Hatton, in press). Both analyses point to the important mediating role of staff support in realizing the opportunities for constructive activity inherent in leading an ordinary life for people with conspicuous disabilities.

LOOKING TO THE FUTURE

Reform in residential services began by looking backward at institutions and deciding to do things differently. Three decades of development later, we have a much clearer view of the design brief for the alternative service. We have learnt that there are no pivotal arrangements which if decided correctly determine all that is important; there are no levers which mechanistically produce quality when pulled. Small size does not guarantee quality and nor does community location, ordinary housing design or adequate staffing. They are certainly necessary to achieving high quality but the relationship between outcome and the nature of the environmental context is mediated by internal organization, working methods and the procedures which shape what staff do. A considerable investment in attitudinal or values training throughout the 1980s proved insufficient to provide sufficient guidance. Indeed, although normalization is concerned with the interpretation of process and outcome, it does not provide a sound analysis of the links between them.

As a consequence, Felce (1991), Mansell and Beasley (1993), McGill and Toogood (1993) and Emerson and Hatton (in press) have argued that the implementation of an 'active support' model through clearly defined structures for planning staff and resident activity and for the delivery of practical help to residents to meet the behavioural demands of commonplace situations is an essential component of high-quality provision, at least for those with more substantial disabilities. This position takes account of the earlier Andover and NIMROD research, together with projects such as that undertaken by the Special Development Team in South East Thames to resettle people with the most severe challenging behaviours into ordinary housing (Emerson *et al.*, 1993). Procedures for day-to-day organization and effective support are reiterated in Figure 11.4. However, they are shown as operative within a context which has developed on from the conceptualization of the 1980s.

Expectations and understanding about providing an ordinary environmental context for people with disability in our society who need service support have continued to evolve. The move from large institutional scale to groupings on a much more human scale has not always been matched by an equal degree of reform to the process by which people come to live together, their status and their rights within their accommodation, their degree of control over their lifestyle and how their needed support is arranged.

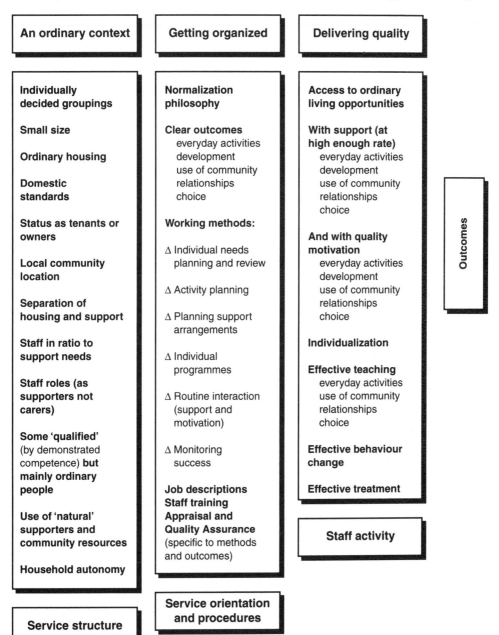

Figure 11.4 *Designing housing services for an ordinary life*

Recent perspectives, exemplified by the 'supported living' paradigm (Kinsella, 1993), have continued to push forward the extent to which people with disabilities are extended choices and circumstances which other people in our society take for granted. Certainly, provision practice has continued to develop in the last ten years: people are more likely to be tenants in their accommodation now than at the beginning of the 1980s; more effort has been given to determining groupings in other than an arbitrary way; and greater flexibility in resourcing has been evident. However, too many services have followed a predetermined size and constrained groupings to fit the chosen number. Too many have adopted a similarly formulaic approach to determining staff support, and too many have maintained the traditional disposition towards service control, seeing direct service provision as the solution to all need. Moreover, too many still provide accommodation and support as an indivisible arrangement, and fail to extend security of tenure to each and every person served.

Supported living emphasizes the primacy of planning for and with individuals, deciding groupings and service size to suit their needs and wishes. It also emphasizes the logic of determining support in relation to individual need and promotes the role of services not only as a direct provider of resources, structures and processes but also as a facilitator to enhance the benefit derived from the individual's network of natural support and the resources of the community. Promotion of typical options over which people normally make choices and the exercise of individual control are also paramount. In this context, separating the provision of housing from the provision of support is an important safeguard to personal determination. It must be possible for people to review and change their support arrangements without having to move and vice versa. The nature of residential services will, therefore, undoubtedly undergo further revision in seeking to help people with learning disabilities attain fulfilling and satisfying lives. However, this does not mean that one should look at past reform with too critical an eye. Understanding about how to act in the best interests of people with learning disabilities has grown as a result of what has been done and will surely continue to do so.

REFERENCES

Bank-Mikkelson, N.E. 1980. Denmark. In R.J. Flynn and K.E. Nitsch, (eds), *Normalisation, Social Integration and Community Services*. Baltimore: University Park Press

Berkson, G. and Landesman-Dwyer, S. 1977. Behavioral research on severe and profound mental retardation (1955–1974). *American Journal of Mental Deficiency*, **81**, 428–54.

Beswick, J. 1992. An evaluation of the effects on quality of life outcome measures for people with learning difficulties (mental handicap) of changes in the living situation from hospitals to community environments. Unpublished PhD thesis, University of Manchester

Beyer, S., Todd, S. and Felce, D. 1991. The implementation of the All-Wales Mental Handicap Strategy, 1983–1988. *Mental Handicap Research*, **4**, 115–40

Blatt, B. and Kaplan, F. 1966. *Christmas in Purgatory*. Boston: Allyn and Bacon

Bowlby, E.J.M. (1951), *Child Care and the Growth of Love*. Geneva: WHO

Bratt, A. and Johnston, R. 1988. Changes in lifestyle for young adults with profound handicaps following discharge from hospital care into a 'second generation' housing project. *Mental Handicap Research*, **1**, 49–74

Brown, H. and Smith, H. 1992. *Normalisation: A Reader for the Nineties*. London: Routledge

Clarke, A.D.B. and Hermelin, B.F. 1955. Adult imbeciles: Their abilities and trainability. *Lancet*, **2**, 337–9 de Kock, U., Saxby, H., Thomas, M. and Felce, D. 1988. Community and family contact: an evaluation of small community homes for adults. *Mental Handicap Research*, **1**, 127–40

DHSS (Department of Health and Social Security). 1969. *Report of the Committee of Inquiry into the Allegations of Ill-treatment of Patients and Other Irregularities at the Ely Hospital, Cardiff.* London: HMSO

DHSS. 1971a. *Better Services for the Mentally Handicapped.* London: HMSO

DHSS. 1971b. *Report of the Farleigh Hospital Committee of Enquiry.* London: HMSO

DHSS. 1972. *Census of Mentally Handicapped Patients in Hospital in England and Wales at the End of 1970.* London: HMSO

DHSS. 1978. *Report of the Committee of Enquiry into Normansfield Hospital.* London: HMSO

DHSS. 1979. *Report of the Committee of Enquiry into Mental Handicap Nursing and Care.* London: HMSO

Donegan, C. and Potts, M. 1988. People with mental handicap living alone in the community: a pilot study of their quality of life. *British Journal of Mental Subnormality*, **34**, 10–22

Emerson, E. and Hatton, C. (in press). *Moving Out: The Impact of Relocation from Hospital to Community on the Quality of Life of People with Learning Disabilities.* London: HMSO

Emerson, E. McGill, P. and Mansell, J.(eds). 1994. *Severe Learning Disabilities and Challenging Behaviours: Designing High Quality Services.* London: Chapman & Hall

Felce, D. 1989. *Staffed Housing for Adults with Severe and Profound Mental Handicaps: The Andover Project.* Kidderminster: BIMH Publications

Felce, D. 1991. Using behavioural principles in the development of effective housing services for adults with severe or profound mental handicaps. In R. Remington (ed.), *The Challenge of Severe Mental Handicap: A Behaviour Analytic Perspective.* Chichester: Wiley

Felce, D. (in press). The quality of support for ordinary living: staff: resident interactions and resident activity. In Mansell, J. and Ericcson, K. (eds), *Deinstitutionalization and Community Living: Intellectual Disability Services in Britain, Scandanavia and the USA.* London: Chapman & Hall

Felce, D., de Kock, U., Mansell, J. and Jenkins, J. 1984. Providing systematic individual teaching for severely disturbed and profoundly mentally handicapped adults in residential care. *Behaviour Research and Therapy*, **22**, 299–309

Felce, D., de Kock, U. and Repp, A. 1986. An eco-behavioural analysis of small community-based houses and traditional large hospitals for severely and profoundly mentally handicapped adults. *Applied Research in Mental Retardation*, **7**, 393–408

Felce, D., Kushlick, A. and Smith, J. 1980. An overview of the research on alternative residential facilities for the severely mentally handicapped in Wessex. *Advance in Behaviour Research and Therapy*, **3**, 1–4

Felce, D. and Perry, J. (in press). The extent of support for ordinary living provided in staffed housing: the relationship between staffing levels, resident dependency, staff: resident interactions and resident activity patterns. *Social Science and Medicine*

Felce, D., Repp, A.C., Thomas, M., Ager, A. and Blunden, R. (1991). The relationship of staff: client ratios, interactions and residential placement. *Research in Developmental Disabilities*, **12**, 315–31

Firth, H. and Short, D. 1987. A move from hospital to community: evaluation of community contacts. *Child: Care, Health and Development*, **13**, 341–54

Fleming, I. and Stenfert Kroese, B. 1990. Evaluation of a community care project for people with learning difficulties. *Journal of Mental Deficiency Research*, **34**, 451–64

Goffman, E. 1961. *Asylums.* New York: Doubleday

Haldeman v. *Pennhurst State School and Hospital.* 1977. 446 F. Supp. 1925 (E.D. Pa. 1977).

Haldeman v. *Pennhurst State School and Hospital.* 1985. Civil Action No. 74–1345. Final settlement agreement (E.D. Pa. 1985).

Hemming, H., Lavender, T. and Pill, R. 1981. Quality of life of mentally retarded adults transferred from large institutions to new small units. *American Journal of Mental Deficiency*, **86**, 157–69.

Heron, A. 1982. *Better Services for the Mentally Handicapped?* London: King's Fund

House of Commons. 1974. *Report of the Committee of Inquiry into South Ockenden Hospital.* London: HMSO

Jahoda, A., Cattermole, M. and Markova, I. 1990. Moving out: An opportunity for friendship and broadening social horizons? *Journal of Mental Deficiency Research*, **34**, 127–39

Jones, M. 1953. *The Therapeutic Community*. New York: Basic Books

King, R., Raynes, N. and Tizard, J. 1971. *Patterns of Residential Care*. London: Routledge & Kegan Paul

King's Fund. 1980. *An Ordinary Life: Comprehensive Locally-based Residential Services for Mentally Handicapped People*. London: King's Fund Centre

Kinsella, P. 1993. *Supported Living: A New Paradigm*. Manchester: National Development Team

Knapp, M., Cambridge, P., Thomason, C., Beecham, J., Allen, C. and Darton, R. 1992. *Care in the Community: Challenge and Demonstration*. Aldershot: Ashgate

Kushlick, A. 1967. A method of evaluating the effectiveness of a community health service. *Social and Economic Administration*, **1**, 29–48

Kushlick, A. 1970. Residential care for the mentally subnormal. *Royal Society of Health Journal*, **90**, 255–61

Lakin, K.L.C., Bruininks, R.H. and Larson, S.A. 1992. The changing face of residential services. In L. Rowitz (ed.), *Mental Retardation in the Year 2000*. Berlin: Springer-Verlag

Lowe, K. and de Paiva, S. 1991. *NIMROD: An Overview*. London: HMSO

Lyle, J.G. 1959. The effect of an institution environment upon the verbal development of imbecile children: I verbal intelligence. *Journal of Mental Deficiency Research*, **3**, 122–8

Lyle, J.G. 1960. The effect of an institution environment upon the verbal development of imbecile children: III The Brooklands Residential Unit. *Journal of Mental Deficiency Research*, **4**, 14–22

McGill, P. and Toogood, A. 1994. Organising community placements. In E. Emerson, P. McGill, and J. Mansell (eds), *Severe Learning Disabilities and Challenging Behaviours: Designing High Quality Services*. London: Chapman & Hall

Mansell, J. and Beasley, F. 1993. Small staffed houses for people with a severe mental handicap and challenging behaviour. *British Journal of Social Work*, **23**, 329–44

Mansell, J., Felce, D., de Kock, U. and Jenkins, J. 1982. Increasing purposeful activity of severely and profoundly mentally handicapped adults. *Behaviour Research and Therapy*, **20**, 593–604

Mansell, J., Felce, D., Jenkins, J., de Kock, U. and Toogood, S. 1983. A Wessex home from home. *Nursing Times*, **79**, 51–6

Mansell, J., Felce, D., Jenkins, J., de Kock, U. and Toogood, A. 1987. *Developing Staffed Housing for People with Mental Handicaps*. Tunbridge Wells: Costello

Mathieson, S. and Blunden, R. 1980. Nimrod is piloting a course towards a community life. *Health and Social Service Journal*, **90**, 25 January, 122–4

Maxwell, J. 1961. *The Level and Trend of National Intelligence*. London: University of London Press

Mental Health Foundation. 1993. *Learning Disabilities: The Fundamental Facts*. London: Mental Health Foundation

Ministry of Health. 1962. *Hospital Plan for England and Wales*. London: HMSO

Morris, P. 1969. *Put Away*. London: Routledge & Kegan Paul

National Development Group (NDG). 1978. Creating a learning environment. Chapter 5 in *Helping Mentally Handicapped People in Hospital*. London: DHSS

Nirje, B. 1980. The normalization principle. In R.J. Flynn and K.E. Nitsch (eds), *Normalisation, Social Integration and Community Services*. Baltimore: University Park Press.

O'Brien, J. 1987. A guide to life-style planning. In B. Wilcox and G.T. Bellamy (eds), *The Activities Catalog: An Alternative Curriculum for Youth and Adults with Severe Disabilities*. Baltimore: Brookes Publishing

O'Connor, N. 1965. The successful employment of the mentally handicapped. In L.T. Hilliard and B.H. Kirman (eds), *Mental Deficiency*. London: Churchill Livingstone

O'Connor, N. and Tizard, J. 1951. Predicting the occupational adequacy of certified mental defectives. *Occupational Psychology*, **25**, 205–11

O'Connor, N. and Tizard, J. 1956. *The Social Problem of Mental Deficiency*. London: Pergamon

O'Connor v. *Donaldson*. 1975. 422 U.S. 563 (1975)

Oswin, M. 1971. *The Empty Hours*. Harmondsworth: Penguin

Perry, J. and Felce, D. (1994). Outcomes of ordinary housing services in Wales: objective indicators. *Mental Handicap Research*, **7**, 286–311

Porterfield, J., Blunden, R., and Blewitt, E. 1980. Improving environments for profoundly handicapped adults: using prompts and social attention to maintain high group engagement. *Behaviour Modification*, **4**, 225–41

Rapoport, N.N. 1960. *Community as Doctor*. London: Tavistock

Raynes, N.V., Pettipher, C., Wright, K. and Shiell, A. 1994. *The Cost and Quality of Community Residential Care*. London: Fulton

Revill, S. and Blunden, R. 1979. A home training service for pre-school developmentally handicapped children. *Behaviour Research and Therapy*, **17**, 207–14

Schumacher, E.F. 1973. *Small is Beautiful: A Study of Economics As If People Mattered*. London: Blond and Briggs

Scull, A.T. 1977. *Decarceration: Community Treatment and the Deviant*. London: Prentice-Hall

Shearer, A. 1968. Dirty children in a locked ward: a children's ward in a mental hospital on a bad day. *Guardian*, 28 March

Sutherland, E. H. and Cressey, D. R. 1960. *Principles of Criminology*. Chicago: Lippincott.

Taylor, J. and Taylor, D. 1986. *Mental Handicap: Partnership in the Community?* London: Office of Health Economics/MENCAP

Thomas, D. 1985. Putting normalisation into practice. In E. Karas (ed.), *Current Issues in Clinical Psychology*. New York: Plenum Press

Thomas, D., Kendall, A. and Firth, H. 1978. *ENCOR: A Way Ahead*. London: Campaign for Mentally Handicapped People

Tizard, J. 1960. Residential care of mentally handicapped children. *British Medical Journal*, **1**, 1041–3

Tizard, J. 1964. *Community Services for the Mentally Handicapped*. London: Oxford University Press

Todd, S., Evans, G. and Beyer, S. 1990 More recognised than known: the social visibility and attachment of people with developmental disabilities. *Australia and New Zealand Journal of Developmental Disabilities*, **16**, 207–18

Tredgold, A.F. 1952. *A Textbook on Mental Deficiency (Amentia)*. 8th ed. London: Baillière, Tindall & Cox

Ward, L. 1986. From hospital to ordinary houses, ordinary streets. *Health Service Journal*, 1 May, 601

Wolfensberger, W. 1972. *Normalisation: The Principle of Normalisation in Human Services*. Toronto: National Institute on Mental Retardation

Wolfensberger, W. 1983. Social role valorization: A proposed new term for the principle of normalisation. *Mental Retardation*, **21**, 234–9

Wolfensberger, W. and Glenn, L. 1975. *Programme Analysis of Service Systems: Handbook and Manual*. 3rd ed. Toronto: National Institute on Mental Retardation

Wolfensberger, W. and Thomas, S. 1983. *PASSING (Program Analysis of Service System's Implementation of Normalization Goals): Normalization Criteria and Ratings Manual*. Toronto: National Institute on Mental Retardation

Wyatt v. Stickney. 1972. 344. F. Supp. 387 (M.D. Ala. 1972)

Chapter 12

Changing Day Services

Gus Gray

INTRODUCTION

> He alone can do good who knows what things are like and what their situation is.
> R. Joseph Pieper, *Prudence*. Translated by R. and C. Winston (1960)

Day services are now receiving criticisms previously levelled at large-scale residential care. Congregation, segregation, isolation, size, lack of individual planning, little use of mainstream services, few links with the community served. There is lobbying for a move away from buildings-based services towards individual day service planning leading to individual programmes. The Social Services Inspectorate report (Department of Health, 1989) on the inspection of day services added weight to the view previously expressed in *An Ordinary Working Life* (King's Fund, 1984) that 'traditional day services have inherent problems which prevent these [ordinary life] principles being implemented'.

This chapter attempts to show what things were and are like. There have been significant changes in services known to the writer during the past 25 years. These have not happened as fast or been as far-reaching as many people wish but, some services do:

- involve users in service planning and development,
- provide individually planned programmes and review them regularly,
- make substantial use of mainstream educational and recreational facilities, and
- maintain close links with their local communities and employers.

It seems important that enthusiasm for exciting new ways of doing things should not obscure the solid achievements of two and a half decades. The incomplete chronology in Table 12.1 may be of value in a brief survey of the past. In turn, this should provide a basis for speculation about the future, and the contribution that day services might make to the goal that is set for the responsible authorities of 'developing a system of care capable of responding sensitively and flexibly to the needs of disabled people and their carers' (Stephen Dorrell (then Parliamentary Secretary for Health) in a speech to a MENCAP conference in 1991).

Table 12.1 *Day services – a brief chronology*

1968	Report of the Committee on Local Authority and Allied Personal Services (Seebohm)
1970	Chronically Sick and Disabled Persons Act. Local Authority Social Services Act. Education (Handicapped Children) Act
1971	*Better Services for the Mentally Handicapped* (White Paper)
1975	National Development Group (to advise Minister on policy and implementation) National Development Team (to advise field authorities on planning and operation)
1977	*Day Services for Mentally Handicapped Adults* (NDG Pamphlet No. 5)
1978	Report of the Committee of Enquiry into the Education of Handicapped Children and Young People (Warnock)
1979	Report of the Committee of Enquiry into Mental Handicap Nursing and Care (Jay)
1983	Mental Health Act
1983	All Wales Strategy for the development of services for mentally handicapped people
1984	*An Ordinary Working Life.* Kings Fund Project Paper No. 50
1985	*Day Services, Today and Tomorrow* (MENCAP)
1988	*Community Care: Agenda for Action* (Griffiths Report)
1989	*Caring for People: Community Care in the Next Decade and Beyond* (House of Commons)
1989	Inspection of Day Services for Mentally Handicapped People (Social Services Inspectorate)
1989	Children Act
1990	National Health Service and Community Care Act
1991	Stephen Dorrell's speech – 'Learning disability' not 'mental handicap'
1991	*The Development of Day Services for People with Learning Disabilities* (new government guidelines)
1992	Supported employment for people with learning disabilities, NDT Real Jobs programme

Three periods will be covered. First, the late 1960s to mid-1970s, a period of optimism and major change, because finance was available, for service development. Second, the later 1970s to the mid-1980s, a period of slower development and consolidation, when changing pressures and financial constraints led to changing priorities. Third, the later 1980s to the present time, a period of waiting, of confusion and contradictory messages, not just from the politicians. Commercial considerations and the language of the market-place suggest a bleak outlook for a client group with little financial or political power. In reality, each period blended into the other – with common themes, such as, individual rights, assessment and reassessment, individual programmes, promotion of independence, fully co-ordinated local services, adequate finance and appropriately trained staff, recurring throughout.

THE LATE 1960s TO MID-1970s: EMERGING FROM ADVERSITY

Many day services were provided by an uneasy coalition between parents, and local authority health departments. Parents anxious that gains at Junior Training Corps or school should not be lost were determined to rebut the extreme views expressed earlier by authors such as Tredgold (1952). Staffing was generally limited. Programmes, often heavily dependent on volunteers, were mainly occupational, repetitive, light industrial work, packaging or simple subassembly tasks. Some services attempted to maintain literacy and numeracy skills but deliberate development of self-help/independence skills was rare. James Cummings, former Director of Education, Training and Employment of MENCAP, wrote of this period that he was 'not alone in having recollections of an ancient church hall in which simple woodwork and weaving were the activity of the more able, whilst the less able sorted strands of coloured wool into matched heaps which at the end of the day were put back into a sack'. 'Activities within occupation centres were rooted in the concept of ineducability' (MENCAP, 1985). A notable exception was the Slough experiment initiated by MENCAP in which James Cummings played a key role. This was described in detail by Eileen Baranyay in *A Lifetime of Learning* (1976) and *Towards a Full Life* (1981).) Advised by Herbert Gunzburg, this largely industrial workshop established assessment and review systems (using the 'progress assessment charts') and developed social training programmes. Slough remained an exemplar into the 1970s.

Other centres were less organized. Most staff were unqualified; managers had little support. The handover to the newly created social services departments in 1972 was achieved with little ceremony. Sometimes files were simply transferred and managers notified that in future they should report to Mr X in Social Services rather than Mr Y in Health. Managers known to the writer included someone who had been a BR stationmaster, another who had been a ballroom dance champion, another a cobbler, another a subpostmaster and proprietor of a village store, one person who was an army warrant officer, another a scientific instrument maker and another a former licensed victualler. In one authority the former ballroom dance champion was the only suitably qualified member of the staff in four centres; one or two others had trade or craft qualifications. In another authority, a manager who used jigs extensively was universally known by colleagues in his own and surrounding authorities as 'Jigger'.

Centres were often housed in church halls, converted outbuildings, large houses, redundant schools or 'temporary' wartime buildings. In one authority, a converted Territorial Army centre offered reasonable accommodation but had to be temporarily abandoned – drainage deficiencies filled the ground floor with raw sewage after heavy rain. It was reoccupied once remedial work had been completed. In church halls, folding tables had to be unchained from walls or taken out of storerooms and set up, and chairs and materials had to be distributed before work could start. The process took from 30 to 45 minutes and had to be reversed before staff and trainees could leave at the end of the day. Some centres had no separate dining or sitting area, midday meals were served in the work area and eaten from a space cleared on work benches. Staff ratios were generally between 1:12 and 1:14 trainees. In practice, emergencies and frequent absences regularly made these ratios much higher. In one case, the manager had been on extended sick leave for six months without replacement, leaving three ladies to cope somehow with 48 'trainees'! The national survey undertaken later by Whelan and Speake (1977) revealed that in some centres ratios were as poor as 1:20.

Work was repetitive and dull, seldom with educational value or related to local employment opportunities. Typical tasks included assembly of aerosol bottle tops packaging of nails, screws, bolts and other small items from a variety of industries, sewing dust covers on to springs (this required nimble fingers), collating mail-outs and directories, stringing reflective plastic strips on to plastic-covered clothes line, sub-assembly work (often using a fly-press), and packing and repackaging boxes of various products, including cosmetic and hair products. Some centres showed great ingenuity in breaking up relatively complex tasks into simple steps.

Working in difficult conditions, often poorly supported, always short of money and given unrealistic target income to generate, most staff remained remarkably optimistic and determined to work to improve things.

Hopes realized

Government responded swiftly to the 1968 Seebohm Report. In April 1971 the legal concept of ineducability was swept away by the Education (Handicapped Children) Act of 1970. A major factor in this significant change was determined lobbying by educationalists including Stanley Segal whose book *No Child is Ineducable* had given renewed hope to many since the 1950s

Also enacted in 1970 was the Local Authority Social Services Act which set up powerful 'one-door' social services departments. It was followed in 1971 by the White Paper *Better Services for the Mentally Handicapped*, which noted (paragraph 149) that many of the practices typical of normal education had already been assimilated by the new special schools, and expressed the hope that this educational approach would influence the work of day services for adults. Paragraphs 153–157 spoke of social and work training or occupation intended to develop work habits and increase self-reliance generally. These paragraphs also said that programmes should include further education and recreational activities. The targets set and the general direction indicated by the White Paper had a significant influence on local authorities. The possibility of additional finance stimulated vigorous interest in *Better Services*. The recommendations about joint planning and development by hospital and local authorities were less vigorously implemented. Separate services continued to develop and train staff in different traditions. In some authorities, local colleges of further education responded to requests from the new social services departments by appointing members of staff to work in adult centres, and some college-based courses were available as early as 1972.

Table 12.2 *Characteristics of centres known to the writer – early-1970s*

Premises	No purpose-built accommodation A large house A church hall Temporary buildings A converted stable block A Territorial Army centre
Programme includes	Light industrial activities Packaging nails, screws etc. Assembly of aerosol bottle tops Reflective strips on clothes lines When work was unavailable jigsaws, puzzles and table games Literacy and numeracy seldom taught
Activities outside centre	To shops or cafes occasionally in groups Coach outings two or three times a year One centre mounted an annual trainees' 'Black and White Minstrel Show' mimed to recorded music
Transport	52-seat coach Taxi Coach and taxi
Staff/trainee ratio	1:12 to 1:14 (including manager)
Number of staff qualified	One manager Two had craft qualifications

The new social services departments took advantage of purpose-built centre developments planned by the health departments. These centres followed the 1968 *Model of Good Practice*. Built on industrial estates, they closely resembled adjacent factories and commercial premises – some had conveyer belts installed to facilitate assembly and packing work. Some social services departments appointed a senior officer specifically charged with day centre development. Recruitment drives, secondment and in-service training were used to improve staffing levels. Output from diploma courses could not satisfy the demand for qualified staff. Jostling to attract qualified staff led to some acrimonious disputes between authorities about poaching. Authorities were seconding two, or sometimes more, staff a year. Some offered secondment to existing students paying their own fees. These measures would have taken an interminable time to remedy deficiencies in knowledge and skill amongst the staff in post. Some social services departments asked local further education colleges to mount courses specifically designed for this staff group. Some responded with remarkable speed and efficiency. In one, a member of staff was recruited, appointed and the first one-day-a-week, 12-week training course for day services staff completed by Christmas 1972. Investment in training led a substantial proportion of managers and staff to adopt a less paternalistic, custodial approach to their work, to debate whether or not activities were meeting the needs of trainees and to question what centres were training people for. One manager known to the writer suggested in 1974 that 'people were being trained to work in training centres'. Contract work remained the main business of day centres and produced appreciable income for the local authority. This money was seldom reinvested in the centres, but was merely used to offset the cost of providing day services. The low earnings limit led to a steadily increasing feeling that trainees were being exploited.

THE LATER 1970s AND MID-1980s: DEVELOPMENT AND CONSOLIDATION

As has been mentioned, a national survey of centres was published in 1977 by Whelan and Speake. Aspects covered included: staffing, staff qualifications, premises, equipment, transport, special care, support from other professionals, perceived functions of the training centre, assessment methods used, work undertaken, payment of trainees (the vast majority received less than £2.00 a week and more than 700 received no payment at all), educational activities, social training, and trainees entering sheltered and open employment. The detailed findings revealed wide variations between centres and the need for national guidelines.

In February 1975 Mrs Barbara Castle, Secretary of State for Social Services, set up the National Development Group (NDG) and the National Development Team (NDT) for the Mentally Handicapped to advise her and encourage the responsible authorities to develop services as outlined in the White Paper.

Moves towards a broadly educational approach stimulated by *Better Services* and improved training received considerable impetus in 1977 when the NDG's Pamphlet No. 5 *Day Services for Mentally Handicapped Adults* (NDG, 1977) was published. In his introduction, David (now Lord) Ennals, Secretary of State for Social Services, reaffirmed the government's commitment to the targets spelt out in *Better Services*, acknowledged that mentally handicapped people were capable of learning and developing to an extent not previously thought possible, said that day services were a key component of community care and announced that Pamphlet No. 5 replaced the 1968 *Model of Good Practice*. The NDG, chaired by Peter Mittler, Professor of Special Education at the University of Manchester, included members such as Mrs Peggy Jay, Mr (later Professor) Stanley Segal and Dr G.B. Simon. They saw the work of day services 'as educational in the broadest sense' and advocated 'an educational approach concerned with the active fostering of skills and abilities, never static but always looking ahead to the next step in development and for new achievements, however small'.

Pamphlet No. 5 dealt in clear, succinct detail with current provision, and offered guidelines on staffing, the admission and assessment process, activities and programmes to meet needs, record-keeping, people with severe and multiple handicaps, work preparation and opportunities, payment and incentives, leisure and recreation, counselling for students and families, and the use of community resources. It purported to be '[n]ot so much about buildings as about what might go on inside them' (paragraph 49).

Proposals for 'social education centres' 'which could meet the needs of a wide range of mentally handicapped people' (paragraph 53) were outlined in paragraph 52:

- the needs of individuals must be the starting point for planning services;
- the process of assessment should identify needs and 'provide a basis for a programme designed to facilitate the person's education and development in the widest sense';
- they must be flexible and meet changing needs; and
- they must offer a range of different but complementary components.

Table 12.3 *Characteristics of centres known to the writer: mid-1970s*

Premises	Mostly purpose-built Some converted property
Programme includes	Industrial work assembly and packing shower attachments, balloon pumps, aerosol bottle tops Wood work, horticulture Centre and college staff running centre-based literacy, numeracy and social skills programmes
Activities outside centre	Use of local sports centres and swimming baths, generally by groups at booked times Shopping for meals. Volunteers' tea-shop manned one day a week Some college programmes open to trainees
Transport	Coach and minibus
Staff/trainee ratio	1:12 (excluding manager)
Number of staff qualified	Five out of six managers DTMHA Some staff DTMHA Some staff have a craft qualification One a qualified teacher Most had done in-service training

This advice had most effect in the 'good' centres already attempting to use objective assessments to develop individual programmes. Other centres simply changed their name to social education centre and continued much as before. However, Pamphlet No. 5 gave an enormous boost to good practice. Much of its sound guidance could be followed with little additional expenditure. Some of its guidance, however, on training, staffing levels and the establishment of special care sections, could not be followed with little expense. In some authorities, joint finance, the only source of 'new' money, was used to create community facilities such as special care sections in day services for people who in the recent past would have been admitted to hospital.

Other influences during the later 1970s and early 1980s included training that encouraged staff and managers to look critically at the continued use of contract work, work which produced substantial incomes for the local authority but was of little benefit to trainees. Ideas from overseas, particularly Scandinavia and the USA, encouraged staff to think of people with mental handicaps as individuals, with the same right to be valued as other members of the community. Authors including Brandon, Craft, McConkey, Myers, Norris, O'Brien, Oswin, Towell, Tyne, Whelan and Speake, Wertheimer and Williams were just a few of the knowledgeable people writing and talking in detail about different ways of doing things. Organizations such as the Association of Professions for the Mentally Handicapped (now BRIDGES), the British Institute of Mental Handicap (now BILD), the Campaign for Mental Handicap (now VIA), the King's Fund, MENCAP and the Rowntree Foundation organized conferences and published information about possible service improvements. The 'Let's Go' television series, a joint venture between MENCAP and the BBC, was closely followed and many centres used the programmes and associated materials as a foundation for new and different activities.

Officers with specific responsibility for day service development had generally disappeared but encouraging developments in the 1980s included:

- An increase in special care units for profoundly and multiply handicapped people.
- Work experience schemes (Pagliero, 1981).
- Employment schemes, Pathway and the Shaw Trust, creating work opportunities in the community.
- Colleges of further education offering opportunities for continuing education to people with mental handicaps, both in centres and in colleges.

The All Wales Strategy recognized the interdependence of services and emphasized the need for them to collaborate with each other and with the people for whom the services were provided. Hopes that a similar strategy would revitalize the scene in England were, however, short-lived.

Some developments resulted from personal initiatives. One manager, frustrated by his failure to provide additional accommodation in his overcrowded centre, obtained the keys of empty, short-life accommodation on a Friday. On the following Monday, he moved ten students and an instructor in. He assumed that the property department would not risk the adverse publicity involved in dispossessing him! That building provided effective and much-needed day services for more than six years and eventually accommodated more than sixty students.

THE LATER 1980s TO THE PRESENT TIME: GROWING CONFUSION

For the most part, the 1980s saw further consolidation, and limited development. Competition for joint finance monies became increasingly fierce. Managers responsible for other client groups became increasingly resentful of the amount being spent on people with mental handicap and competed fiercely for available funds. As budgets became increasingly tight, some planners, managers and direct-care staff became confused and stuck to well-worn routines. On the one hand they were being urged to develop services and on the other hand they were having to make savings.

The Mental Health Act 1983 had little direct effect on day services. The new concepts of mental impairment and severe mental impairment it introduced confused rather than clarified issues around programmes on personal relationships and sexuality, which some centres had begun to introduce. Some legal advice given in all seriousness to one authority was that on the whole it would be safer (for the authority) if people with a mental handicap did not have personal relationships!

Table 12.4 *Characteristics of centres known to the writer: early 1980s*

Premises	All but one centre in purpose-built accommodation
	Special care sections contrived within centres or in separate accommodation
Programme includes	Virtually no contract work. One centre continued to make footpath signs, stiles and bridges for the county council
	Social skills and self-care programmes including personal relationships
	Horticulture, garden centres
	Wooden craft work
Activities outside centre	Literacy, numeracy, as part of adult or further education
	Swimming and other sports at local leisure centres
	College courses for special school-leavers
	Shopping service
	Tea-room manned twice a week
	Music and drama in local arts centre
	Work experience
Transport	Minibuses
	Increasing use of public transport (road and rail) where available
Staff/trainee ratio	1:10 (excluding manager and deputy)
	1:4 in special care
Number of staff qualified	All managers and deputies qualified
	CSS replacing DTMHA
	All staff have some qualification
	Care assistants in special needs with experience

In 1984 the King's Fund published *An Ordinary Working Life* (Project Paper No. 50) (King's Fund, 1980). This examined the application of 'ordinary life' principles to vocational services, and evaluated current employment and day services using the principles expressed in *An Ordinary Life* (King's Fund, 1980). It recognized that day services were overstretched but concluded that they had inherent problems that prevented 'ordinary life' principles being implemented. The group argued that service design derived from the 'ordinary life' principles required a shift from the 'readiness' or 'continuum' service model, ably developed by authors such as Whelan and Speake, to a model which moved 'directly to providing whatever support the person needs in the integrated setting which is desired'. The group found no rational or coherent vocational policy for people with mental handicaps in the wide range of services they identified. A number of employment options in the UK and the USA were examined. The paper did not specify job descriptions or organizational arrangements but 'gave a list of' essential ingredients for local services to follow. It was assumed that vocational services would be developed 'within the context of a plan for comprehensive services designed to ensure that the full range of needs of people are met'. In one authority by 1985 a successful work experience scheme in one centre had spread to its other five centres. Work experience officers were appointed, and they formed links with local employers, specialist careers advisers, youth training schemes and the Shaw Trust to build a network of successful placements, a number of which led to sheltered or open employment.

The Independent Development Council for People with Mental Handicap, an association of leading voluntary organizations in the field of mental handicap which aimed to fill the gap created by the abolition of the NDG in 1980, tried to establish an effective means of providing information and strategic advice on a national level and promoting good practice and action at local level. Their pamphlets supported the approach to day services of the NDG's Pamphlet No. 5 but increasingly emphasized the wisdom of involving people with mental handicap and their families in service planning, the importance of 'real' work in the community rather than 'pretend' work in centres, and the need to make the fullest possible use of further education facilities. *Next Steps* (Independent Development Council, 1984) recognized that training centres had 'an almost impossible role to play. It is rather a series of roles which may at times overlap, but which frequently results in no single function being performed adequately.' In *Living Like Other People* (Independent Development Council, 1985), the Independent Development Council reviewed Pamphlet No. 5 and acknowledged its beneficial influence on day services, but suggested a move away from centre-based services, which often failed to provide the services their users wanted, towards services intended 'to promote integration and community participation'. It actively supported the views put forward by the Campaign for Mental Handicap and the King's Fund's *Ordinary Working Life* in 1984. However, in *Cinderellas Again?* (1990), the Independent Development Council assessed the likely impact of the 'care in the community' policy framework on the lives and families of people with learning disabilities and expressed anxieties that the broad policy framework failed to safeguard the interests of people with learning disabilities and that services to people with learning disabilities had lost their priority in the face of other pressures.

By the mid-1980s even local authorities committed to the development of services for people with mental handicaps found commitments increasingly difficult to maintain. In one, a joint health authority/local authority strategy for a comprehensive range of services overcame an initial barrage of criticisms but made little progress because the two main agencies could not afford 3 per cent growth per year for ten years. Research in the same authority revealed that day services were underproviding for the most handicapped and the most able but overproviding for clients of 'average ability'.

The client-centred approach to day services was heavily supported by *Day Services, Today and Tomorrow* (MENCAP, 1985). It was described by Sir Brian (now Lord) Rix as 'a first attempt at defining and qualifying policy and practice issues which will be relevant to day services provision, possibly until the end of the century'. Its recommendations included 'a comprehensive revision of the ATC' (p. 19) moving towards 'a comprehensive Day Services Agency which will be capable of facilitating provision to meet the needs of individuals' ... 'The Individual Programme Plan forms the basis for planning and provision of appropriate services for individuals with mental handicap' ... 'Day services ... should be available 5 days a week' ... 'a more extensive service should be provided for profound and multiply handicapped adults' ... 'Greater co-ordination and co-operation between social services, voluntary bodies, Health, Education and other statutory agencies at all levels from local to national' (pp. 20 to 21).

During this time the commitment of senior managers and local government politicians to services for people with learning disabilities began to be diverted. In one authority, meetings between centre managers and staff, which had been recommended in Pamphlet No. 5 (paragraphs 356 to 359), were discontinued. They were said to serve no useful purpose and to be an unjustifiable expense.

At this time two works had been published, connected with the concept of community care. They were: *Making a Reality out of Community Care* (Audit Commission, 1986) and the *Second Report on Community Care with Special Reference to Adult Mentally Ill and Handicapped People* (House of Commons, 1984/5). They served as a basis for Sir Roy Griffiths' review of the way in which public funds were used to support community care policy, which was published early in 1988. It was entitled *Community Care: Agenda for Action* (House of Commons, 1984/5) In it he made no direct mention of day services except as part of 'packages of care best suited to enabling the consumer to live as normal a life as possible' (1:3:2 and 1:3:3). The government response in 1989, *Caring for People: Community Care in the Next Decade and Beyond*, talked of providing a 'coherent framework to meet present and future challenges' but made no reference to day services which were now attended by more than 50,000 people each week. In 1977 David Ennals had referred to day services as 'a key component of community services'. The lack of a reference to day services in the government paper seemed a curious omission and was of no help to planners or day service staff.

Philip Seed's book *Day Care at the Crossroads* (1988) clarified some of the confusion about day services. (Research was conducted in Scotland but the findings were said to be 'likely to be equally relevant for England and Wales' (p. 1).) Day services/centres were victims of their own success. As financial constraints had produced a shortage of other resources, they had been encouraged to do more and more. Seven different, but not mutually exclusive, models were identified and discussed in detail. Seed suggested that three basic models existed for day centres:

1. The work resource centre, providing work experience and sheltered or open work opportunities.
2. The further education resource centre, jointly managed by social work departments and further education colleges providing further education.
3. The community resource centre, promoting patterns of living using normal community facilities. Clients make a recognized contribution to the community and may move out of the parental home.

In 1989 the Association of Professions for Mentally Handicapped People, concerned that national guidelines for day services were 12 years old, arranged a weekend conference. Discussion of the Social Services Inspectorate report on day service was prevented by delayed publication but a wide-ranging series of discussions including service users, parents, planners and providers was initiated by Peter Mittler asking 'Whatever happened to Pamphlet 5?' He concluded that its influence, considerable at the time of publication, had been severely affected by 'severe malnutrition and lack of interest by service managers and central government'. Existing services were full, and many more severely handicapped people required day services (two out of five school-leavers). Some progress had been made. Involvement of further education colleges was patchy but promising and integrated opportunities were increasing. The Manpower Services Commission Training Agency, and Youth Training Schemes, were offering some help with employment. There was a greater awareness of philosophy and values, and of normalization – the 'ordinary life' model influenced practice. MENCAP was right to campaign for statutory services for adults. Committed staff showed many examples of good practice. Access to ordinary community activities was increasing. It was important that people with learning difficulties were engaged in community activities and provided services to the public. Who should run day services? Pamphlet No. 5 had concluded social services departments, but it could be Education. However, colleges were now independent of local authorities, and were unlikely to give priority to people with mental handicaps. A specialist Mental Handicap Development Agency which was part-Health, part-Social Services and part-Education would be likely to provide separate services rather than integration into mainstream services.

Working groups considered a range of topics and issues including the role of day care officers in building social networks. Resources other than day centres were discussed, as were people with learning disabilities in further adult education, self-determination, empowerment, personal relationships and sexuality, self-advocacy, working with families, code of practice for staff, work experience, employment and community services, and some implications of special care day services. The published account of the conference revealed the active interest and initiative of many involved with day services and their commitment to good and improving practice. A collection of papers describing the discussions, 'Developing Day Services', demonstrated this commitment but did not provide a blueprint for future services.

The long-awaited Social Services Inspectorate report on its inspection of day services for people with a mental handicap was published in 1989 (Department of Health, 1989). At lacklustre launch meetings in London and Manchester, inspectors said that they believed it was a factual account of services in the 150 units provided by the 13 local authorities studied during 1986 and 1987. Confusion and lack of direction amongst day services and the responsible authorities was revealed. What are day services? Who should they serve? What is their purpose? Is there a clear coherent statement of policy at local level? The NDG's Pamphlet No. 5, making recommendations for policy at national level, had neither been understood nor fully implemented. Good and imaginative practice at unit level was often frustrated by lack of understanding and support at departmental level. Islands of good practice were identified, but were more often in special care than in mainstream units, and were seldom the result of departmental initiatives. There was little tranfer between units. Good practice was seldom stimulated by planned staff development programmes. Day care staff were unlikely to receive adequate levels of management information and support. Five pages of desirable recommendations about policy, planning, management, staffing, training, function, assessment, the involvement of families, social workers, volunteers and voluntary agencies were prefaced by the statement: 'SSI expects local authorities will wish to consider the following recommendations as resources allow'. Properly critical of unsatisfactory service, the report recommended that authorities should take immediate steps to remedy manifest deficiencies, but it promised no financial support. The report could have been constructively used as a base to translate such wishes as those expressed by service users at Hannibal House in November 1989 to:

- develop a common vision of the function and purpose of day services, as part of a range of services for people with a mental handicap removing obstacles, at local and national level to the development of effective day services;
- provide appropriate training and support for all levels of staff;
  listen to the people who use the service; and
- review progress at all levels and remedy revealed deficiencies without delay.

By this time services for people with mental handicaps were almost forgotten by politicians, policy-makers and planners. The Children Act 1989 and the National Health Service and Community Care Act 1990 meant that senior managers and planners whose sustained support is necessary for effective service development were bound up with the multitude of unproductive problems and negotiations that inevitably accompany major reorganization – the senior manager who has just been told he/she must apply for a job in the reorganized department is unlikely to give wholehearted attention to the needs of any client group!

Table 12.5   *Characteristics of centres known to the writer: later 1980s*

Premises	All in purpose-built accommodation All with purpose-built special care facilities
Programme includes	Virtually no contract work Social skills, self-care Stimulation and physio & speech therapy Personal relationships Horticulture, garden centres Literacy and numeracy Wooden craft work
Activities outside centre	Literary and numeracy as part of adult or further education Sports at local leisure centres or sports clubs College courses for special school-leavers Work experience and sheltered employment Tea-room manned twice a week Music and drama in local arts centre
Transport	Minibus Public transport (road and rail) where available
Staff/trainee ratio	1:10 (excluding manager) 1:4 special care
Number of staff qualified	All managers and day care officers with some appropriate qualification Care assistants with experience

The momentary optimism produced by Stephen Dorrell's announcements at the MENCAP conference in June 1991 that 'we have decided that the Department of Health will, in future speak of "people with learning disabilities" rather than of "the mentally handicapped" ' faded in the face of ominous phrases like 'as resources allow', 'as far as is practical', 'what resources are available' and 'there will always be practical constraints', later in his speech. It was almost extinguished by the draft guidance on day services – *The Development of Day Services for People with Learning Disabilities* (Department of Health, 1991). This used 'as resources allow' in its second paragraph and appeared to be directly derived from a mixture of Pamphlet No. 5, *An Ordinary Life* and the Independent Development Council pamphlets. It stated: 'The Special Care Section should act as specialised resource area, offering intensive treatment and support, which can be used as a base by the most severely handicapped students, but from which they are exposed to increasingly demanding tasks and experiences in the rest of the centre.' The punctuation differs and 'the rest of the centre' is substituted for 'elsewhere' but otherwise it is all there, just as the NDG wrote it 14 years earlier. It seems to confirm the accuracy of Peter Mittler's assessment of lack of public interest and ministerial and government indifference. It was beginning to look as though the anxieties expressed by the Independent Development Council in *Cinderellas Again?* could be justified.

Despite the problems, pillars of good practice stand out above the muddy waters. Some of these had been described before by Ann Shearer in *Building Community* (1986). She reported on a number of different ways of opening up choices and opportunities in employment and leisure for people with learning disability, including such schemes as:

- The Shaw Trust
- Centre-based outreach developments using mainstream community educational and employment opportunities (Camperdown Tyne and Wear)
- A three-centre service with a successful vocational service based in one of them (Newcastle)
- The Wedge where a working community produces high-quality craft goods by weaving, modelling in reconstituted stone, producing wooden articles and engaging in rug work (L'Arche in Lambeth)
- The Gillygate wholefood bakery which sells a whole variety of goods and foods and provides a cafe where you can sit and eat them (York initiatives by Camphill Committees).

Not mentioned in *Building Community* are centres in two cathedral cities, Salisbury and Hereford, where people with learning disabilities assist in cleaning the cathedrals. In Hereford they also work in the cathedral shop and cafe. In Winter they keep the cafe open whilst other volunteers take their holiday.

Encouraging developments in Solihull at about this time are reported by McEvoy *et al.* (1993). A service with an operational policy based on 'ordinary life' principles provided a comprehensive packages of individualized care for 48 people. The range of activities varied from client to client according to needs and preferences identified in individual programme plans. A network of community-based work, leisure and education resources were used. Clients were also supported in the 'ordinary life' activities. Staffing levels were higher than those usually found in social education centres. One day care officer was attached to each of 13 three- and four-bedroomed houses in the scheme. For every two or three houses, an assistant day service manager facilitated the work of the day care officer, networking contacts with resources and providing access to them. The quality of the service was influenced by the working relationships between the day care officers and the residential staff. Positive effects of inter-agency working were the development of good relationships and an increasing variety of activity undertaken by clients, day care and residential staff. The service was flexible and could accommodate a range of abilities, ages and needs. Reported difficulties included travelling and an initial overdependence on educational resources. Despite the largely good relationships between day and residential staff, some clarification of their roles was still required. No details were given of costs.

The work of the FEU (Further Education Unit) on behalf of learners with disabilities and learning disabilities through the Training Enterprise and Education Directorate has developed and enhanced employment-led provision in colleges of further education. A project which ran from September 1990 to August 1992 had important messages for all further education colleges and Training and Enterprise Councils about ways of responding to the White Paper *Education and Training for the 21st Century* and the key role colleges can play in providing people with disabilities and learning difficulties with employment skills. The project explored amongst other things how colleges tutors could develop the new skills needed and tested the use of the development pack *Learning Support*.

The Real Jobs initiative, a partnership between the NDT, Training and Systematic Instruction (TSI) and the Joseph Rowntree Foundation set up in 1990, is an important development to encourage the development of supported employment opportunities for people with moderate or severe learning disabilities. Supported employment is 'Real work in an integrated work setting with on-going support provided by a social service agency', as has been stated by the Canadian Council on Rehabilitation and Work.

A survey of supported employment schemes was undertaken by Tim Lister of TSI and fellow authors from November 1991 to January 1992. It canvassed over 200 services. Of these, 79 claimed to meet the survey criteria. No information was received from the Shaw Trust, and limited information was received from MENCAP Pathway services. Independently operated services which had numbered 8 prior to 1987 numbered 79 in 1991. The following statistics were compiled:

- 79 schemes: 60 English, (nine in Greater London, six in Lancashire and Cheshire, between one and four in other authorities), 15 Welsh, 6 Scottish
- 1,619 supported workers, aged under 18 to over 65
- About 73 per cent assessed as moderate to borderline
- About 28 per cent assessed as severe to profound
- Weekly working hours from less than 15 to full time
- Annual support costs (based on 23 responses) ranged from £1,980 (little or no intensive support) to £4,919 (mostly intensive support)
- Most frequently cited problems – security of funding, staffing levels, current (1992) recession, the benefit system

Other details in the survey included: time in post, levels and patterns of support, types of employer, job and work site, referral sources, client characteristics best predicting success, pay policy and so on. The authors believe that people with a learning disability could now be taken seriously when they said that they wanted a job. Lack of effective strategic planning and a solid management infrastructure was likely to impede the spread of supported employment. Some of the 14 recommendations were felt to be optimistic, particularly if social services departments continued to retreat behind the 'rhetoric of financial realities'.

Seven randomly selected case studies of people in supported employment were reported separately:

- 3 men, 4 women, age range 22–53
- 4 exhibited behaviours described as challenging
- 3 were non-verbal
- hours worked: from 1 hour per week to full-time employment
- jobs – franking mail
            paper shredding
            grass cutting and factory work
            assembly work
            cleaning
            onion peeling
            clerk typist

It seems a pity that this interesting survey dismisses work experience as 'indefinite periods of unpaid work with no apparent goal'. Numbers of work experience staff in different parts of the country do work out clear goals with each client before arranging a placement and regularly review placements and, when the clients wish it, support them in obtaining full- or part-time, sheltered or open employment.

DISCUSSION

Speculation about the possible effect of the current economic and political climate on personal services for disadvantaged people is tempting but beyond the scope of this chapter. Recent experience of reorganization in Health and Social Services suggests that imminent reorganization of local government will mean that day services and their future will not be high on the agenda of national or local policy-makers or senior managers for some time. An extended period of hard work may be necessary to defend and maintain the status quo before any serious developments can begin.

Much of the content of this chapter is the result of personal recollection and reminiscence. It was exciting to be involved in day services in the 1970s. Things were changing and improving all the time. The pace of change has slowed and many issues have yet to be adequately addressed:

- How and by whom should day services be provided?
- How should the client group be defined?
- How can people with learning disabilities be supported when they become parents?

Centres have much in common yet the outcomes for clients are often very different. Thinking about what factors enabled centres to produce better, more valued outcomes for clients led to the polarities set out in Table 12.6. The polarities set out in this table are not new or original. With minor modification they apply to other services for other client groups. However, they are informed by an extended involvement with day services and may be of use to managers and staff who want to think about what they are doing, who they are doing it for and how it will be done. Good managers and managers in good authorities will almost certainly be involved in some kind of annual establishment review, and this may help some of them to look differently at a process that can so easily become a convenient excuse for doing more of the same – again and again. The factors are not in any rank or order but factor 12 which sees day services as an important, integral part of a local system of services must rank very highly. Ideas about a comprehensive system of accessible local services are not new. They were implied rather than spelt out in *Better Services*, and were developed in some detail by the NDG and further developed by the Independent Development Council and MENCAP.

Homeward Bound (Audit Commission, 1992) showed that working relationships between different agencies and professions and even between members of the same agency was 'not all that it should be' (paragraph 42). People working in different settings, even where there is a system of individual planning, seem to have difficulty in subordinating personal, professional and sectional interests to the task of working, in consistent ways, towards agreed goals for individual service users. Paul Taylor observed this phenomenon and suggested that it stemmed from lack of model coherency between services. It seems important to find some way of helping all those involved with services to move towards a shared vision of

- what should be done
- how it will be done
- who will do it
- where and when it will happen

There is no room here to describe model coherency in full. A chapter 'Conceptualising Service Provision' by Emerson *et al.* (in *Severe Learning Disabilities and Challenging Behaviour*) points out that:

> work is needed to think through the model of community based services, to clarify how staff should work together to meet the needs of the people they serve, and what kinds of organisation they should adopt to do so. This needs to be done partly at the level of the placement ... but it is also required at the level of the service system, to integrate the placement within the wider network of other services and the rest of the service-providing organisation.

When this work is done a shared vision of day services might look something like this: As an integral part of a range of provision offering day, residential and other support (to people with learning disabilities, and their families), day services should enable people with learning disabilities to:

- experience and engage in activities (including work) valued by ordinary members of their community;
- learn more about things that interest them;
- develop and maintain skills and competencies; and
- make informed choices about how they wish to spend their time.

Such a definition might help to avoid the trap of the neat and tidy single service solution (so beloved of administrators) that produced in turn the large-scale, long-stay institutions and the present, mainly segregated, day centres. Is it too fanciful to imagine that eventually it will be possible to appoint staff to a service – not to this day centre – that home – or the other community team – so that they could work to support individual service users wherever support was required? What a challenge for the twenty-first century!

Table 12.6   *Some factors which make day services more or less successful*

Likely to be more successful	*Likely to be less successful*
1. Local policy-makers and senior management give committed knowledgeable support to a developmental approach	1. Local policy-makers and senior management show little interest in client group
2. Unit manager gives consistent competent leadership	2. Unit manager inconsistent, frequently changes, does not lead
3. Shared vision of the purpose and function of the service and its limitations	3. Few shared perceptions about purpose and function. Limitations unrecognized
4. Staff support and training well structured and appropriate	4. Staff support and training lack structure. Most training external and sometimes inappropriate
5. Active students with influence on services and vision	5. Student influence on services and vision limited or non-existent
6. Established, effective process of assessment, individual programming and review	6. Process of assessment may exist as a paper exercise, seldom affects programmes
7. Acceptable risk levels of activities agreed and reviewed for individuals and groups	7. Activities organized to minimize risk
8. Planned, extensive use of mainstream community resources, including employment	8. Occasional, generally unplanned use of community resources
9. Good relationships with other services cultivated and maintained	9. Contact with other services limited
10. Involvement with and service to local communities	10. Token involvement, often in groups, with local communities. Seldom any attempt at service
11. Regular exchange of information (and staff) with other providers	11. Occasional exchange of information when people happen to meet
12. Day services seen as important integral part of local system of services	12. Involvement with other services only at crisis case conferences

REFERENCES AND FURTHER READING

Association of Professions for the Mentally Handicapped. 1990. *Developing Day Services*. London: APMH

Audit Commission. 1986. *Making A Reality out of Community Care*. London: HMSO

Audit Commission. 1992. *Homeward Bound: A New Course for Community Health*. London: HMSO

Baranyay, E. 1976. *A Lifetime of Learning*. London: MENCAP

Baranyay, E. 1981. *Towards a Full Life*. London: MENCAP

Department of Education and Science. 1978. *Report of the Committee of Enquiry into the Education of Handicapped Children and Young People*. Cmnd. 7212. London: HMSO.

Department of Health and Social Security. 1969. *Report of the Committee of Enquiry into Allegations of Ill Treatment at Ely Hospital, Cardiff*. London: HMSO

Department of Health and Social Security. 1971. *Better Services for the Mentally Handicapped*. London: HMSO

Department of Health and Social Security. 1979. *Report of the Committee of Enquiry into Mental Handicap Nursing and Care* (Chair: P. Jay). London: HMSO

Department of Health and Social Security. 1980. *Mental Handicap: Progress, Problems and Priorities*. London: DHSS.

Department of Health. 1989. *Inspection of Day Services for People with a Mental Handicap*. (Social Services Inspectorate). London: DoH

Department of Health. 1991. *The Development of Day Services for People with Learning Disabilities.* London: DoH

Department of Health. 1993. *Services for People with Learning Disabilities and Challenging Behaviour or Mental Health Needs* (Chair: J. Mansell). London: HMSO

Dorrell, S. 1991. Speech to MENCAP conference.

Emerson, E., McGill, P. and Mansell, J. (eds). 1993. *Severe Learning Disabilities and Challenging Behaviour.* London: Chapman & Hall.

House of Commons Social Services Committee. 1984/5. *Second Report on Community Care with Special Reference to Adult Mentally Ill and Mentally Handicapped People.* London: HMSO

Horobin, G. (ed.). 1987. *Why Day Care?* London: Jessica Kingsley

Independent Development Council for People with Mental Handicap. 1984. *Next Steps.* London: King's Fund Centre

Independent Development Council for People with Mental Handicap. 1985. *Living Like Other People.* London: King's Fund Centre

Independent Development Council for People with Mental Handicap. 1990. *Cinderellas Again.* London: King's Fund Centre

Inglis, K. 1987. To believe in a single solution is dangerous. *Social Work Today*, **18**, 2 March

King's Fund. 1980. *An Ordinary Life: Comprehensive Locally-based Services for Mentally Handicapped People.* Project Paper No. 24. London: King's Fund Centre

King's Fund. 1983. *An Ordinary Life: Issues and Strategies for Training Staff for Mental Handicap Services.* Project Paper, No. 42. London: Kings Fund Centre.

King's Fund. 1984. *Planning for People: Developing a Local Service for People with a Mental Handicap.* Project Paper, No. 47. London: King's Fund Centre

King's Fund. 1984. *An Ordinary Working Life.* Project Paper No. 50. London: King's Fund Centre

Leighton, A. (ed.). 1988. *Mental Handicap in the Community.* Cambridge: Woodhead Faulkner.

McEvoy, J., Dagnor, D., Thomas, R., Ashton, P. and Trower, P. 1993. A pilot evaluation of a new approach to day services in Solihull. *Mental Handicap*, **21**, 54–8

Martin, J.P. 1984. *Hospitals in Trouble.* Oxford: Blackwell

MENCAP. 1985. *Day Services, Today and Tomorrow.* London: MENCAP

MENCAP 1987. *Patterns for Living: Shared Action Planning.* Milton Keynes: Open University Press.

Ministry of Health. 1968. *Local Authority Adult Training Centres for Mentally Handicapped Adults: Models of Good Practice.* London: Ministry of Health.

National Development Group for the Mentally Handicapped (NDG). 1977. *Day Services for Mentally Handicapped Adults.* London: DHSS

O'Brien, J. and Tyne, A. 1981. *The Principle of Normalisation: A Foundation for Effective Services.* London: Campaign for Mentally Handicapped People.

O'Brien, J. 1986. *A Guide to Personal Futures Planning.*

Pagliero, V. 1981. *Work Experience Scheme, Bracknell.* Reading: Berkshire Social Services Department

Porterfield, J. 1984. *Positive Monitoring.* Kidderminster: British Institute for Mental Handicap

Seed, P. 1988. *Day Care at the Crossroads.* Tonbridge: Costello

Shearer, A. 1986. *Building Community*, London: Campaign for People with Mental Handicap and King's Fund Centre

Thomas, D. *et al.*, 1978. *ENCOR – A Way Ahead*, London: Campaign for the Mentally Handicapped

Thompson, T. and Matthias, P. 1992. *Standards and Mental Handicap.* London: Baillière, Tindall.

Tredgold, A.F. 1952. *A Textbook on Mental Deficiency (Amentia).* 8th ed. London: Baillière, Tindal & Cox

Welsh Office. 1981. *All Wales Strategy for the Development of Services for Mentally Handicapped People.* London: HMSO.

Whelan, E. and Speake, B. 1977. *Adult Training Centres in England and Wales.* London: National Association of Teachers of the Mentally Handicapped

Whelan, E. and Speake, B. 1979. *Learning to Cope*. London: Souvenir Press
Whelan, E. and Speake, B. 1981. *Getting to Work*. London: Souvenir Press
Wolfensberger, W. 1980. A brief overview of the principle of normalisation. In Flynn, R.J. and Nitsch, K.E. (eds). *Normalisation, Integration and Community Services*. Columbus, Ohio: PRO-ED.

Chapter 13

The National Development Team: Continuity and Change

Derek Thomas

INTRODUCTION

This chapter is about the National Development Team (the NDT as it is usually known) – its past, its present and its future. It is about the part played by the team as an agent of change and about change in the agency itself. It is essentially an interpretative 'insider' account by someone who was not part of its early history, but who has led it for its last five years as a governmental body and its first three years as an independent not-for-profit agency. The recency of the events and my personal involvement have both advantages and disadvantages.

Why write about the NDT anyway? Because in a text that is about advocacy on behalf of people with learning disabilities during the last twenty to thirty years, the NDT has and continues to perform a distinctive leadership role in helping to change policy and services. This in itself is worth celebrating. But also understanding its history may help decide what might maintain a process of positive change. At this stage I want to mention just three distinctive qualities of the NDT – its longevity, its values and vision and its emphasis on supporting innovation and implementation.

There are few who would dispute that the last two decades have been a time of fast and furious change – in technology, in the economic and social structures of our communities and in the way we manage and organize our public and private agencies. At a time when the old certainties are no more, it is perhaps reassuring to discover some continuities. The NDT is an institution which, whilst not static in terms of ideas or leadership, has *longevity*. It is 20 years old, as of 1995.

Secondly, the NDT is an agency that is not ashamed to express its *values* and to energetically articulate and promote its *vision* of how life should and could be for people with learning disabilities and their families. Its current vision is about opportunity and inclusion. In the early days it stood for more local, dispersed services, better partnership with families and good multi-professional working.

But thirdly, it is an organization that, both in the way it is designed and in the way it operates, seeks to facilitate and support *innovation and implementation* of these dreams.

This chapter first looks at the NDT's roots. Secondly, it looks at key ideas and methods of working during the first two phases of the NDT's life – from 1976 to 1986, and then from 1987 to 1992. Finally, it looks at the way the NDT has been working and changing itself so that it is in better shape to help others with both the new opportunities and the challenges that are a feature of the closing stages of the twentieth century.

ROOTS

The main reason for the establishment of the NDT was a continuing concern about the quality of life and the quality of service available to children and adults with learning disabilities living in hospitals. To this was added a new related concern about the slow pace of development of alternative community services. *Better Services for the Mentally Handicapped* (DHSS, 1971) had been published but soon it was realized that national policy and capital and revenue finance were not enough. If significant change was to occur in management and in care practice, *support for implementation* was also required at a local level. Consequently, early in 1975, Barbara Castle – then Secretary of State for Social Services – announced the establishment of:

- the National Development Group (NDG);
- the National Development Team for the mentally handicapped (NDT); and
- the Committee of Enquiry into Mental Handicap Nursing Care (the Jay Committee).

Whilst the NDG was to provide advice and guidance that would assist in the implementation of government policy and advise the government on policy, the NDT was to work *directly with field authorities*, advising on implementation, albeit only in England. It was also expected that the NDT would thus be in a good position to act as the 'eyes and ears' of the government in monitoring progress and problems in the implementation of national policy.

The roots of the NDT lay in the Hospital Advisory Service, established in 1969 by Richard Crossman. The problem here again was poor practice within long-stay hospitals. The result was neglect and abuse of vulnerable individuals and, in turn, political embarrassment. Central policy in itself had been shown to be a relatively weak lever for local change and the arrangements for informing and forewarning ministers had been shown to be inadequate.

The answer was seen to be a semi-independent body that was within the Department of Health, who funded it, but not *of* the Department of Health. Such a body would need to be able to face in two directions – to the centre and to the field – and to be able to offer knowledgeable, experienced advice to both. To do this it would need to be led by a senior practitioner rather than an administrator. This person would account to the Secretary of State but would work with providers and planners at the local level. The team would be serviced by civil servants.

It was from the Hospital Advisory Service, which since its inception had been visiting mental handicap hospitals, that the NDT was to take much of its methodology. This included large-scale on-site visits to services by teams of seconded professionals and managers: also a focus on review of services, plans and structures.

FIRST PHASE: 1976–1986

Leadership and membership

The first director of the NDT was a psychiatrist specializing in learning disabilities. He was Dr Gerry Simon, who was also deputy director of the NDG. This latter role, together with a close personal relationship with Peter Mittler who was chair of the NDG, ensured a good two-way flow of information between the team and the group. His position as director of the British Institute of Mental Handicap also ensured a strong link with training and dissemination activities.

As with the Hospital Advisory Service, it was believed that practitioner rather than administrative or general management leadership was required. Moreover, it was *medical* leadership that was thought to be the most appropriate for this particular job at that time. But the multidisciplinary nature of the task was also recognized and three assistant directors were also appointed, with educational, nursing and social work backgrounds.

One of the intended outcomes was to encourage a greater sense of priority at a local level. But there was also a sense of possibility – a growing optimism that inter-disciplinary and inter-agency working could be an engine of change, at least in services for this client group.

The administrative support provided from within the Department of Health was to prove both a strength and a weakness. On the one hand, it had the possibility of ensuring a close working relationship with the Department of Health's own policy advisers. But it also had potential for compromising the 'independence' of the agency. Here were career civil servants who needed to develop strong affiliation and loyalty to the non-departmental leadership, but whose careers and performance appraisal lay within the department!

The central team of director and assistant directors was augmented by invited 'panel members'. The panel, whose names were to appear in the overview reports of the team, consisted of professionals such as psychiatrists, nurses, social workers and members of the remedial professionals working as practitioners and/or managers. These people were drawn mainly from health authorities and local authorities, but some were from voluntary agencies. In addition, there were some panel members with research and academic backgrounds. Importantly there were also some people who were parents/relatives of people with learning disabilities.

Methods

The team's main approach to its work was to review services and plans through visits to particular localities involving teams drawn from the panel and led by the director or assistant directors. The assumption was that the best way of influencing practice was through advice and pressure from peers who are thought to be knowledgeable, experienced and had demonstrated a record of positive change in their own localities. This idea has remained a persistent one. It is still to be found as a core notion in the Health Advisory Service, as the Hospital Advisory Service was retitled. It was to be replicated in the national monitoring exercises established when it became apparent to ministers that their key 'community care' reforms would not be implemented on time in certain localities without extra pressure and extra 'how to do it' advice. It was seen again as a central concept in the operation of the Mental Health Task Force that has recently completed its central leadership task. Finally, it has continued to be a central tenet in the operation of the NDT.

Moreover, the involvement of peers to review methods and outcomes is inherent in the idea of peer audit that has gained ground over the last few years – particularly in medicine and in the audits that commissioners are now beginning to require as part of their arrangements for quality monitoring.

In this context it should also be noted that the use of peers who are still in practice – i.e. not full-time consultants – has an additional potential advantage in mediating change. It allows leaders to renew and refresh themselves: also to reflect on their own practice and strategies, and sometimes to take back completely new ideas to their own work settings.

By 1984 the NDT had been rechristened the National Development Team for Mentally Handicapped People and from January 1985 the local reports of the team were published and available, not just to the commissioning agencies.

Ideas and models

The overview reports prepared by the team's first director (DHSS, 1978, 1980; 1982; 1985) make interesting reading. They reveal that certain challenges endure and persist whatever the organizational structure, culture or resource context.

Since the primary intention in establishing the NDT was to sustain momentum and quality in the implementation of national policy, it was expected that the team would advise in a way that was consistent with *Better Services*. But herein was to be found one of the dilemmas that were to remain with the team throughout its first phase of life.

First, *Better Services* looked simultaneously in two directions. It looked to improving quality of services in hospitals – which at that time were seen as having a long-term role – and it looked to the development of more local alternatives. Arguably – at least in terms of review visits during the early years – the result was too much focus on the current hospital services.

Second, *Better Services* represented a strategy for the development of small-scale services that were more local, but for the most part buildings-based, rather than a strategy that promoted social integration and community responsiveness. The NDT, during the first two phases, failed to break this particular mould in continuing to advocate for centres, hostels and community units. Consequently it was left to others such as Campaign for People with Mental Handicap (CMH), the Jay Committee and the King's Fund to develop a significant critique of the policy and the models and to promote more strongly the concept of an ordinary life for all, irrespective of the degree of their disability.

But the NDT did develop the idea of community teams as a key element in a local service. *Better Services* had talked about individual assessment and planning, but had not made it clear how this was to be undertaken or by whom. The NDT was also very emphatic about the need for joint planning, as well as multidisciplinary teamwork. It also strongly advocated the development of the voluntary sector in a provider role alongside Social Services and Health long before this was to become a central element in the government's NHS and local authority reforms.

Achievements

What then were the team's achievements during the first decade?

First, its presence at a local level helped to ensure that some priority was accorded by health authorities and local authorities to this underresourced, undervalued service for a sector of society that was severely disadvantaged. Likewise its national reports to ministers ensured that at least junior ministers of Health holding mental handicap as part of their brief were made aware of the continued underresourcing of this service and the failure in many parts of the UK to develop joint strategies and better practice. In particular, the team's continuing interest in services for children and families, together with the NDG's advocacy, amplified the voice of external pressure groups who were campaigning to get children out of hospital. This culminated in Patrick Jenkin's speech in 1981 in which he declared that no child should have to grow up in a mental handicap hospital. So the team not only helped to maintain priority, but also helped in a shift in policy.

Secondly, there is evidence that the team shaped in significant ways the pattern of community services. In particular its continuing advocacy and explanation of community teams led to their adoption and implementation in many parts of the UK.

Thirdly, it seems likely that the team did improve the quality of existing service, at least in some hospitals. For example, by supporting local arguments for improved staffing ratios, and the provision of better physical environments and more therapists, the team played its part in making life better for many people. This should not be overstated. In most hospitals, quality of life as measured by key indicators remained very poor.

Fourthly, in promoting joint planning the team laid the basis for much collaboration and local innovation that might otherwise have not occurred.

Weaknesses

The team did have weaknesses. Arguably, despite the claim that it was not an inspectorate, its insistence on visiting all wards in each hospital gave a contrary message and those visited often experienced the review as an inspection.

Again, although community teams and community units represented 'interpretations' and 'development' of policy, the team failed to really grasp the significance of the 'ordinary life' movement, and few people who were part of this movement were invited to join the panel. The team was progressive without being visionary. Moreover, whilst community teams continued to enjoy popularity, community units – with their multiple functions as office base, short-term care and a home for some people – were subject to criticism and eventually became discredited as a model.

Whilst stretching the edges of policy with community units and community teams, the team developed a reputation for being prescriptive. It failed to realize that different localities would and should develop mechanisms and processes with which local people were comfortable.

Change of leadership

During the latter years of the first decade, a new director was appointed – Dr George Kerr. Again it is interesting that someone with a medical background in the psychiatry of mental handicap should have been appointed. Unfortunately he had to retire soon after taking the post on the grounds of ill-health. Then followed an interregnum when the assistant director – nursing acted as director.

SECOND PHASE: 1987–1992

The period from 1987 to 1992 is probably best viewed as a period in the agency's history of extended transition that culminated in the decision to reconstitute it at 'arm's length' from the Department of Health. But transition did not mean consolidation and stability. On the contrary, it was a period of experimentation and progressive change.

Context

It is important to grasp the context for this transitional phase. First and foremost, it was a time of major structural change within the NHS. Roy Griffiths' first report recommending the introduction of general management at a local level and an overall executive board at the national level had been accepted by the government and was being implemented. These structural reforms and a change in the culture of the NHS were both to take the time of senior officers at the Department Of Health and to influence their and their ministers' thinking. This was also a transitional period for the NHS, although few expected or predicted that these reforms were to be rapidly superseded by Margaret Thatcher's more radical attempts to create internal markets within the NHS.

But there were also other priorities coming on to the national agenda – in particular a long overdue recognition that mental health services were not working. This, together with a belief that mental ill-health was a major contributory factor to the politically embarrassing visibility of homeless people on the streets of London, was enough to capture the attention of ministers at the Department of Health. Since there was also an unwillingness to increase the civil service workforce, this meant that learning disabilities were inevitably to be given a lower priority.

Later in this period, Roy Griffiths' second report, this time on community care, was produced, heralding the community care reforms that were subsequently to be introduced at the beginning of the 1990s. Leadership within the Department of Health was inevitably to shift from the Priority Services Division to the Community Services Division, with its more generic community care remit and with a particular focus on elderly people. Again, learning disabilities was to take a back seat.

So it is against these major changes in priorities and in structure that the change in policy and services for people with learning disabilities has to be understood. It also has to be understood in the context of cultural change. The Department of Health, both ministers and civil servants, were unsure whether they wanted to 'manage' the shape and pace of change in local service. If it was to be left to those out there to get on with it in a spirit of decentralization, then what was the role for a central development team like the NDT? But if the public was likely to call central government to account, then it would need ways of supporting the implementation of its policies.

In fact many field authorities had run ahead of national policy. Although the centre has not fully embraced 'ordinary life' principles, many health authorities and social services departments had. Likewise, several regional and district health authorities, encouraged through the process of ministerial regional reviews, were beginning to talk about closure of their mental handicap hospitals – ahead of an explicit national policy to this effect.

A time for change?

It was against this backcloth that in 1987 I was appointed as the first director without a medical background. In putting the team not just under new management but in appointing an 'outsider' who had previously not been associated with the NDT as an assistant director or panel member, the Department of Health was indicating a willingness to embrace change. Exactly what kind of change was wanted or expected was not clear!

It seems reasonable to speculate that at the time of my selection in 1986 the administrative and professional team within the Department of Health:

- wanted again to maintain the momentum for change in learning disabilities in the face of emerging new priorities;
- wanted the change to be broadly in line with the policy of decentralization of services outlined in *Better Services*; and
- wanted to move a little more firmly away from an NHS led service.

Leadership and membership

What of the additional leadership within the NDT? What was its extended member-ship? Who now constituted the team?

My first steps towards introducing a change in direction were to introduce new people into the management team. Instead of making full-time appointments, I looked to establish several associate director posts that enabled new people to work with me on a seconded, part-time basis. This included someone with senior management experience within social services, someone with a senior position within the voluntary sector, someone with a qualitative research background and someone with organiza-tional development expertise.

In making these appointments, I was departing from the precedent of a nurse, social worker and psychiarist team. Whilst the commitment to multi-professional working that had been a hallmark of the NDT was maintained, shared core values and vision and ability to engage confidently at all levels with the NHS, the local authority and the independent sector were now of more importance than professional balance in the core team. These were also to be key criteria in bringing in new blood to the panel. Some of the existing panel were retained, but many new people were recruited.

Values and vision

Better Services had provided a key central impetus that was subsequently well supported by the NDG and the NDT. Within the parameters it set there has been a
significant change in the nature and location of services, together with a gradual shift in
management responsibility from the NHS to local authorities and voluntary or private
agencies. It had also been strong on service principles, such as the need for a
comprehensive assessment of each individual and the co-ordination of professional
skills. Here again, the NDT had been influential in adding to the case for greater
individualization.

Better Services was, on the other hand, weak in projecting a positive image of people
with learning disabilities, and in making key positive values explicit. Those stated tend
to be expressed negatively, e.g., 'should *not* be segregated unnecessarily from people of
similar age, nor from the general life of the community'. Even important subsequent
developments of policy for children with learning disabilities were expressed in this way
– 'should *not* have to grow up in large hospitals' rather than 'should have a right to grow
up in a family'. It was also weak on its vision of the opportunities that people should
have and in its vision of a more inclusive community.

The new NDT, on the other hand, sought to be clear and explicit about its core values
and to express these in positive terms:

- people with learning disabilities should be treated as having equal value as human
  beings;
- people with learning disabilities should be encouraged to develop as individuals and
  this means that their specific learning disabilities must be recognized and addressed;
  and
- people with learning disabilities should be enabled and supported not just to be *in*
  communities, but to participate as citizens.

The framework that the NDT found helpful was one that gradually achieved
widespread currency throughout the UK. It sought to express these values in terms of
'accomplishments'. This was the word chosen by John O'Brien; to describe essential life
experiences which people tend to value and to seek.

The key accomplishments identified by O'Brien were:

- community presence;
- relationships;
- competence;
- choice; and
- image and status.

Here therefore was the beginning of a *reformed* national agency that could review
services – still at the request of field authorities, rather than as part of a mandatory
process – but against 'ordinary life' values and principles. Here was a team and a
network of associates, many of whom, like myself had been strongly influenced by
Wolfensberger's development of the concept of normalization, by examples from
Nebraska (Kendal and Firth, 1978) and by O'Brien's framework of 'accomplishments'.
Reviews of services and of strategy continued to be a major part of our programme, but
we were far more likely to want to assess quality in services by reference to the

experiences of those who used them. The NDT had from the very early days set a very positive example by including parents and relatives as part of its service/strategy review visits. This was a precedent that I followed. Parent members were able to offer a powerful and influential critique of services.

Prior to 1987, the visiting teams were more likely to spend significant amounts of time with front-line staff than with those who used the services. The audits were more likely to concentrate on process variables, such as staffing level, multi-professional mix and joint planning mechanisms, than on outcomes for people with learning disabilities. Previously the reviews had attempted to be comprehensive. For example, it was standard practice to visit all the wards in a particular hospital. But our new practice was to spend more time in a few settings and to get more of a feeling of what it was like to use the services: what opportunities for ordinary living were being created: and how were the healthiest, most lively, more innovative parts of the service performing? It was felt important that best practice was identified so that it could act as a benchmark for progress elsewhere in their locality.

The team also began to experiment with different kinds of work. For example, we began to invite commissions, not for independent assessment and review of the existing services, but for help in designing or redesigning services. Here the customer already knew that the current service failed to meet the wishes and needs of people with learning disabilities, but was unsure what should be offered.

Gradually we also began to act as facilitators – helping to shape the local agenda, set priorities, build teams, strengthen alliances. Often we were acting as process consultants, but with up-to-date strategic vision and knowledge about what was possible in practice. In some localities, we also began to undertake project management in which we, in effect, became members of the client organization.

Weaknesses

Looking back, my main regret is that I did not fully exploit the very considerable resource opportunities available to me with a base budget of around £500,000. We could and should have invested more at that time in the development and training of associate consultants, who would subsequently have led field and project work. We should, in particular, have invested in the recruitment and training of consultants from black and other ethnic minority communities. Finally, we should have begun to involve people with learning disabilities more centrally in the life and work of the NDT.

Achievements

But during the second phase the NDT achieved a number of things. As before, it helped to maintain a sense of priority at the centre in the face of competing pressures. Whilst it was Res-Care's arguments for village communities that were to create the occasion for time and resources to be allocated by the policy division, the NDT exerted effective pressure and was able to influence the content of the two subsequent circulars (Department of Health, 1992a; 1992b). Even though the Department of Health maintained its line that a range of residential options were desirable, it sent strong signals to field authorities that it had little enthusiasm for village communities. It announced no new initiatives and no new resources for such communities: nor did it make any commitment to slowing down the momentum of hospital replacement. However, here was an NDT that had an inside tack and that was able *quietly* to provide arguments that civil servants were then able to use with ministers.

This low-key influencing was to be a continuing feature of this period. There was no need for us to raise the profile of the agency or to trumpet our views when these could be expressed directly to those responsible for policy implementation and development. Often during this period we were shown early drafts of Department of Health papers relevant to both adults and children with learning disabilities, and were able to shape internal advice to ministers. The NDT, therefore, can take some credit for maintaining the momentum for hospital replacement at a national level. More specifically, its fieldwork in several parts of the country proved valuable and its advice to close particular hospitals was heeded.

Another achievement during this period was the introduction of the term 'learning disabilities' to replace 'mental handicap' in the new circulars.

During this period the NDT also effectively supported and endorsed those who were developing more individualized options in terms of accommodation and employment. Through its Real Jobs initiative (NDT, 1991; 1992a; 1992b; 1992c) it also exerted a positive influence on the Department of Employment's and the employment services' thinking and policy.

Two main tensions were to persist throughout this period, right up to the decision in 1990/91 to spin off the NDT as an independent agency. The first related to the independence of the team. As director, I was employed as a Crown servant with a reporting line to the Secretary of State. However, the advice to field authorities was expected to be consistent with national policy. There had always been some tension, as the early NDT pushed its interpretation of policy, particularly with regard to community units. But now an NDT with 'ordinary life' beliefs began to test policy and to test the relationships with the department's officials.

But perhaps the more significant challenge related to whether there was now a need for an NDT at all. Within days of my appointment, arguments were being put along the lines that general management when implemented, together with the monitoring and review activities by Regional Health Authorities and the Social Services Inspectorate were probably sufficient to sustain the momentum towards more and better community care.

This questioning of the necessity of a body such as the NDT was to continue and was eventually resolved in 1991. It was decided that there *was* a continuing need for a national development agency such as the NDT, but that it should be at arm's length from the Department of Health. This move was consistent with a push to create various 'next steps' agencies. Given that the main customer was field authorities rather than the Department of Health, it made sense that they should pay for the service. It also meant, since there were competitors out there, that the value of the NDT would be market tested. It also put a degree of distance between the department's pragmatic policies and what was seen as the NDT's idealism.

Consequently the department encouraged a 'management walk-out' by myself, Simon Whitehead, my deputy director, and Margaret Pearson, the team secretary and formerly an assistant secretary within the learning disabilities branch. The NDT was reconstituted from April 1992 as an industrial and provident society with a tapering subsidy from the Department of Health. We were to generate income that would compensate for the reducing core grant through fee-earning consultancy and through specific grant applications to government departments and to charitable foundations.

THIRD PHASE: 1992–1995

This has arguably been the most exciting and innovative period in the NDT's history. We were being supported by the government in establishing ourselves as a small social business with a national role at a time of radical change in the structure and culture of the NHS, local authorities and the independent sector.

This is a venture that we entered with a good degree of anxiety. We did not know whether field authorities would be willing to pay for a service that was previously provided at no charge. We did not know how we would fare in securing specific grants from government departments and charitable foundations, and we were unhappy that no assurance of long-term core funding could be given. We were also concerned that an inner track on policy would be lost and that important relationships with the centre would be weakened.

At the same time we realized that there were important new opportunities. We were now free to work not just in England, but in the UK and, if we wished, internationally. We had freedom to design and manage the organization in the way we wanted and, most important, we were able to manage our own finances. The NDT had come of age.

My annual report (Thomas, 1993) covering the first year as a non-governmental agency was headed 'Time for Change'. I described it as a time in which we were beginning to establish a new strategic direction, a new identity, new capacities and new energy to take a lead in promoting the inclusion of people with learning disabilities in our communities.

I went on to note that as an advisory and development agency, with governmental roots, our objectives inevitably continued to focus on improving services, systems, policy and leadership. But we recognized that we needed to work in partnership with more informal coalitions that include people with learning disabilities, their relatives and ordinary citizens.

I described our core values as equal opportunities; the empowerment of those who are disabled and disadvantaged; individuality and diversity; and emphasizing the importance of community. I outlined our vision of services that can respond to the wishes and needs of individuals, and which offer the person-to-person support and other technical supports needed for ordinary living, and of organizations that are focused, but flexible, collaborative, trustworthy and reliable over time. I stated that they must also be committed to continued investment in innovation and in learning.

In the same report I outlined key elements in the NDT's strategy in the way shown in Table 13.1.

Leadership

One requirement was to increase the volume of our local advice and consultancy. It was here that the main source of our income lay. The decision to stay small in terms of core staff meant, in turn, that we needed to increase the number of associate consultants working under contract to the NDT. This was a process that was to continue throughout

Table 13.1. *Key elements of NDT strategy*

Continuity	Change
• A central *focus* on people with learning disabilities and those who provide specific or dedicated services, and/or on disadvantaged people	• Partnership with others to achieve benefits for *all* who are disabled
• A clear *vision* based on explicit values and up-to-date knowledge of what is possible	• Commitment to working with both public and independent sector agencies to *implement* better services
• Commitment to *equal opportunities* for people with learning disabilities	• Action that establishes the NDT as an exemplary *equal opportunities employer*
• *Accountability* to people who use services and a *commitment to consult* and involve them	• *Careful assessment of* the requirements of our customers and their *satisfaction* with us
• Seeking to influence both *practice and policy*	• Increased emphasis on *networking and dissemination*
• Staying *small* at the centre	• *Enlarging our immediate circle* of associate consultants; improving *communication* within our network; and a commitment to enhancing the quality of services
• Continuing and building on our relationship with the *Department of Health*, and with health authorities and social services departments	• Extending our work to other major public agencies and associated departments concerned with *education, employment, housing and transport*, as well as the voluntary and commercial sectors
• *Retaining the NDT's image* as an influential national body with vision and a history of promoting change	• *Developing an effective marketing strategy* that raises the NDT's profile; creating a positive image that is businesslike and can help people implement and manage change
• *Innovation* that allows for ...	• *Investment* in innovation and in learning
• *Retaining the knowledge, skills and expertise* we have built up over the previous five years	• Investment in developing new competencies and capacities as an independent non-governmental agency

this period. During the first year as a not-for-profit agency we recruited two associate consultants and by April 1995 there were eleven.

Another requirement was to create the organizational and financial infrastructure that would allow us to develop as an efficient and effective social business. This led during 1993 to the appointment of a general manager with an accountancy and managerial background.

Thirdly, we now had a management board. This was an important opportunity to bring in influential people who would add to the agency's status, help us to network and ensure good corporate governance. Four people – a director of social services, a chief executive from a county council, a regional general manager within the NHS and an organizational psychologist – were recruited as non-executives to join me, Simon Whitehead and Philippa Russell on a single-tiered management board.

Local consultancy

The requirement to charge field authorities for our services meant that the NDT had to enhance its profile and credibility. The Department of Health had argued that the only proper way to test the NDT's value as a development agency working at a local level was to subject it to market forces. If it was needed and if it was good at what it did, people would be willing to pay for it. Our aim was to undertake high-quality work relevant to national learning and to demonstrate that this could be fee-earning and could increase in volume.

During 1992/93, the NDT began to offer more varied forms of advice and consultancy. The team visits, providing external review and audit, continued but were augmented by much more one-off consultancy or advisory exercises involving one or two consultants. We are increasingly likely to act as facilitators for local teams and groups, helping to shape local agendas, design and plan new services and build new alliances.

We were diversifying not just in terms of the nature of our local work, but in terms of territory. We began, for the first time, to work in Wales. Training and Enterprise Councils (TECs) and independent sector agencies, in addition to health authorities and social services departments, began to commission work from us. During the first year as an independent agency we worked in over 30 localities with over 40 agencies.

During 1993/94, we increased the volume of our fee-earning consultancy to nearly 700 days through over 100 contacts in over 40 localities. This growth in volume and diversity was to continue during 1994/95.

By our third year as an independent agency, social services departments had overtaken health care providers as the NDT's main customer. This trend followed the emerging leadership role expected of social services departments. Likewise a gradual growth in the commissioning from the voluntary agencies indicated the growing importance of the independent sector as a service provider.

Whilst external service reviews continue to be an important activity, we are much more likely to act as consultants to self-audit review by other parties such as health commissions. Work aimed at enhancing local quality assurance systems is becoming more important. Finally, we are increasingly asked to take on the complex business of reviewing practice and procedure *after* allegations of neglect or abuse have been investigated locally. It is salutary to reflect that such investigations are still needed over twenty years after the first examples of abuse were drawn to our attention.

Policy work

During 1993/94, the NDT began to pilot the idea of development projects designed to create a national focus on a particular issue or topic. The first such initiative was 'Real Jobs'. Here was a programme designed to support the initiation and spread of supported employment as a viable alternative to day services. Here was the NDT beginning to act in support of new leadership and as a catalyst for new networks and alliances. The consultancy work we had undertaken put us in an excellent position to understand the policy and the issues and, in turn, to present arguments for change to those responsible for benefits and employment policy.

Whilst the NDT continued to respond to various major consultative documents, increasingly we are organizing our policy work around major themes. By 1995 we were no longer working on supported employment, but were prioritizing:

- Supported Living
- Day-time Opportunities
- Services for Children and Young People
- Primary Health Care.

Dissemination

In the early days the team disseminated ideas through its period overview reports and from 1985 through the publication of its local reports. Now we publish reports (NDT, 1993a; 1993b; 1993c) relating to main themes/programmes of work. Where customers agree, we also publish local reports.

In addition, the NDT now regularly organizes workshops and conferences to disseminate ideas and experience. Action Learning Networks constitute another fast and effective way of helping people to learn from each other.

Achievements

Looking back over this period, I believe that we have been influential and had a real impact in a number of ways. For example, the Real Jobs programme has provided a national focus and stimulated debate about the future of day services. I believe that the number of people in supported employment has increased as a result of the NDT's consultancy and other work on this topic. More specifically, I believe that we have played an important part in encouraging the Department of Employment's leadership around supported employment.

In many localities where a major focus was people with challenging behaviour, we have made a difference. Our evaluations have highlighted poor-quality physical and social environments, and reinforced the resolve and efforts of managers, practitioners and parents to initiate improvements.

A major objective has been to help public agencies respond to key challenges and opportunities arising from the new 'community care' policies and organizational frameworks. Our work on strategy development and purchasing/commissioning was designed to do just this. Here I believe we have helped promote awareness of the need for a much more individualized approach to purchasing and the importance of both inter-agency strategies and a joint approach to commissioning.

Given that many district health authorities currently lack the capacity, time and experience to develop their purchasing role in relation to community care for people with learning disabilities, we have welcomed the emergence of close joint working with social services departments and the growing recognition of their major role in bringing about the development of community care. This should allow health authorities to focus on their continuing specialist contribution to learning disabilities services, and to develop strategies that ensure health gain through better health promotion in primary, secondary and tertiary health services.

Through our Supported Living programme, we are succeeding in shifting the debate from size of homes towards the more important question of 'Is this what the person wants?' Is the individual being enabled to live as they wish? Managers and practitioners in social services departments, the NHS and the independent sector now have a much clearer vision of what flexible, more individualized accommodation and support should and could look like, and how this can include those with the most severe disabilities.

We have also shown that much more flexible short-term opportunities are desirable and possible (NDT, 1994).

LOOKING TO THE FUTURE

How will the NDT fare in the future? Will it survive and continue to have a positive influence on policies, services and opportunities for people with learning disabilities and their families?

The challenges are very considerable if core funding from the Department of Health is not continued beyond 1996/97. Significant specific grant income will have to be secured to offset, in part, the core costs of the agency. However, as we saw with the collapse of Baring, charitable funding is fragile and the demand for such grants far outstrips supply. Specific grants from central government are also very limited and many are competing for this scarce, time-limited finance.

I believe that there are four strategic challenges which, if we embrace them successfully, will ensure the continuity of the NDT.

The first is a strategic objective about becoming a *forum* – networking with others and supporting the work of others. We believe that this is the best and only way to achieve our vision. We want to stay small – at the centre – but to grow in terms of associates and partners.

Here the signs are good – we are learning how to organize successful conferences, workshops and action learning sets. We are developing strong partnerships with other major national voluntary organizations, such as the King's Fund, the Council for Disabled Children and MENCAP, and with the research units and centres which major on learning disabilities.

A second challenge is that we want to be a creative, flexible and friendly learning organization.

We are already fast and flexible. Good ideas generated in one-to-one conversations and meetings between core team members and between core staff and associates are shared quickly. They often shape and influence our behaviour in a very immediate way, and then get expressed in policy and procedural form. Many people, both in the core group and in the associate group, can and do perform several roles. Individuals have shown that they can adapt to changing roles and expectations,. But we need to get better at anticipating the changes that are likely to be most difficult and stressful.

And we are creative – there is never any shortage of ideas. The problem is prioritizing and implementing them,. We are committed to learning. We take risks, make mistakes, and change our practice in the light of experience. The work that is developing around allegations of abuse that seeks to help other organizations learn from these stressful experiences is a good example of this. But we still struggle with capturing and sharing the very considerable experience that we have.

A third challenge is that we want to be an exemplary equal opportunities agency.

We have made significant improvements to our national office in Manchester in terms of mobility and internal access.

Women now constitute two-thirds of the management team (although the two senior managers in the agency are men) and undertake over two-thirds of the consultancy by core staff. They constitute four of the eleven current associate consultants and undertook just over one-third of the fee-earning days. They constitute just over 60 per cent of the wider network of consultants we use, and undertook over two-thirds of this fee-earning consultancy. More women are leading consultancy projects than formerly, but not yet in a way that properly reflects their presence in the workforce.

Women are now well represented in all the advisory groups for our various development projects, and Helen Platts and Margaret Flynn are acting as project managers for short-term respite, listening to offenders and providing short-term care for adults. All the project workers are women.

We have also made significant progress in increasing the involvement of people with learning disabilities in the life of the NDT. We have made the decision to invite their participation in the management board. Our workshops and conferences are now co-chaired, as a matter of policy, and people with learning disabilities are involved in some, but not yet all, of our advisory groups. We now employ two people with disability. We also now have consultants who have learning disabilities.

As to involving people from black and ethnic cultures, our performance remains very poor. We have used only one black person as a consultant this year, and only one other black person as a member of an advisory group. The management board remains white, the management and support teams likewise; the same can be said for the associate consultants, and the other consultants we use. All this must change and is set to change!

Finally, the fourth challenge. We want to improve our business efficiency and develop a more systematic approach to quality – beginning with a better account of what we have to offer, particularly to field authorities, but also improving our competencies. Only if we do these things will we able to justify our case for continued core funding and increase the volume of our fee-earning consultancy.

CONCLUSION

The NDT has completed its transition from governmental agency to non-governmental agency. We have a clear and exciting vision of what kind of agency we want to be and what we do best. We have a record of positive achievement.

We will need to sustain balance in our overall programme so that we make time for development work, policy-influencing and dissemination, as these activities extend our network, renew our knowledge and increase our profile. But we must also ensure quality and growth in our local consultancy.

The NDT remains a major force for change. It now has knowledge, practical experience and motivation to continue to play its part in promoting better services and better opportunities for people with learning disabilities within a fairer, more inclusive society.

REFERENCES

Department of Health. 1992a. *Social Care for Adults with Learning Disabilities (Mental Handicap). LAC(92)15.* Heywood: DOH

Department of Health. 1992b. *Health Services for People with Learning Disabilities (Mental Handicap).* HSG(92)42. London: DOH

DHSS (Department of Health and Social Services). 1971. *Better Services for the Mentally Handicapped.* London: HMSO

DHSS (Department of Health and Social Services). 1978. *Development Team for the Mentally Handicapped.* First Report: 1976–1977. London: HMSO

DHSS (Department of Health and Social Services). 1980. *Development Team for the Mentally Handicapped.* Second Report: 1978–1979. London: HMSO

DHSS (Department of Health and Social Services). 1982. *Development Team for the Mentally Handicapped.* Third Report: 1979–1981. London: HMSO

DHSS (Department of Health and Social Services). 1985. *Development Team for the Mentally Handicapped.* Fourth Report: 1981–1984. London: HMSO

National Development Team. 1991. *Real Jobs.* Report of a conference for supported employment agencies sponsored by the Real Jobs initiative. Manchester: NDT

National Development Team. 1992a. *Survey of Supported Employment Services in England, Wales and Scotland* by Tim Lister. Manchester: NDT

National Development Team. 1992b. *Changing Lives: Supported Employment and People with Learning Disabilities* by Alison Wertheimer. Manchester: NDT

National Development Team. 1992c. *Real Jobs Initiative: An Evaluation*, by Alison Wertheimer. Manchester: NDT

National Development Team. 1993a. *Group Homes – An Ordinary Life? A Look at Why These Services Are Not Meeting the Needs of People Who Live in Them* by Peter Kinsella. Manchester: NDT

National Development Team. 1993b. *Supported Living – A New Paradigm?* by Peter Kinsella. Manchester: NDT

National Development Team. 1993c. *What Can We Do: The Legal Framework of Community Care Services for Adults with Learning Disabilities in England and Wales* by Gwyneth Roberts and Aled Griffiths. Manchester: NDT and MENCAP

National Development Team. 1994. *Taking A Break: Liverpool's Respite Services for Adult Citizens with Learning Disabilities* by Margaret Flynn with Liverpool Self Advocates. Manchester: NDT

O'Brien, J. 1987. A guide to life-style planning: using the *Activity Catalog* to integrate services and natural support systems. In G. T. Bellamy and B. Wilcox (eds) *A Comprehensive Guide to the Activities Catalog: an Alternative Curriculum for Youth and Young Adults with Severe Disabilities.* Baltimore: Brooks.

Thomas, D., Kendal, A. and Firth, H. 1978. *ENCOR: A Way Ahead.* London: Campaign for Mentally Handicapped People

Thomas, D. 1993. A time for change. *Soundtrack*, Issue No. 1. October 1993. Manchester: NDT

Chapter 14

Alternative Communities

Charles Getliffe

The history of the development of services for people with learning disabilities tends to be vague and inaccurate, at least until the end of the nineteenth century. Even where it is available from public records, it tends to present a particular point of view of what went on rather than an accurate assessment of the total provision.

There are accounts of residential initiatives, often of a religious nature, dating back over a thousand years. Although there are many instances of care and education being provided before and during the first half of the nineteenth century, most credit is given for the expansion of residential care to Johann Guggenbahl in Switzerland who set up the first residential home for children suffering from cretinism in Abendberg. As a result of Guggenbahl's work, Abendberg was hailed throughout Europe as a major reform. Institutions modelled on it were opened in Germany, Austria and Great Britain. However, it would not be right to give him too much credit for the expansion which occurred during the latter part of the nineteenth century because the process was now under way – motivated by other pioneers following the industrial revolution and a desire to provide for people inappropriately placed in poor law institutions and hospitals for the mentally ill. In England, inspired by a report of a visit to Abendberg in 1840, the Misses White started in 1846 a small school for four children in Bath which eventually developed into a hospital.

By the first half of the twentieth century each country in the UK and all the states in the USA had set up similar institutions which differentiated between the mentally ill and the mentally handicapped. In the case of large connurbations, these institutions were located in the country, thereby making community links impossible. The notion that residential care and training would bring about a state of normality had to be given up. The institutions became more or less permanent places of segregation. The superintendents found themselves being pushed into the roles of general administrators. Segregation was encouraged by the credence given to Darwinism causing alarm during the second and third decades of the twentieth century. Kanner describes the period from 1910 to 1930 as 'the great lull' when further institutions were built but little was achieved. However, some institutions thrived and persisted; in some cases this was the result of dissatisfaction with existing facilities or because of the pioneering work of individuals.

I suspect this was because of their specialism. For example, in the UK four communities were set up for people with epilepsy during the early part of this century, initially colonies for adults, later developing into specialized centres, two becoming specialized schools latterly with further education facilities. The capacity to adapt and specialize seems to be one way in which communities continued to survive and develop.

However, much has been blamed on the medicalization of asylums, schools and colonies which really only led to their remaining as hospitals in the UK in 1948 with the introduction of the National Health Service (NHS).

In the early 1950s some UK parents were attempting to change services in a most practical way. In 1954 a group of them approached Karl Konig with the question of what could be done for their children with special needs, particularly when they reached adulthood. The hospitals provided by the NHS did not allow for people with special needs to have any quality of life. Goffman's 'Assylums' eventually highlighted what many parents already knew, i.e. that they were not places of safety and protection. The need of parents and their growing maturing children coincided with an inherent Camphill ideal to establish village communities in which men and women with special needs or otherwise would work together and create new forms of social and cultural life. These parents set out to find the funds and a property suitable for a first village community of the nature envisaged by Karl Konig and his friends in Camphill. In 1955 Botton Hall was purchased and the Camphill Movement embarked on a new venture – the Camphill Village Communities. Botton Village became the model for many other village communities throughout the Camphill Movement both in the UK and abroad, which in turn have inspired others outside the Camphill Movement to find new ways of living for and with people with special needs.

Another group of parents were ahead of those at Camphill and had already bought a house in Berkshire called Ravenswood. The Rudolf Steiner approach which underpinned the thinking behind Camphill was to effect this albeit small initiative. Originally with only four children and volunteer staff, they were in need of a philosophical direction. It is poetic that this small Jewish venture should embrace the Christian approach of Steiner.

As the earliest intake grew into adults, the founders of Ravenswood decided to admit other adults as well as children. This stimulated the creation of a village-type community. The estate grew from a few acres of land to more than 100 acres. Its founders refused to narrow its function to those of a small residential school, as they had the needs of their own growing children forever in front of them.

Ravenswood Village today is made up of 20 residential homes where the 179 residents live in small groups. Each resident has an individually planned programme which is designed to maximize skills and encourage independence.

The village has its own school which residents attend up to chronological age 19. As well as offering the educational curriculum, speech and music therapy together with physiotherapy and occupational therapy are also based within the school premises and provide a service to the whole village. Residents enjoy the benefits of a hydrotherapy pool which is also situated in the school.

From the age of 19, residents attend Ravenswood's Day Opportunities Centre. A full programme of education and training is offered, including work-related and employment skills where appropriate. Specialized equipment and a high staff ratio ensure that residents with multiple and profound learning disabilities are also able to take full advantage of the courses on offer. The residents and staff are supported by a psychologist and a consultant psychiatrist.

A leisure programme is offered daily within the village and residents are also encouraged to take advantage of the facilities which are available in the local community.

From its early beginnings in the 1950s, this village has evolved into the Ravenswood Village and Suhar David Centre of Special Education. (Suhar David was one of the founder parents.) Firm links have been forged with the local college of further education, with Kings College Medical School and with Bulmershe College of Higher Education where some of the teaching staff obtain their special diplomas. Ravenswood Village is part of the Ravenswood Foundation, an organization of international renown which offers a network of caring and educational services for over 1,500 people with learning disabilities. In the voluntary sector Ravenswood Foundation is unique. This is because no other organization has such a wide range of services.

The development of Camphill, Ravenswood and others was a direct reaction to the horrors of the long-stay hospitals. Nevertheless at first glance the concept of a village community might seem directly opposed to the normalization ethos. The negative aspects often highlighted by the normalizers compare to those of the worst long-stay hospitals in that parallels are drawn with labelling, devaluing, institutionalization, segregation and so on. Indeed, when comparisons are made with the quality of life for people who move from hospital to community, we do see the following measurable improvements: 'a greater degree of normalisation, increased personal independence, more contact with friends and relatives, greater integration of activities, more time engaged in constructive activity and an improvement in attitude towards their living situation' (Aston Hall/Derby Scheme).

But villages are not hospitals and indeed the counter-argument is that there are many people with learning disabilities that have a far better quality of life in a village community than many people who live in the wider community. For some people, so-called normalized living can only mean a denial of their needs and it is imperative that as a society we have a variety of options and choices available. What is needed is a research project that will compare quality of life opportunities for people with learning disabilities living in a village with those living in the community.

Normalization and integration are central concepts in the discussion of service provision for people with learning disabilities. The historical importance of these principles cannot be overlooked. Even today, they play an important role in the battle against the inhuman conditions found in many large institutional settings. Following the normalization movement, however, alternative service providers, such as village communities, have been placed in the background. Such alternative systems have suffered from the negative associations with large institutions. Because the discussion in the past few years has tended to centre on such issues as the number of places or the central location of a service on quite a superficial level and neglected the broader issue of 'quality of life', alternative models have had little chance to demonstrate their special contribution.

The normalization movement is a response to the inhuman services for people with learning disabilities in large institutions, especially psychiatric clinics and hospitals. The focus is on the deficits and risks of the services provided in many large residential institutions (e.g., isolation, labelling, devaluation) which was important at the beginning of the normalization debate and remains important today. For many people with learning disabilities, completely new opportunities for a life in the community are now available. The advantages of this cannot be overlooked after three decades. However, the time has come not only criticize what was or is problematic in the large institutions but also to define carefully what is meant by 'quality of life' in the community.

In many countries including the UK, the normalization movement has brought with it a selection process – with the result that centres for persons with very profound handicapping conditions (e.g., profound learning disabilities, severe behaviour disturbance, special medical needs) have developed which in turn can take on the character of a 'clinic'. Hence, the aim of undoing the worst aspects of the old systems can be thwarted, with former models being re-established and perpetuated in the new system. On the other hand, model services are operating which attempt to implement the integrated model even for very severely handicapped people. They try to compensate for the difficulties of integration by focusing on the provision of intensive personal support. This model is based on the belief that all problems can be solved by professional services alone but neglects the essential question of adequate social structures.

With the above approach, an important goal may not be reached. This concerns the question of 'personal autonomy'. Autonomy is the ability to cope competently in one's social environment with little or no support. This includes relationships between handicapped people themselves; it includes furthermore the possibility of influencing one's own living conditions; it includes the opportunity to undertake valued social roles and to obtain the feeling of social safety.

Autonomy understood in this way cannot be accomplished simply by the provision of more caring staff. The degree of autonomy is dependent on not only developmental level and education but also on the surrounding social structures themselves. We all live within a social context of political economy, culture and the institutional and ideological frameworks of society as a whole. A social structure is 'normal' for an individual if he or she is able to cope competently alone. The reduction of all possible and necessary social structures to a 'norm' for people with learning disabilities actually leads to a reduction of autonomy and perhaps a diminishing of the quality of life.

From the outset of the normalization debate, these weaknesses have been pointed out but have so often been regarded as irrelevant. People with learning disabilities and their parents should have a choice. Options for different lifestyles should be available. Moreover, alternatives do continue and flourish, e.g., L'Arche Communities, the Camphill Movement, Ravenswood Village.

Not only do they exist but they thrive and all have extensive waiting lists of people who want places. Even when funding agencies indicate that ideologically they do not want people with learning disabilities living in villages, we still see a steady stream of people queuing for places.

Why is this? We think the answer must lie with the parent/relative lobby groups who are keen to find alternatives to both the hospitals and the community care solutions for their more severely disabled family members. Concern is often expressed about the lack of resources made available to meet the identified needs of some people with learning disabilities in the community.

In Sweden in the mid-1970s there were as many people in residential care as there were in care in London. The difference was that in Sweden the hospitals were between

100 and 200 in size compared to the UK's which still average 1,000. Furthermore, in Sweden they had been broken down into small living groups of around four people. Sweden also devoted 13 per cent of its social and health budget to the care of people with disability, compared with 5 per cent in the UK.

Obviously villages are not the only form of residential provision required. They must form part of the range of provision. The majority of families have no desire for their members with disabilities to reside elsewhere. It is nevertheless significant that villages have been created by a range of caring voluntary bodies – as well as parent initiatives – in a number of countries.

It is also interesting to note that in Australia they see the village concept as part of this spectrum of provision. This is also the view of the Ravenswood Foundation. Besides Ravenswood Village, the Foundation has a unique range of community-based services located in north-west London and Essex. The village community therefore is a major challenge because it does not sit comfortably within the framework of normalization.

Stanley Segal along with others questioned Wolfensberger's principles of normalization on the basis of their first-hand experience of working and living with people with severe, profound and multiple handicaps in village communities. At a conference on villages in 1989, Segal stated: 'Our focus must never be diverted by norms, away from the human beings who are our concern. There is no civilised society which is so tolerant and flexible that it has NO NEED of special provisions; provisions which protect the vulnerable from the society or the society from its members'.

Is there a significant role for special villages within a climate of community care? If so, how can it best be promoted? I suggest that the notion of options between lifestyles is best evaluated not by the inputs but by the outcomes as they affect the quality of life for people with learning difficulties. Therefore the debate revolves around issues of freedom and independence for the individual. The concept of autonomy also appears to require more in-depth analysis.

Publications of the Prince of Wales's Advisory Group of Disability give support to the belief that autonomy is an aim for all. In the guidelines called Learning Options, which deal with the needs of people with 'moderate and severe learning difficulties, those with severe and multiple impairments and those with social and emotional difficulties', as well as those with physical or sensory difficulties, this key principle, under the heading 'Individuality and Choice', is asserted: 'Like everyone else, disabled people have individual attitudes, abilities, preferences, likes, aspirations and fears. As individuals, they have the right to make choices and decisions concerning their lives.'

If this assertion is correct, then the belief that for some severely or multiply disabled people autonomy is an over-ambitious and inappropriate aspiration must be consigned to the same dustbin as the notions of unemployability and ineducability. Of course this is not to deny that, at any given time, the condition of many disabled people is so far from autonomy as to make any but the most modest expectations seem unrealistic; not infrequently, all progress in the direction of autonomy may appear to be blocked for considerable periods. However, the insistence that there is always a way forward is of paramount importance.

Autonomy is an integral part of the aim for all people with disabilities. From this in turn it follows that all systems in provision will have to be evaluated by assessing not the quality of input in terms of education and care but the standard of output in terms of the total quality of life of which autonomy is an essential part.

Can villages contribute towards progress in that most difficult of areas, that of options? Can they help to get rid of 'choice' as a mere slogan and actually develop some theory and practice of life-choices?

This does not at all imply a view which is at heart anti-integrationist; on the contrary, it acknowledges that the integration of all minorities is the long-term aim: 'surely the crowning proof of integration's rightness is society's need for both the enrichment and the healing which minorities and above all disabled people, have to offer' (Daunt, 1990).

The executive and directors of Ravenswood Foundation recognize that the staff of Ravenswood Village have undergone major changes in their attitude towards the residents in recent years. The developments towards support in choice and decision-making are now a fundamental feature of the services provided. The changing role of the Adult Day Service is a significant contributory factor in this process. Residents of the college are encouraged to make decisions about the kinds of learning options they would like. This has led to a widening of the options available.

Residents from the village are also supported in a significant number of mainstream educational classes at local colleges and adult educational centres, though there have been some problems in the process of integration. I mean here that there has been the discovery of a mismatch, which may be fundamental, between the priorities and values of the general adult education system and the specific needs of those whose integration is being attempted. My conclusions from the Ravenswood experience are that although problems of procedure and resources can never be overlooked and may sometimes be severe, they are difficulties of a second rank, not at the heart of the question. What really matters for the future of integration for people with disabilities into colleges and adult education classes are the values and priorities of those establishments themselves, their present character and even more important, the direction in which they are going. Wherever the normal system presents, or is moving in such a way as to present, a generally unfavourable environment to integration, then whilst it is true that integration may continue to progress, the pace of its advance is likely to be reduced; it follows that in those conditions separate provision can be perceived not as something marginal with a merely short-term future, something simply to be run down, but as something that has an essential, significant and active contribution to make, at least in the mid-term. This must therefore be relevant to the concerns of Ravenswood which is involved in the lifelong provision of education and care.

I believe that special villages should not 'give in' but must 'reach out' in order to contribute to the complex process of integration in a gradualist and positive spirit.

Some of the ways in which Ravenswood Village is currently orientating itself in order to have a wider impact are by:

1. Developing its in-service training programme to benefit professionals who will be working in the wider community. Training packages leading to NVQ Levels 2 and 3 are being offered.
2. Involving the local community in activities and adult education classes within the village.
3. Developing cafes and a self-service store that people from the locality can use.
4. Capitalizing on leisure opportunities in the wider community.
5. Training volunteers from the locality to take on advocacy roles.

6. About a quarter of the residents – some 40 or so – have little or no contact with their families. Much work by the social work team has been undertaken to create foster links but still this significant number remain. A working party was established to discuss how these residents could be helped. What has followed is the establishment of a separate charity totally apart from Ravenswood which is committed to providing citizen advocates for all these residents.

The Ravenswood Village, along with other special villages, should continually strive at being an open community which embraces its locality in a positive, creative and dynamic way for the benefit of all concerned.

In addition, Ravenswood Village is supporting and developing services to directly impact on residents. These are immensely important as it is necessary continually to fight against institutional practices. Continual nurturing of the services and close monitoring are seen as vitally important by managers.

The areas of activity are:

1. Developing a wide range of community-based opportunities and experiences.
2. Encouraging access into the community in small groups or on a one-to-one or individual basis.
3. Being proactive in developing the concept of circles of friends.
4. Facilitating residents having their own bedrooms unless they want to share with someone special.
5. Devolving budgets so that revenue income is close to the residents ensuring that they are empowered within the decision-making processes that affect their lives.
6. Offering a wider variety of living environments to meet residents' individual needs and wishes.
7. Involving residents in the meetings where decisions are made that effect their lives, e.g., committees, working parties. It is vital to engage residents in the consultation processes around change in service provision.
8. Involving residents in choosing the staff they want to have engaged.
9. Supporting residents in choosing their own keyworkers.
10. Supporting the resident voice whether that be in the day-to-day decisions as to what to eat, what to wear (so long as residents are making informed choice) or via the IPP (Individual Programme Plan) process and self-advocacy groups, i.e., developing awareness and skills in facilitating choice and decision-making.

Major challenges are presented to villages to develop appropriate services based on individual needs within the income available. Clearly these challenges exist for all services based in the community as well. Proponents of residential communities argue that people with learning disabilities should have a choice and that options of different lifestyles should be based on real experiences which instruct the decision-making process for people with learning disabilities.

When being retrospective about service provision, it is always easy to be critical. We should remember that not all was bad about hospitals, nor is everything bad about 'community care' and villages. There are good aspects to all provision though admittedly I cannot see much that was good about hospital life when comparing it to the options. We must be aware of what works and learn from the mistakes of the past. Options must be kept open and rigid ideological paradigms rejected.

Villages are part of the community and should not be perceived as being separate. Villages could then radiate out to 'community care' initiatives by offering specialized support and expertise. If we could take this cognitive leap, then we would go a long way towards facilitating centres of excellence that could develop services in a most innovative and creative fashion.

ACKNOWLEDGEMENTS

Much of the thinking and the ideas expressed in this chapter came from the mind of the late Professor Stanley Segal who was the principal of Ravenswood Village for many years. However, in presenting this thinking I have attempted to develop it in many different and practical ways to improve the quality of life opportunities for the residents of the village community which he so loved. Amongst his many activities Stan organized numerous conferences of which two in particular focused on alternative communities. Papers from these conferences have assisted greatly in drawing together the threads of my argument. Of these I highlight those of Professor John Corbett and Patrick Daunt.

REFERENCE

Daunt, P. 1991. *Meeting Disability: A European Response.* London: Cassell

Part III

Changing Attitudes

Chapter 15

Seen Through a Glass Darkly: Modifying Public Attitudes

Roy McConkey

People we now label as having 'learning disabilities' have been present in every human society down through the centuries. In pre-Christian Ireland, for example, the fifth-century Brehon Laws identified the following distinct categories: 'idiots, fools and dotards; persons without sense and madmen'. These groups were exempt from certain punishments and protected from exploitation. Moreover, under Brehon Laws, it was the responsibility of the community or the clan to look after the deprived child.

Over one thousand years later but still four hundred years ago, the writer Daniel Defoe argued for the setting up of 'public fool houses' to care for idiots and proposed that this be paid for by a tax levied on the authors of books. This he saw as a kind of natural justice! However, his vision of publicly provided facilities was not to become a reality until the mid-1800s by which times the industrial revolution and the spread of universal education had swollen the number of perceived 'idiots'. The eugenics movement hastened the growth of mental institutions with the aim of protecting society as much as serving their patient population. Moreover, with the spread of the British Empire, this 'enlightened' thinking was exported throughout the 'civilized' world (Ryan and Thomas, 1980).

A century and a half later, we still struggle against this Victorian legacy. And not just in terms of the social death it brought to hundreds of thousands of British citizens but also in the attitudes and perceptions of the wider public who still see these people through a glass darkly. Folk memories linger on; are these people fully human ... are they a danger to society ... a threat to me ... are they a curse on their families ... are they eternal children?

As this collection amply illustrates, the past three decades have produced a revolution in our services for people with learning disabilities. This was fuelled by the doggedness of parents who did know what was best for their child and channelled by visionaries such as Stanley Segal, who dared to question conventional wisdom.

In a short time, the re-formation of services was well under way, spearheaded by a burgeoning professional workforce. With hindsight we can see that this was both a strength and a weakness. The diversity of people's needs were now recognized and in varying degrees, were attended to, but the growth of specialisms did little to change the attitudes of the public. If anything, they only served to reinforce the notion that ordinary people could not cope with this disability.

Even the shift of services into community settings was not accompanied by any systematic attempt to make the resource one that local people had any stake in. Repeated surveys in Ireland and the UK have highlighted the limited contact neighbours have with community residences or day centres (McConkey, 1987). These are still perceived as belonging to the service and for people who by definition are not like them. Most of our so-called community facilities are surrounded by a glass wall through which the public sees but darkly.

THE NEED TO EDUCATE COMMUNITIES

Arguably the need to make the public better informed and better educated about learning disabilities has never been greater. First, the aspirations of young people with this disability and of their parents have been bolstered by the ordinary childhood which many have experienced, e.g., through a happy family upbringing, attendance at mainstream schools and membership of youth organizations. The extension of this 'ordinary life' philosophy into the adult years means people living in ordinary houses albeit with support from paid staff, joining in neighbourhood leisure pursuits and finding employment in local businesses (Sutcliffe, 1990). Antagonistic reactions from an uneducated public threatens all of these initiatives. Likewise the successful resettlement of former patients from mental handicap hospitals is dependent on a welcoming community.

Secondly an informed community is an important outcome in its own right but more significantly it is a step towards an *involved* community. The quality of life for people with learning disabilities living in community settings is enhanced by having a circle of acquaintances and friends. At present, loneliness is a common complaint (Richardson and Ritchie, 1989). However, survey findings and experiences from various demonstration projects have shown that there are people from the community who are willing to share their lives in some small way with people who have a disability. It is just that often no one has invited them (McConkey, 1994). Professional services are often so preoccupied with their clients' *dis*-abilities that ordinary, yet basic needs for companionship, enjoyment and relaxation are neglected.

Finally, there is growing recognition that ordinary men and women are capable of providing a better quality of service to individuals than can established service agencies. The best example is family-based respite care which many users rate as preferable to hospital-based or hostel-based care. Likewise, employment schemes in local businesses which use co-workers to support the person with learning disabilities 'on-the-job' have been much more successful than the traditional vocational training centres in generating paid, productive work (Tackney, 1992). Once again, the spread of schemes such as these both locally and nationally is dependent on members of the community being prepared to join.

The common springboard in these three reasons for educating communities is the needs of people with learning disability. Ironically, as long as we believe that professionally resourced services are the best way of meeting their needs, we have no incentive to involve the community. Instead our energies are put into getting more money to employ more staff and planning yet more programmes and therapies to meet their special needs. The humility required to acknowledge our limitations is the start to clearing the darkened glass that separates so many services from their community. Then local people can begin to see people with disabilities as they are, and not as they think them to be.

MISTAKEN MYTHS

How then should we set about the task of educating communities? As good a starting point as any is to dispel some commonly held myths about this endeavour.

First, there is little evidence to support the widely held belief that national advertising campaigns on television, radio or billboards make the public any better informed or disposed to helping. Indeed, the people most likely to attend to such messages are those already involved and interested, such as family members or staff. Precisely the same phenomena is found with car advertisements. People read more avidly the adverts for the cars they have just purchased. In both instances, the advertising helps to confirm our choices and beliefs. We cannot justify the expense of national advertising campaigns on the grounds that it will change the minds of others who think differently.

Worse still, such publicity can *perpetuate* negative images of disability. Particular criticism has been levelled at the fund-raising posters produced by national charities. Unwittingly their appeal for the public's sympathy has led them to promote unflattering portrayals of people with disabilities. The most infamous of these was MENCAP's poster campaign in the early 1980s which showed a sorrowful child with Down's Syndrome and the caption; 'Some families have a cross to bear this Christmas' (Doddington, Jones and Miller, 1994).

Likewise, national television programmes which feature the 'plight' of disabled people may distance the viewer from ever helping by increasing the feeling that 'they couldn't cope' and 'aren't the parents or staff marvellous who do that sort of work'.

A second myth is that information changes people's attitudes and behaviour. For years, people have been bombarded with health education messages about the dangers of smoking, the need for exercise and the benefits of a healthy diet and yet millions of people persist with their unhealthy behaviours. Hence, telling the public about the rights and needs of people with disabilities is unlikely to have much impact on their attitudes and behaviour.

Once again, information can feed prejudices. For instance, a common request from the public is to know the causes of 'mental handicap' and how it can be prevented. In responding to this need, we can inadvertently devalue the person with a disability and heighten the public's wish to avoid contact with such people. Folk beliefs of infection through contact still linger on.

A favoured way of challenging these and other mistaken beliefs has been inviting the public to visit centres and residences for people with disabilities. The most common tourists have tended to be parties of schoolchildren or trainee professionals along with groups of officials and local politicians interested to see how public money is spent. Such visits can change people's attitudes but paradoxically it is their opinion of the staff and facilities which goes up whereas their perceptions of the clients worsens (LeUnes, 1975). In hindsight, this is understandable. Packaged tourists rarely get to meet the natives.

The final myth is probably the most pernicious of all – that educating communities is a specialized task which requires particular skills and resources. Such beliefs are expressed in various ways: by creating special projects such as Mental Handicap Week; by setting up a short-term (research) project on the topic; or by making work with 'the community' one person's responsibility. Such methods rarely result in any long-term gains and sadly this myth is perpetuated as a self-fulfilling prophecy – we don't have the skills so we can't educate communities!

EFFECTIVE EDUCATION

So what does change people's beliefs and behaviour? One consensus emerges from all the international research which has been done on changing attitudes towards people with disabilities, and that is that enjoyable interactions with a peer who is handicapped invariably produces positive changes. Researchers note too that it is the *quality* of the contact rather than quantity which is important and they do warn that certain contacts may actually increase rather than decrease the public's negative impressions.

Such contacts can come about by ensuring that from a young age children and adults with disabilities are part of community life:

- babies and toddlers with disability attend local groups with their mothers;
- pre-schoolers are enrolled in neighbourhood playgroups and nurseries;
- children with a marked disability may attend the same primary school as their brothers and sisters;
- youngsters join youth organizations and sports clubs;
- young adults attend colleges of further education and find places on work experience schemes;
- people with disabilities are employed in local businesses; and
- men and women live in ordinary housing, either on their own, with their partners or in small groups.

Research into the effects of various meeting experiences has helped to identify the contexts most likely to promote a change in attitudes.

Successful contacts are more likely if:

- People meet in ordinary places rather than in specialist centres. Hence in a short programme on mental handicap used in Irish secondary schools, a group of trainees from the local centre came to visit the pupils in their school rather than the more usual arrangement of pupils visiting special centres (McConkey and McCormack, 1983).
- People share an activity together rather than relying solely on conversation. Business executives who shared a two-day 'wilderness' expedition with people who had physical disabilities were more willing to consider employing such a person in their firms (McCleary and Chesteen, 1990).
- The public's first contacts are with people with whom they can communicate relatively easily. As their confidence increases they can be introduced to people with more severe handicaps (Antonak, 1980).

- There is a 'mediator' present. This should be someone who knows the person with disabilities, can help smooth introductions, identify topics of mutual interest, set up activities, overcome communication difficulties and more generally act as a role model for the person who is not used to interacting with people who have disabilities.
- People have the opportunity to interact in small groups. Pairing unfamiliar people with one or two individuals who have a disability is preferable to meeting in large groups.
- The people meeting are about the same age, from the same area and ethnic background and so on. The attitudes of teachers in mainstream schools were more affected by meeting peers with disabilities than children from special schools (Donaldson, 1980).

Indeed, the evidence is now indisputable that creating contacts of this sort does make the public – employers, neighbours, teachers – change their behaviour and attitudes (e.g., Harrison and Tomes, 1990; McConkey, Walsh and Conneally, 1993). Hence such initiatives must be to the fore-front in our services. Equally, they force us to redefine what we mean by educating communities, a theme to which we will return later.

INTERESTING AND RELEVANT INFORMATION

Although negative attitudes may stem from inaccurate information, the corollary of creating more positive attitudes by giving information holds true only under a number of conditions (Shearer, 1984):

- The information needs to emphasize the personal attributes of people with disabilities rather than the features of the impairment. For example, 'Andrew is a Ranger's Supporter with Down's Syndrome. His extra chromosome doesn't stop him from cheering on his team ... '
- An emphasis needs to be placed on people's abilities in order to counter the public's stereotype of dis-ability being *in*-ability. Abilities can include a sense of humour; memory for names; love of the seaside; and so on.
- The information needs to be relevant for the target group and to address their particular concerns. Information targeted at primary school youngsters needs to be different from that provided for potential employers.
- People with a disability, or parents of a child with a disability, are amongst the best providers of information as they can speak from their personal experience and in ways to which an audience can relate. Likewise, people from the community who have experienced a change of attitude themselves can be used to share their experiences with others; for instance, neighbours living beside a group home.
- Information must be easily understood. Short sentences using simple words and plenty of examples will communicate your message more effectively than textbook prose (Sturmey, 1993).

This said, there is very little evidence that information *per se* changes attitudes. Equally, if not more important, is the way information is presented.

MULTI-MEDIA PRESENTATIONS

The advice here is simple: do not rely on one method to get your message across. Videos, talks, leaflets, posters, cartoons and discussions can all be used to good effect.

- Video has the advantage of portraying people with disabilities in a range of ordinary settings whilst also providing implicit role models for viewers as to how they might interact with them. Locally produced videos have added appeal.
- Leaflets and posters must contain illustrations. Colour photographs are preferable to black and white. The advent of colour photocopying has helped to reduce the costs.
- Puppet shows and drama productions have also been used to convey serious messages about discrimination and disability in a fun and appealing way.
- Use can be made of 'activity learning' techniques such as having to use signs to communicate or shopping around the town in a wheelchair. Although used more frequently with children and young people, they can be used with all ages.
- Mock 'debates' in which people are allocated adversial roles have also produced changes in expressed attitudes, e.g., swimmers complaining to management about the number of people with disabilities using the pool. Time must be allowed for guided discussion of the issues raised, otherwise the learning value of the activity can be lost.

TOWARDS A STRATEGY FOR EDUCATING COMMUNITIES

Looking back over the past twenty years or so to when educating communities about disability first started to emerge as a specific endeavour, a number of fundamental shifts can be detected in the way in which the task is now conceived. These are:

- *A focus on the person not the disability.* Priority is given to creating enjoyable, face-to-face meetings rather than providing formal talks or literature.
- *Educating communities is a process rather than an event.* Sustained changes in the public's attitudes and behaviour do not come about from a single event. Instead they result from a range of initiatives and from a diversity of sources so that members of the public accumulate experiences and knowledge.
- *The goal is to build inclusive communities rather than to give information.* Educating the community is not an end in itself, nor should it get distorted into a charity appeal. Rather it is the essential complement to all the careful planning which goes into preparing young people with a learning disability for living in the community. Such programmes may develop their talents but equally necessary are the creation of openings and opportunities within communities which they cannot produce by themselves.

Many factors have brought about these changes: the advocacy of the people with disabilities and their families; the change in service systems from institution-based systems to community-based systems; and the results of earlier efforts at educating communities.

However, old thinking still lingers on. In an attempt to give it the kiss of death this section describes a strategy for educating communities which embraces all the 'stakeholders' – people with learning disabilities, family carers, professional workers, service providers and politicians – and makes the task everyone's responsibility whilst recognizing that the various players can contribute in different ways according to their opportunities and talents. The result is a multi-facet task which never ends because people's needs change and new members join communities.

ESSENTIAL ELEMENTS OF THE STRATEGY

The essential elements of the strategy are these:

- The needs and aspirations of local people with learning disabilities determine the agenda for educating communities.
- The priority is to create opportunities for enjoyable interactions between people with disabilities and their peers in a range of community settings.
- Information about disability is conveyed in a way that promotes positive images of people with disability, corrects misconceptions and addresses the concerns of communities.
- An analysis needs to be made locally of the various 'communities' who can contribute significantly to the lives of people with disabilities and educational initiatives are then targeted specifically at them.
- The task can be undertaken by various groups of people but their efforts may require support and should prove more effective when co-ordinated around common goals.
- The success of such initiatives is reflected in the increased participation of people with learning disabilities in community activities.

The rationale for the first three elements has been covered earlier so here we concentrate on the idea of target communities; we identify the range of people already involved in educating communities and tackle the thorny issue as to how this strategy can be put into practice.

A COMMUNITY OF COMMUNITIES

The old notion of geographical communities – people living and working within a common locality – is fast breaking down in modern society and in cities especially. Replacing it are communities made up of people with common interests drawn from quite wide areas. Defined in this way, the public are members of many different communities albeit with varying degrees of allegiances. Hence a 30-year-old woman could belong to various communities – badminton club; playgroup committee; labour party; the police; residents' association; and the supermarket!

Conceiving of communities in this way makes it easier to identify those sections of the community which are a priority target in any educational programme. For example, you may chose to focus your energies on certain influential groups, who by the nature of their work come into contact with people who have learning disabilities – leisure centre attendants, local bus drivers/conductors, police constables and officials in housing departments. All of these people could make life easier if they had a better understanding of the disability.

Or attention might be focused on groups who in turn could become educators of others – newspaper reporters or local radio presenters; senior pupils in secondary schools; apprentices; and students in training.

More specifically, the common needs of people with learning disabilities will identify priority groups. For example, if several people wish to work in cafes or restaurants, the owners of such businesses might be targeted for special attention.

A focus on 'target groups' also makes the task more manageable in that the different but particular needs of each group are more easily identified and addressed. What local councillors want or need to know about learning disability can be quite different from the concerns of workers in a playgroup about to enrol a child with Down's Syndrome.

Last but most significantly, the focus on specific groups can make the task more manageable, if the educators involved in the endeavour are already members of the targeted groups or know someone who already is. Such 'circles of friends' as they have become known are potent ways of introducing people with disabilities into communities.

From my experiences, the most popular 'target' groups singled out for educational initiatives in Scotland are: schools; employers; neighbours of community residents; the media; politicians; and churches. Hence in a recent publication, I have summarized what has been done, or could be done, to address the particular needs and concerns of these communities (McConkey, 1994).

COMMUNITY EDUCATORS

The image of the 'expert' lecturer lingers on, unintentionally perpetuated perhaps by the many professionals who earn a livelihood in the disability services and who are invited to talk about their work to community groups. In reality, this sort of contribution appears to have little impact except to boost the morale of the lecturer, and their time and talents are better deployed in other ways.

More importantly though, the education of communities does not need to be done formally, nor even identified as such. Much effective work is already being carried out by a range of people as they go about their usual routines. For instance, the parents of a toddler with Down's Syndrome who enrol their daughter in a neighbourhood playgroup may not label it as an initiative in community education. For them the driving force is the well-being of their child. Yet such an experience is deeply educational for the leaders, children and parents associated with that group.

It is most important that the talents and opportunities of a wide range of people are harnessed if a widespread impact is to be made on people's perceptions and beliefs. I am thinking of the following groups of people.

- *People with learning disabilities*. They are often their own best advocates if given the chance. Their involvement in the enterprise should break down the 'them' and 'us' mentality that so pervades current thinking.
- *Parents and relatives*. They have the emotional involvement and the direct experience which can silence the sceptic. As most are already connected into local

communities through family and friends, they can help gain access to many community groups.

- *Sympathetic people from the community.* This includes 'volunteer helpers', employers who have taken people on work experience and next-door neighbours to community homes (Hogan, 1986). They are creditable witnesses to others in the community; people with whom they can easily identify. Through their contacts, they too are able to link into other groups.
- *Front-line service staff.* Their role may already involve contacts with the community – neighbours, shopkeepers and health centre staff – and much can be gained from their experiences. They are aware too of the particular needs amongst people with disability. Other professional workers may have a special expertise they can share with others, e.g., how best to communicate with certain people; what to do if a person has an epileptic seizure; and so on.
- *Status figures in the community.* Such as doctors, councillors, clergy. Their advice and ability to open doors into communities may prove valuable even though they may be the first to admit that they know nothing about learning disabilities. It is what they know about the local community that makes their contribution valuable when planning local initiatives.

WHOSE JOB IS IT TO EDUCATE COMMUNITIES?

The above list is a reminder of the possibilities as to who can be engaged in educating communities. However, nothing will be done if each is leaving it up to the others! Also, how can the efforts of these groups be brought together in a common endeavour? In sum, who's taking the lead in educating communities?

In Scotland, an Educating Communities Network was established with assistance from the Mental Health Foundation with the aim of providing mutual support and information exchange amongst people interested or involved in this task. Of the 60 or so active members, all but a handful were employees of regional council social work or education departments (48 per cent), voluntary sector services (32 per cent) or health boards (17 per cent), and they were working in a range of services, including day services and employment schemes, residential services, leisure and befriending schemes and community education.

However, when asked to identify the most common obstacles they had encountered in attempting to educate local communities, the most commonly mentioned were: 'too much other work' (66 per cent) and 'no organizational policy or agreement on what to do' (34 per cent).

The network members were, however, under no delusions concerning their own importance to the process. They considered the people best placed to undertake the job of educating communities to be:

- people with learning disabilities (with support),
- teachers in primary and secondary schools, and
- families of people with learning disabilities.

Generally they rated themselves in fourth place!

Similarly they assigned *responsibility* for ensuring that education of communities takes place to:

- central government – Scottish Office,
- social work departments, and
- community education.

Very few rated it the responsibility of service providers.

What then should be the role of professional, i.e., paid, staff in disability services if they disclaim responsibility for the task and feel that others are better at undertaking it?

For me the answer is simple: They are the instigators of action and mobilizers of resources. They know well the particular needs and aspirations of the people with disabilities; they are employed to meet these needs; and through their employing agencies they have access to contacts with other people and resources. None of the other possible educators are so well placed.

However, for front-line staff to undertake this new role effectively, organizational support is essential.

First, the funding agencies – central government and social work departments especially – must make a clear commitment to the education of local communities and allocate resources for this endeavour. Community care plans, for example, could specify local targets and set out strategies for how these could be attained.

Second, service providers in both the statutory and the independent sectors should include commitments to community involvement and their operations should reflect this. Certain posts might be designated to further these objectives or the job descriptions of workers widened to provide for greater involvement with local communities. Needless to add, managerial support and guidance in such endeavours is vital in order to establish and sustain new work practices, as are opportunities for in-service training.

Making a serious commitment to educating communities requires changes to the policies and practices at all levels within our existing service systems. The fact that this is still the case is an indication of the changes still required for them to truly become community, rather than disability, focused.

PARTNERSHIPS

The emphasis on services as instigators of community education is not to suggest that this is done solely by service personnel. On the contrary, the expectation is that they will work in partnership with others, especially people with learning disabilities, their family carers, and local 'allies' from the community. Indeed, their efforts could sensibly be directed towards facilitating and supporting such groups to undertake their own initiatives and joining with them in lobbying for the necessary resources.

In time, too, other groups could take over the responsibility, especially as they gain expertise and confidence in the task. I am thinking particularly of self-advocacy groups of people with learning disability. Although some may be well equipped to do this already, our experiences in Scotland suggest that this is not generally so. However, people with physical and sensorial disabilities are increasingly to the fore in promoting greater community awareness.

Ultimately the hope would be that communities themselves take the initiative in consulting and adapting to the needs of people with disabilities. This would recognize their status as full and equal members of that community. But without being unduly pessimistic, that day seems far off.

EVALUATION OF COMMUNITY INITIATIVES

The strategy promoted here emphasizes the importance of local initiatives. This means that it is unlikely that people from outside the district will undertake this work although regional or national initiatives could supply useful support. Such an approach has many advantages but it can also be wasteful in the sense that local groups through naivety may make the same mistakes as others have done elsewhere. Too often decisions are made on false presumptions.

I end then with a plea for local groups to document their experiences in a way which can be shared by others. This can be done most simply through team reviews – when all members of the team share their perceptions as to what worked and what they feel needs changing.

More ambitiously, reactions can be collected systematically from the targeted group by means of questionnaires or interviews. Enquiries can be made as to what was got out of the programmes and their suggestions for changes. Particularly useful would be their perceptions before and after the programme started. There is a real dearth of published material on changing community perceptions from which others can learn.

UNRESOLVED ISSUES

Thus far, our attention has been exclusively focused on people with learning disabilities. But on many issues they have much in common with other disability groups. Still there is a great reluctance to join forces – often on the premise that 'we are not like them'. People with physical disabilities do not want to be associated with people who have learning disabilities while they in turn are keen to emphasize that they are not mentally ill. The real danger is that one disability group devalues another in their keenness to project themselves. We still have much to learn about working together towards a common community.

Another unresolved issue is the future role of specialist services and their trained workforces. Put simply, there will be less need for both as local communities develop their competence at coping with people who have learning disabilities. Is there a conflict of interest which prevents existing services working wholeheartedly towards the involvement of their service users in local communities? (Schwartz, 1992)

Finally, British society has changed radically during the last thirty years and will continue to do so. What if these changes lead to the breakdown of communities as we know them, which could happen if British society becomes more self-centred and competitive, if lawlessness and exploitation of the weak increases and if family networks become more fractured. Indeed, some would argue that already in many city areas community life barely exists. What then are the prospects for people with learning disabilities under these conditions?

I accept that these three issues would have major ramifications for the UK's present social policy in regard to people with disabilities. However, I am not sufficiently foresightful to anticipate the consequences. Suffice it to say that being aware of them is at least some safeguard to the complacency which comes from thinking that we have got it right. Rabbie Burns put it more poetically when he wrote:

The best laid plans o' mice an' men;
  Gang aft agley [often go awry]
An' lea'e us nought but grief an' pain;
  For promis'd joy!

As you embark on the task of educating communities – an option incidentally you cannot refuse if you have accepted my arguments thus far – I trust you are spared the grief and pain; experiencing instead the promised joy.

ACKNOWLEDGEMENTS

Much of the content of this chapter is taken from the author's book *Innovations in Educating Communities about Learning Disabilities* (1994), and is reproduced here by kind permission of the publishers, Lisieux Hall Publications.

REFERENCES

Antonak, R.F. 1980. A hierarchy of attitude toward exceptionality. *Journal of Special Education*, **14**, 231–41

Doddington, K., Jones, R.S.P. and Miller, B.Y. 1994. Are attitudes to people with learning disabilities negatively influenced by charity advertising? An experimental analysis. *Disability and Society*, **9**, 207–21

Donaldson, J. 1980. Changing attitudes toward handicapped persons: a review and analysis of research. *Exceptional Children*, **35**, 5–22

Harrison, B. and Tomes, A. 1990. Employers' attitudes to the employment of people with mental handicaps: An empirical study. *Mental Handicap Research*, **3**, 196–213

Hogan, R. 1986. Gaining community support for groups homes. *Community Mental Health Journal*, **22**, 117–26

LeUnes, A. 1975. Institutional tour effects on attitudes relating to mental retardation. *American Journal of Mental Deficiency*, **79**, 732–5

McCleary, I.D. and Chesteen, S.A. 1990. Changing attitudes of disabled persons through outdoor adventure programmes. *International Journal of Rehabilitation Research*, **13**, 321–4

McConkey, R. 1987. *Who Cares? Community Involvement with Handicapped People*. London: Souvenir Press

McConkey, R. 1994. *Innovations in Educating Communities About Learning Disabilities*. Chorley: Lisieux Hall Publications

McConkey, R. and McCormack, B. 1983. *Breaking Barriers: Educating People About Disability*. London: Souvenir Press

McConkey, R., Walsh, P.N. and Conneally, S. 1993. Neighbours' reaction to community services: Contrasts before and after services open in their locality. *Mental Handicap Research*, **2**, 131–41

Richardson, A. and Ritchie, J. 1989. *Developing Friendships: Enabling People with Learning Difficulties to Make and Maintain Friendships*. London: Policy Studies Institute

Ryan, J. and Thomas, F. 1980. *The Politics of Mental Handicap*. Harmondsworth: Penguin

Schwartz, D.B. 1992. *Crossing the River: Creating a Conceptual Revolution in Community and Disability*. Cambridge, MA: Brookline Books

Shearer, A. 1984. *Think Positive: Advice on Presenting People with a Mental Handicap*. Brussels. ILSMH

Sturmey, P. 1993. The readability and human interest of information leaflets from major British charities: an unintelligible and boring replication? *Mental Handicap Research*, **6**, 174–83

Sutcliffe, J. 1990. *Adults with Learning Difficulties: Education for Choice and Empowerment*. Milton Keynes: Open University Press

Tackney, J. 1992. The pathway to success. In R. McConkey and P. McGinley (eds), *Innovations in Employment Training and Work for People with Learning Difficulties*. Chorley: Lisieux Hall Publications

Chapter 16

Think Positive! Advice on Presenting People with Mental Handicap

Ann Shearer

WHY IS PRESENTATION SO IMPORTANT?

All of us, every day, are forming our own ideas of people we do not know and deciding 'what they are like'. We may not even be aware that this is happening. But we are influenced by:

- pictures we see of them
- what people say and write about them
- how people behave towards them

The way people are presented, in all these different ways, has a very important effect on the way others perceive them. This is true of both individuals and whole groups. The idea of 'what they are like' can be so strong that even if we meet an individual who is very different from our preconceived 'image', we may feel that that individual is an exception and not representative of the 'group' at all.

This is as true of people with mental handicap as it is of anyone else. So societies of their parents and friends have a special responsibility to think about how they present them. In a world where many people still do not accept fellow citizens who have a mental handicap as equally respected members of their communities, these societies could play a special part in combating old fears and prejudices and in presenting a new view of 'what people with mental handicap are like'.

We all know that such fears and prejudices can be very powerful, learnt by children from their parents and other adults across generations. The prejudices can be so deeply engrained that people are not even aware that they hold them – until, perhaps, some people with mental handicap move into their neighbourhood.

There is no such thing as a neutral image of a person who has a mental handicap. Unless it is deliberately made positive, people will see it as confirming their negative preconceptions – whether that is intended or not. And because negative images are so powerful and deep, it takes very deliberate thought and action to combat them.

People will express these preconceptions in different ways, according to the traditions and teachings of their particular culture. But most will have one or more of the following images of people with mental handicap deep inside them:

- as and or pathetic, destined to lead a tragic life and bring sadness to all who know them
- as eternal children, unable to grow or develop beyond childish understanding and dependence
- as 'sick' and in need of medical supervision
- as 'mad', incapable of reason or even of noticing their surroundings
- as superhumanly strong, and dangerous physically and sexually
- as especially chosen by God – which may be another way of saying that they're 'not like us'

Societies of parents and friends of people with mental handicaps are now trying to present a positive image of them in place of these fears and prejudices. They want others to see them as:

- individuals who are more like any other individuals in their normal feelings and needs than they are different from them
- individuals who can enjoy life and can bring happiness to those who know them
- individuals who, with the help they may need, can grow in understanding and ability, and make their own contribution to their family and community
- individuals who are worthy of the same respect as any other human person

This chapter is about ways in which societies of parents and friends can build this positive image of people with mental handicaps.

CHANNELS OF COMMUNICATION

Images and ideas of 'what people are like' are communicated in ways that are subtle and unintentional, as well as in ways which are obvious and intended. Sometimes societies working for and with people with mental handicap will be clear what they want their message to be. But they may also send messages which they did not intend.

Messages are sent through three main channels:

- *Public education programmes*
  Here the people sending the message know what they are setting out to do. They may use poster advertisements, or other advertising techniques, and/or try to place stories with radio, TV, newspapers and/or magazines as part of a special programme of education. Or they may try to place stories with the media as often as they can as part of a more general and non-specific attempt to get their educational message across. Often, they use both approaches.

- *Fund-raising campaigns*
  Here the main aim has nothing to do with presenting an image of people with mental handicaps at all. But the way they are referred to in the written material that goes with the campaign, and the pictures of them that are used to persuade people to give their money, will still carry powerful messages about 'what people with mental handicaps are like'. So it is important to remember that a fund-raising campaign is really 'successful' only if it both brings in the money *and* presents a positive image of people with mental handicaps.

- *Behaviour towards individuals with handicaps*
  Here again there may be no conscious intention to send a message or to create an image of 'what people are like'. But by the way we talk about them and to them, and by our behaviour in their company, that is exactly what we do.

So messages are sent through pictures/visual images, through written and spoken words and through behaviours.

'PICTURES CAN SPEAK LOUDER THAN WORDS!'

The visual images we see of people play a major part in constructing the 'view' we have of them. It is not just the picture itself that is important. It is all the different connotations that the picture brings and the way that it can confirm deep fears and prejudices unless these are actively combated.

So whether the pictures presented of people with mental handicaps are for advertising, fund-raising or public education, the same general rules apply:

DON'T present pictures of people with mental handicap who look

- *sad or pathetic*
  This just confirms the old prejudices that 'there's no point in trying to help' – and the view that people with mental handicap are not enjoyable to be with.

- *ill-dressed and badly cared for*
  This will confirm the view that people with mental handicap are not to be valued and respected – and the idea that 'they aren't the sort of people we'd like to identify with'.

DON'T use pictures of people with mental handicaps who are

- *isolated from the world or alone*
  A picture of a single mentally handicapped person against a plain black background carries the message that 'they aren't part of our world' and 'they don't belong in our ordinary community'.

- *just sitting or lying, doing nothing*
  This confirms the view that 'they can't do anything'.

- *doing something odd or lacking in dignity*
  A picture of an adult playing with a child's game will confirm the view that these are 'eternal children'. A picture of a person naked in circumstances where others would be clothed, or in the bath or on the lavatory, will confirm the idea that 'these people do not deserve respect'.

- *in an unusual environment*
  A picture of a mentally handicapped person in a bare hospital ward will encourage others to believe that 'these people are sick'.

DO present pictures of people with mental handicap who look
- *happy and interested*

This will help others think 'There's someone attractive' before they think 'and they're handicapped ... !'

* *normally dressed and cared for*
Pictures of people who are dressed not especially well but in ways that are typical for their age group in their community will encourage identification with them as 'like me' or 'like someone I know'.

DO use pictures of people with mental handicaps who are

* *interacting with other people*
This will help people think 'There's someone who enjoys company – and who brings enjoyment to those they're with'.

* *doing something 'ordinary'*
This may be school or play for children, or work or leisure for adults. It will show that people with mental handicaps enjoy participating in at least some of the activities open to other members of their communities.

* *in an ordinary environment*
Schools, shops, streets, parks, houses ... These are all places with which anyone can identify and seeing handicapped people in them helps others think 'Here are people who do the same sort of things as I do'.

* *interacting with people who are not handicapped as well as with those who are*
This encourages the idea that 'These people are really people after all!' and helps combat the old prejudice that they're better off spending all their time with others who also have handicaps.

These 'dos' and 'don'ts' can be quite hard to follow in choosing pictures for fund-raising or public education campaigns. Societies of parents or those involved in public education need to get across the message that they need money to improve services – and so want to show pictures of bad conditions. They may want to show pictures of people with mental handicaps who are unhappy and ill-treated, neglected, isolated and doing nothing, because this is the truth of the situation and they want to help to change it.

But if you do show such pictures, *do* always try to show positive pictures as well – to give a contrast and to underline your positive message. It is not enough to show negative pictures and then talk about alternatives to what they portray in either written or spoken words. The power of the visual image is too great. People will usually just remember the negative picture that confirms their own deep prejudices and fears.

WORDS MATTER TOO!

Words don't just carry the messages we intend. They may carry other more subtle ones as well – and the effect may not be what we intended at all.

Words describe people

How do we describe people with mental handicaps – whether we are talking to others, either directly or on radio or TV, or writing about them?

- *Are they 'the mentally handicaped', 'the retarded', 'the subnormal', 'the defectives'?*
  Words like this put people into a – usually devalued – grouping. They blur their individuality and so conjure up those old prejudices and fears. Try instead: 'people/persons/individuals with mental handicap' or 'people who have a mental handicap'.

- *Are they 'patients', 'residents', 'clients'?*
  Words like this sound 'professional' and confirm the prejudice that people with mental handicaps need special 'treatment' – because they are sick or totally dependent or receivers of services all the time. Try instead: 'the people who live here', 'the people who use our services' – or simply use individuals' names!

- *Are they 'the children', 'the kids', 'the young people'?*
  This is an accurate description of children and adolescents. But if used for adults, it just confirms the image of people with mental handicaps as 'eternal children'. Try instead: 'the people/individuals/persons' or use individuals' names.

Words are positive or negative

The way we put words together can carry messages which are themselves positive or negative. If we talk or write about what people with mental handicaps *can't* do, we will just confirm those old prejudices. If we talk about what they can do, we will help others realize that they are growing and developing individuals.

This does not mean being unrealistic

It does not help people with mental handicaps at all if we convey a false impression of what they are able to achieve. But it does mean emphasizing the positive things about people.

As an example of negative and positive presentations, look at this piece of copy, written as part of an (imaginary) fund-raising campaign:

NEGATIVE

Peter will be eight for the rest of his life
Peter is eight. But he can't walk properly or talk. And in another eight years he won't be looking forward to dating girls or getting a job.

Like thousands of other children, Peter is severely mentally handicapped. Like them he will need loving care from specially trained staff for the rest of his life.

POSITIVE

Peter is eight and growing up fast!
Last year, Peter took his first independent steps. He's growing more adventurous all the time as he explores his community and makes new friends. He's enjoying learning to sign to them on his signboard, too.

Like other children with severe mental handicap, Peter is learning more than we thought possible only a few years ago.

Help us to go on giving that care, by sending your donation to:

Help us to help him find the skilled help he needs to go on growing – and the friends who make his hard work worthwhile.

What does this advertisement convey?

NEGATIVE

- *Peter is an eternal child*
- *He will never develop*
- *He won't make relationships*
- *He will always be 'useless' and dependent*
- *He is just like thousands of others, not individual*
- *You can't do anything except send money because he needs 'specially trained' staff*

So this advertisement confirms many negative stereotypes about people with mental handicaps. It invites readers to pay the society which is advertising to 'keep them away from us'.

What does the other advertisement convey?

POSITIVE

- *Peter has a severe handicap and is clearly not nearly as capable as others of his age*

BUT

- *He is learning to talk and communicate*
- *He has friends*
- *He enjoys life*
- *He can go on progressing if he gets the help he needs*

This presents a realistic but positive picture of children with severe mental handicaps. It invites readers to contribute to the society which is advertising in ways which do not exclude volunteering their time as well as sending money.

What is true about descriptions of individuals with mental handicap is equally true of descriptions of the situations they may find themselves in. Here again, there are negative and positive ways of presenting information. Compare these two approaches to writing a statement for the press and other media:

NEGATIVE

Conditions in Anywhere Hospital are 'shocking and disgusting', the Society for Subnormal Children says today. It calls on the Government to act immediately.

In its new report, 'Twilight Lives' the Society gives details of conditions which it says are 'not fit for animals'.

These include:

- lack of toilets and baths
- inadequate bedding
- inedible food

It also details 'unacceptable' practices which include:

- lack of stimulation and activity
- inadequate staffing

The Government, it says, should remedy these defects immediately.

This statement conveys that the society is concerned about conditions in the hospital. But it does not explain *why* it is concerned and *what* the government should be doing. The statement assumes that readers will understand a whole lot without being told. It underestimates, though, the weight of prejudices and negative images that people may be carrying. And by the way it is written, it risks confirming these.

Key words and images:
shocking, disgusting, animals, subnormal children, lack of hygiene, inedible food, 'twilight lives'.

These are all very negative images and associations. It would not be surprising if readers turned away from this statement – and the people it is about. And that is what the statement is inviting them to do. By saying 'The Government should act', it is saying that 'this is nothing to do with you'.

POSITIVE

'Hundreds of our fellow-citizens are being denied their rightful opportunities for growth and enjoyment, the Society of Friends of People with Mental Handicaps said today. It sets out a programme of action for Government and community members to improve the lives of people now living in Anywhere Hospital.

In its new report, 'New Opportunities for People with Mental Handicaps', the society contrasts the deprivation of people in the hospital with the opportunities of those living in their own homes and using its programme. In the hospital, it finds totally unacceptable conditions which include:

- lack of elementary hygiene
- inadequate bedding and 'inedible' food
- inadequate staffing

This means that people with mental handicaps are becoming far more handicapped than they need be, the society says.

In its own programme, by contrast, it offers:

- support to families
- individual education in the skills of everyday living
- education in skills which will help people contribute to family and community life.

Since its programme started, the society says, the people who attend have grown in ability, self-confidence and enjoyment of life – and so have their families. Now, it says, the Government and community groups should build on its experience to bring those opportunities to more people with mental handicaps in the ways outlined in its recommendations.

This statement also conveys that the society is concerned about conditions in the hospital. But by contrasting these with its own programme and the effects of hospital life with life in the community, it explains *why* it is concerned. It also indicates that it has worked out a plan for what should happen next. It conveys positive information about how families and people with mental handicaps can live more happily together, and invites readers to play their part in making this possible for more people.

Key words and images:
fellow-citizens, growth, enjoyment, friends, *people* (with mental handicaps), action, community, opportunities.

These are positive images and associations. They invite the reader to engage with the people involved. And the statement shows them that they have the chance to do that.

Positive presentations about people with mental handicaps do not, of course, just show different ways of using words to convey a message. They also convey two different approaches to helping those people. That underlines an important point. Words and actions have to go together in any fund-raising or 'public education' campaign. The best way to encourage others to think and act positively towards people with mental handicaps is to show them evidence that you are already doing so yourself?

ACTIONS CARRY MESSAGES!

The third main way in which people form their view of 'what people with mental handicap are like' is through observing the ways in which those who know them well behave towards them. The way society members and staff behave towards the people they serve will play an important part in setting standards and expectations of behaviour for others.

Parents as advocates

This is particularly true of parents. Usually, it is they who know their own child best, and can better than anyone else convey their child's individuality. It is parents who can best give a realistic picture of the joys as well as the difficulties of living with someone who has a mental handicap. It is parents who can most eloquently explain why particular help may be needed.

But, like anyone else, parents can sometimes send messages about their child that they don't intend to convey.

- Perhaps they never introduce their child, even when they are with them – or perhaps they worry incessantly about what their child is doing, so that others can neither meet the child nor talk to the parent.
- Perhaps they never mention their child in conversation – or perhaps they talk about him or her only to complain or only to talk about 'special' services that are needed.

The message of actions like this is that it is a real burden to have a handicapped child. This confirms the old prejudices. It also discourages people from getting to know the child – and from helping the parent.

Other parents behave differently towards their child.

- They have the child with them when other children are present, in a natural and appropriate way.
- They behave towards their child in public as far as possible as they do towards their other children – so that others have a chance to meet the child and converse with the parent.
- They talk about their child as they do about their other children – with pictures of the child, perhaps, as they show of others. They take the chance to explain how their handicapped child is different in a casual and relaxed way.
- They show, by the way they speak of and to their handicapped child, that there are happy times as well as difficult ones, and that their child is very much part of the family and of the community.

The message of actions like this is that people with mental handicaps share many needs and enjoyments with everyone else, and that though they need special help, they are true members of their own family and community, valued and loved for themselves. It is messages like that which make parents such good advocates for people with mental handicap.

Service providers as advocates

Many societies of parents and friends of people with mental handicaps organize different programmes for them. The ways those who introduce others to the programmes act towards the people who use them carry messages as well.

When people visit your society's programme . . .

Are they introduced to the staff only
OR
to the staff AND the people with handicaps who use the services?

The message of the first: 'The staff are the people who matter here – the handicapped people don't matter.' This may leave the preconceptions of the visitors untouched – or their negative views of people with handicaps reinforced.

The message of the second: 'We regard everyone here as equally worthy of respect – and we expect others to do the same.' This gives the visitor a clear expectation for their own behaviour and this also gives them the chance to dispel their own preconceptions about people with mental handicap.

Are staff introduced by their full name and title, and handicapped people by their first name only?
OR
Is everyone introduced in the same way – either by full name and title or by first name?

The message of the first: 'The staff are the important people here.' The message of the second: 'We value everyone here equally and expect others to do the same.'

Are people with mental handicaps 'spoken for', with others answering questions that they could well answer themselves?

OR
Are visitors encouraged to talk to them directly?

The message of the first: 'The views of people with handicaps don't matter. They can't speak for themselves – we must speak for them.' The message of the second: 'Very many people with mental handicaps can speak for themselves and it's important that we listen to their views and respect these.'

If a handicapped person can't speak, are visitors told, in their presence, all the things they can't do?
OR
Is there emphasis on what they are learning to do, however slowly, given in ways that include the person concerned – by touch and gesture as well as words – in the conversation?

The message of the first: 'This person isn't any use and doesn't have ordinary feelings either.' The message of the second: 'This person is developing and growing and worthy of respect.'

In a residential home, are visitors taken into the bedroom of the people who live there as a matter of course?
OR
Is it a rule that only the person whose bedroom it is can invite others into it?

The message of the first: 'Handicapped people don't matter enough to have ordinary privacy.' The message of the second: 'We value the privacy and dignity of the people we work with and expect others to do the same.'

Every time a visitor comes to see a programme, there are many opportunities to help them change the way they value and perceive people with mental handicaps. If those opportunities are not taken, there is a danger that the visitors will simply have their own fears and prejudices confirmed.

People with mental handicaps as self-advocates

Every time a parent encourages someone to speak directly to their mentally handicapped child instead of communicating through them, that parent is recognizing that people with a mental handicap have their own views and perceptions which deserve to be respected. Every time a service provider introduces one of the people who use the service to a visitor, they are recognizing that the consumer's voice is important. Those recognitions are the first step towards encouraging self-advocacy amongst people who have mental handicaps.

Sometimes self-advocacy is quite informal. People with mental handicaps, for instance, may explain their own preferences and needs to others in the course of conversation. Sometimes, self-advocacy is quite formal. There is a growing number of groups organized by people with mental handicap, together with their helpers and advisers. And it is becoming easier for people with mental handicaps to speak on behalf of friends and colleagues through interviews on radio, TV and in the press.

Societies of parents and friends of people with mental handicap will want to encourage the growing self-advocacy movement in any way that they can. Self-advocacy is probably the most effective way that there is of building positive and realistic images of people with mental handicap as individuals with their own gifts and needs.

GUIDELINES FOR ACTION

Whether people with mental handicaps are being introduced to others face-to-face, or indirectly, through advertising or media stories, the guidelines to follow are the same.

1. *Try to present people with mental handicap in ways that other people would find acceptable for themselves*
   This helps others to see them as having normal human dignity.
2. *Try to present people with mental handicap in ways that are positive rather than negative, active rather than passive*
   This helps dispel the old myth that 'nothing can be done' and that they are 'useless', 'sad' or 'pathetic'.
3. *Try to present people with mental handicap in situations that are ordinary or typical for their community*
   This helps people see them as 'more like us' rather than 'different from us' and raises expectations that they will participate in the ordinary life of their community.
4. *Try to present people with mental handicap in situations that are typical for others of their age in their community*
   This helps counter the view that they are 'eternal children' and raises expectations that they will participate in ordinary life and activities.
5. *Try to present people with mental handicap in situations where they are enjoying the company of others, not all handicapped*
   This helps people to see that they have something to offer and to break down the barriers of fear and ignorance that lead to segregation.
6. *Try to present people with mental handicap in situations and ways that exaggerate neither their abilities nor their disabilities*
   This helps people have a realistic view of what they can achieve and dispels myths about their 'special' as well as their 'useless' differentness from others.
7. *Try, whenever possible, to enable people with mental handicaps to speak for themselves*
   This enables others to see them as individuals with their own views, preferences and needs. It dispels so many myths. It is hard to see people as 'sad', 'useless', 'eternal children' and 'not really like us at all' when they are speaking about their hopes and their lives. It is hard to dismiss what anyone is saying when they are speaking simply and directly from their own experience.

HELPING OTHERS SPREAD THE MESSAGE

However hard a society works, other people will continue to have their own, often negative, views of people with mental handicap. Often, too, the people who express these views in public are influential members of the community – like politicians and professional workers. So they will get a lot of attention from the media. And so other people will identify with these views – and pass them on to a new generation of children.

Here are a few ideas about how societies could help these opinion-formers to give a more positive message:

- When someone gets publicity for a negative statement about people with mental handicap, organize a letter campaign to that person from individual parents and friends, giving a more positive view. Politicians will often respond more to many letters from individual constituents than they do to a single letter from a society whose views are well known – especially if those individual letters seem to be quite spontaneous and have nothing to do with the society at all! The society can, separately, write its own letter, inviting the individual concerned to come and meet some of the handicapped people with whom it is doing positive work.

- Remember that negative messages sometimes come in subtle ways. Politicians may call each other 'idiots' or 'morons' in debates, for instance, and this may be widely reported. Radio dramas or fiction stories in magazines may carry negative references to people with mental handicap. Here are other chances for letter campaigns to give more positive views.

- Children build up fears of people with mental handicap from what they hear from their parents and other adults. If societies hear of parents passing on negative or inaccurate views, they could invite a few of the key parents in the community to visit their service and learn a different way of seeing things. Then, with the parents' agreement, they could invite small groups of children to spend time with people with handicaps who use the service.
When organizing such meetings, it is important to remember that:
- large groups do not usually achieve as much as small meetings and individual encounters;
- people who do not know people with mental handicap may be awkward, embarrassed and curious, and may need help to express their feelings; and
- meetings should be enjoyable for everyone concerned, not a 'duty'. People need occasions to get to know each other in a relaxed atmosphere, perhaps over a meal. They learn more this way usually than through 'tours of inspection' or 'lectures'.

Remember to reinforce the positive as well as work on the negative! Appreciative letters to politicians, for instance, who make a positive public statement about people with mental handicap, will encourage them to do so again. (They'll be even more likely to listen if the letter does not also ask them for a favour, or for support for a project. That can come later!)

WORKING WITH THE MEDIA

However hard a society works, much of the presentation of people with mental handicap will be out of its hands. Newspapers, radio, TV and magazines will have their own ideas about what mental handicap is about – and usually far greater resources to spread their ideas than any society can hope to draw on. Even when the society has 'worked hard to present a "good story"' about individuals or its own work, that story may appear in a distorted form, giving the 'wrong' message.

It is important to remember that to an extent this is inevitable. The media do not see themselves as being in the business of giving free advertising, and will want to put their own interpretation on material offered to them. Reporters, photographers and editors have their professional pride – and, like any other member of the population, they may themselves be ignorant and fearful of mental handicap. But there are still things that a society can do to help the media present people with mental handicap in a positive way:

- Let the media know that the society thinks what they say about people with mental handicap is important – and why. If a media story perpetrates one of the negative myths about them (that they are 'mad' or 'dangerous, for instance) or refers to them in disparaging ways (like calling people with Down Syndrome 'mongols'), organize a letter campaign as described above as well as a letter from the society pointing out their error. The media want to be popular with their readers, listeners and viewers, and in the end they are likely to take notice of this reaction.

- Take the initiative by offering stories of the sort the society would like to see. Local radio stations and newspapers may be particularly receptive to these.
  But first, prepare the ground:
  1. Get to know the key person who will be responsible for the stories you offer. This may be the editor of a local newspaper, or the head of a local radio station, or, in big cities, a particular reporter who has the duty of working on 'social welfare' issues. Arrange a meeting with this person, to find out what sort of material would interest them and how they would like it presented. Invite them to visit the society's programme or service to meet some of the staff and people with mental handicap involved – just a relaxed, social occasion. Remember that media people are also members of the public and may need some help with their own fears, ignorance and awkwardness. Do not wait for them to own up to these. Try a few gentle conversations that begin, for instance, 'One of our difficulties is that so many people think people with mental handicap are unable to learn and grow', and see whether you get a response!
  2. When you have a story to offer the media try to think ahead about how you would like to see it presented, and whether it will create a positive impression of people with mental handicap.
  3. Will publicity given to one particular person who has achieved something look and sound as if that person is very 'special' – and so carry the message that most people with mental handicap could not have achievements of their own? Remember that there are other ways of presenting achievements than singling out one individual. And that there are other positive messages to send as well – like instances of co-operation with community groups and joint activities which everyone enjoys.
  4. Will publicity given to shocking conditions end up reinforcing negative images of handicapped people? Remember to accentuate positive aspects of their lives in different settings to give a more balanced and hopeful picture.
  5. When a reporter and/or photographer come to visit the society or its project, they may not be the people with whom educational work has already been done.

Remember that education has to happen all the time, and that each new reporter and photographer may need help to understand the image that the society is trying to get across. And remember too that they also have their professional pride and will not relish being told what to do. Keep it gentle and persuasive and explain your concerns.

6. Remember that feedback is important. An appreciative letter when a story has turned out 'well' will help build up a positive climate for the next one.

7. And if a story has turned out 'badly', try to find at least one good thing to say about it before you complain. Media people are people too!

8. Remember that others are also working to help the media present more positive images of people with mental handicaps. The local media people may respond to knowing that this is an international concern.

   The United Nations' document *Improving Communications about People with Disabilities* is designed specifically to encourage positive presentations in the media. The society might think of working together with other local organizations of and for people with disabilities to draw this to their media's attention. Order the document from:

   United Nations
   Division for Economic and Social Information
   Department of Public Information
   New York, N.Y. 10017
   USA

   It may form the basis of some interesting discussions.

9. Keep on trying even when the going seems difficult! The influence of the media is too important to ignore. Working with its representatives has to be an important part of any society's overall goal of improving the lives and opportunities for people with mental handicap.

ACKNOWLEDGEMENT

This chapter has been adapted from a document under the same title published by the International League of Societies for Persons with Mental Handicap (now Inclusion International), 1984.

Part IV

Advocacy in Action

Chapter 17

Stanley Segal

Valerie Sinason

My father was the sixth of seven children born to a Russian-Jewish immigrant couple in the East End of London on 11 October 1919. His mother spoke Yiddish and only slowly learnt English while his father, who had received more education, read and spoke several languages. However, his father died when Stan was only 2. 'To be a Professor of Mental Handicap', he wryly said, the week before he died, 'the best qualification is to have a mother who is illiterate'.

Although his early childhood was very different from that of his older brothers, as they had had an experience of being fathered until past school-leaving age, he was aware from their accounts that his father was a gentle diplomatic man who was a skilled organizer. Indeed, he achieved rapid promotion to management rank in the Welsh mining village he first went to (after escaping the Russian pogroms) because he maintained such excellent labour relations. It was the pit closures that led to his move to the East End.

His wife had no formal education but was renowned for her sharp wit and courage. As a ten-year-old she had led a strike in Russia in the boiled sweet factory she worked in, leading to an improvement in the conditions for child workers. She also helped her husband escape from Russia. However, whilst her older sons and daughter had the memory of her as a vivacious woman before her husband's death Stanley's memories were of her depression.

He had two memories from earliest childhood that he regularly mentioned to my brother and me when we were little. For me, they show something of the external and internal experiences that led to his public concerns and ability in lobbying.

The first memory was of his father dying when he himself was only two years old. He remembered his father's polished shoes by the side of the bed. His second memory was holding his mother's hand while she wailed by her dead husband's graveside. He was desperate to comfort her and worried how she would manage looking after him.

Stan always enjoyed polishing our shoes when we were late for school. It seemed that instead of being angry with his father for dying when he was so young, he used that precious rare memory to create a positive attachment. In taking pride in keeping everyone's shoes polished he was, as he continued to do, enjoying finding a strength in someone that could be identified and identified with and applied. His memory of his mother's painful loss, left with seven children in the East End of London, was of wanting to comfort her and of prematurely having a sense of emotional responsibility and, soon after, an awareness of the need for social responsibility.

Even as a young child he saw the schools he attended, and other public institutions, as having a family role – making up for the fathering he had lacked. When he repeated so often in his speeches that 'what a wise and good parent desires for his own child we as a nation should desire for all our children', it was an important emotional truth for him. At the heart of all his lobbying was a belief that Parliament did have the best interests of citizens in mind if he only could communicate well enough!

From earliest childhood he was sent to Hebrew classes daily after school and on Sundays. Despite the savagery and lack of training of many of these teachers, he was impressed with the fact that because they were willing to teach daily, widows, like his mother, could get some support. Again, instead of seeing it as another poor experience, he was quick to appreciate whatever positives could be found in it.

At 11 he was interviewed for a scholarship to a grammar school. However, the presence of his mother at the interview, making quite clear how his salary would be needed once he reached school-leaving age at 14, stopped that chance of a more direct academic experience. He therefore went to Jewish Free Central School.

As well as noting where individual or community action led to improvements, he was also quick to note its omission. On being apprenticed at 14 to a printer and signwriter, he discovered that firms were quick to sack 14-year-olds just before their fifteenth birthday to avoid paying them a higher salary. He started a union, became a shop steward and fought for the rights of 14-year-olds to be kept on after their birthday. He received a Tolpuddle Medal for establishing a union in such an unpromising place and succeeding in his aim. However, he also lost his job! He never put economic security or anything above moral principles.

He met my mother, Tamar, when he was 17. From the moment he saw her walking down the street swinging her tennis racquet, he fell in love with her and they were to be a rare life partnership, sharing political and personal aims. She had to become used to his political agenda from the start. At the beginning of their relationship, fascism was becoming more and more noticeable and when fascist meetings were held publicly in the East End he would be in those audiences and publicly challenge them.

He organized major meetings through the Workers' Education Association (WEA) at Toynbee Hall and at only 17 managed to gain speakers of the calibre of Sir Stafford Cripps. As Secretary of the WEA he felt good speakers could help influence people to create a more humane society.

During the Second World War he served in the 8th Army in the Middle East, Italy and North Africa whilst Tamar was a Forces Red Cross auxiliary nurse in Newmarket. Stan edited the 8th Army Log Book as well as developing his boxing skills. He was well aware of the need for personal strength when fighting an enemy as well as the need for mental strength and the hope to aid enemies to become allies. He was mentioned in dispatches for a personal act of courage.

For the five years Stan and Tamar were separated during the war they maintained their relationship through daily writing. Stan carried throughout his army period a typewriter he had captured and that aided him in his literary tasks! For the rest of his life he was never to be far away from a typewriter or a computer and I considered it to be the transitional object I inherited from him!

After the war he and Tamar married and he decided to train as a teacher. He went to Goldsmith's College which he deeply appreciated, though, as at 11, economic needs meant he passed his teaching diploma with distinction but could not afford the extra year to gain a degree. At the same time he became aware both of the numbers of houses left empty and the enormous numbers of people in overcrowded circumstances and he lobbied for the utilization of the empty homes. His sense of purpose can be seen in his description of his first teaching practice (in *Society and Mental Handicap*, Costello, 1984). 'Spurred on rather than perturbed by the bombed buildings, the grey shabby streets and the soulless depressing exterior of the building, enthusiasm, art and literature seemed to me to offer major tools which could help to illuminate all school subjects ... Here was an opportunity to do something.'

Very soon, he realized that the lowest stream children were unwanted by all the staff, that there was no suitable provision for them and that the books for use with them 'must have been unattractive even when new'.

Meanwhile, to his shock, fascist speakers were still holding street-corner meetings. When I was one year old and my mother was pregnant with my brother, Alan, she remembers him challenging these meetings and taking over the platform. He said that he had not fought all those years in the war to allow fascists to continue spouting their poison. 'I felt worried but I knew he had to do it', said Tamar. He made clear to her right at the start, 'If I am going to live in this area where these things are happening, I have to be involved.'

In Carpender's Park Stan and Tamar formed the first ever Junior Community Association in the country which dealt with further education classes, street lighting, and safe leisure activities. All three parties asked the two of them to consider being parliamentary candidates. However, despite a lifelong personal commitment to socialism, Stan was always a lobbyist to all parties on behalf of the subjects that mattered to him.

My first vivid memory of him, when I was four, crystallizes the way personal and professional values were fused in him. We had gone to Australia where he was offered his first headship. Of additional importance to us as a family was that a house came with the job. When it turned out that there were squatters living in the house my father would not take the job. He did not think that it was right to deprive people of a home when they would not be able to find one as easily as he and my mother could. In fact my parents did not find a home easily and for a while we lived in the Wimmera – in a wooden hut attached to an old disused schoolhouse – without electricity, sewage or running water. His sense of purpose was strong. However, I date my preference for luxury hotels to this period!

My four-year-old consciousness not only had impressed on it the position of the squatters but also the position of aborigines and indeed all those who were dispossessed. In the short period in Australia when my father taught intellectually gifted pupils, he not only chose to produce 'The Merchant of Venice', he also wrote a powerful poetic prologue to it on the nature and meaning of prejudice. I can still remember that production and the opening lines

'Out of the darkness of the mediaeval mind
was conjured up a myth – the Jew ...'

He chose to produce that play because the Melbourne Jewish community was incensed by a leading Shakespeare company portraying Shylock in a particularly anti-Semitic way. He did not want children and adults to throw the Shakespearean baby out with the bath water and he had found, as always, a way of responding that was creative and empowering.

Our journey to Australia began with his unwillingness to dispossess anyone and our return to England three years later was to provide a home for my maternal grandmother who was ill and whom Australian immigration would not allow to join us. The ship we sailed on deviated from its chosen route in order to pick up more passengers. Overcrowding, poverty-stricken pilgrims sleeping on board and poor sanitary conditions led to outbreaks of illness and outright mutiny. Stan was elected as a passengers' delegate to negotiate with the captain. As always, he was concerned for all classes of passenger and his clear but non-polarizing attitude was greatly valued as well as his personal courage. He was threatened with the hold if he persisted representing people on board or a first-class cabin if he changed his mind. He kept to his moral task despite the threats and bribes.

Returning to a council flat in King's Cross in London in 1954, he and my mother speedily created a tenants association. They were concerned that there were no suitable play facilities for little children or club activities for older ones. Soon a sense of community built up. 'It was like a Citizen's Advice Bureau in our flat – there were a range of committees – welfare committee, health, education, leisure ... ' said Tamar. From his teaching experience Stan had realized that the more responsibilities class members had the more they cared about the morale and functioning of the group. He delegated tasks as widely as possible to both children and adults! In his first teaching post on his return to London he created the post of 'class captain' that lasted a month and which could not be held for a second term. This meant that everyone in the class had a chance to be the captain and experience some responsibility and success. His motto was 'ARM' – Accept, Respect, Motivate. With these emotionally disturbed, conduct-disordered boys with learning disability, he also created a class court.

These ways in which he expected the outer social agencies to help change he therefore set up in microcosm within his schools. Indeed, once he began to create school councils, he even succeeded in gaining mayoral visits and, what is more, a ride in the mayor's coach for the school 'mayor'! It was not surprising that Barbara Wootton asked to meet him and suggested he became a juvenile magistrate which he did, including becoming a chairman of the bench. He saw the law as a means of providing provision rather than punishment. This was years before the concept of school councils was established.

From 1954 to 1974 he and my mother would help to organize holidays for deprived children and Alan and I would be helpers. Not many children could see their parents look after rough and deprived 6- to 16-year-olds not only without being made fun of but instead being held in high esteem and affection. When I was first a teacher and then a school psychotherapist I remembered the way he managed to get deprived and disturbed parents interested in coming to visit their children's school and the way he removed the stigma of special education at a time when many teachers for this group were the least able of teachers. He was one of the first to raise his voice against the abuse of physical punishment. He ordered the canes, the 'educational instruments' he was provided with in one school, to be broken into small pieces by the children to be made into a globe of the world.

He lobbied for uniform grants so that children from poor backgrounds would not feel shamed in the school setting and he created social evenings for deprived parents so that they would see the school as a friendly place, as a part of their lives. He held the first art exhibition of handicapped pupils' work in the town hall and inspired MENCAP to take up the idea. He also liaised with the National Book League to organize major exhibitions on reading material for disabled pupils as he found that there was so little material for them. He produced his own series of textbooks, the *Space Age and Working World* series.

Space travel was new and exciting and not yet part of school syllabuses. By making colourful space books for learning disabled readers he was also making the 'C', 'D' and even 'E' streams a cultural centre for education. His classroom with its bright and complex space models was visted by the able children when he taught in a comprehensive and I remember his pride in telling us about a 'D' stream boy who was able to provide some facts on space travel to an 'A' stream pupil.

He never complained when he saw something was lacking. If he had the ability to fill the need, he would do so. Otherwise he would lobby or bring in the talents of others. He helped creative musicians develop in this field – the Nordoff Robbins training had some of its origins in meetings at his school.

When we moved to Loughton he created the Guild of Teachers of Backward Children which he took over from Ablewhite's Guild for Diploma Teachers. He created the journal *Forward Trends* and got Cyril Burt and Neil O'Connor to contribute to it.

His conferences were a part of our family life and we helped on the bookstall of all the early Guild meetings. We especially liked going to the post office proudly carrying sackfuls of letters knowing we were part of something that really mattered. Now that I am an adult working in the field of learning disability, I have the regular pleasure of putting a face to the name I knew on the envelope.

In the last fifteen years I have been involved in psychoanalytical psychotherapy with handicapped patients. As my interest in this group has increased and I have read more, I have had the pleasure of reading my father's books again for professional as well as personal pleasure. His writing always mattered to us as a family and we would hear all his speeches before they were printed or read. When Alan and I were in our teens, the lounge would be filled with the clacking of typewriters and a spread of paper. My mother, once he retired from Ravenswood, gave up the unequal struggle and added a typewriter and paper of her own. Although for Dad a holiday was him carrying his typewriter to a different environment, he could switch instantly from preparing a conference speech if we needed his help, always having the space to respond to the needs of the child or the grandchild!

In my work I have been struck by the way handicap can be a state people move in and out of so that you need expectancy for the highest anyone is capable of and provision for the least. When my father came home from school he would speak to Alan and me in a very slow voice. It took an hour or so before he gained his usual speed. I built up a very powerful image of this handicapped kind of step-sibling who needed to be spoken to so slowly and carefully. I knew it was not the whole story. As a therapist I identified as the most disturbed state that which provoked the gentle tones of my father. In other words, he was able to stay with the lowest point of functioning, without becoming irritated and impatient. He could wait. Indeed, for a man who can wait for children so long, he was amazingly fast over securing adequate provision for them and for a gentle man he was most forceful at pushing for adequate legislation.

Indeed, following the powerful impact of his book *No Child is Ineducable* in 1967 a climate was produced in which legislation was possible and he was acknowledged as a major influence on the Plowden Report. In some circles the 1970 Education (Handicapped Children) Act was referred to as the Segal Act. Professor Ronald Davie, Past President of the National Association for Special Educational Needs, commented

> Stanley Segal's second contribution was in large measure to persuade the government to set up in 1974 a committee of enquiry into the educational needs of handicapped children. This committee, chaired by Mary Warnock established the term 'pupils with special educational needs' to characterise these children; and the committee's report set out the twin principles of maximal integration of disabled children into ordinary schools and of a partnership between their parents and the professionals involved. These principles were later to be embodied in the 1981 Education Act and then further developed in Part III of the 1993 Education Act.

Professor Davie saw my father's third major contribution as his ability to collect and organize people around major themes – hence the Guild of Teachers of Backward Children and the National Council for Special Education (of which he was made a Life President). In 1992 a further fusion created the National Association for Special Educational Needs. Professor Davie's account of his life reached my father while he was still alive and moved him to tears.

He lobbied for the school-leaving age to be raised so that teenagers would not enter an abyss of no provision on leaving school. Indeed, he moved to become principal of Ravenswood Village in 1969 because he was concerned that change could not be adequately effected by the school working hours. He considered that the 24-hour environment needed changing and enriching. With his philosophy, what he meant by education was anything you did to help a child to feed, to go to the toilet, anything that improved life and life quality was educational. He had concerns at leaving the mainstream to go to Ravenswood, a Jewish organization. However, he felt that it could show the way for village development. He appreciated the friendship of Lord and Lady Jacobovitz (who visited him right through to the end) and repaying his debt to the Jewish community that helped to bring him up in his childhood. He saw Judaism as an ethic for living rather than as belief and ritual observances. Indeed, the passage from the prayer book that Reverend Turner read so beautifully and aptly at his funeral service sums up his philosophy – 'It is not our duty to complete the task; neither may we desist from it.'

He was awarded an OBE for his services to special education in 1978 and appointed visiting professor of education at Bulmershe College, now part of Reading University, in 1981. When he retired from Ravenswood in 1985 he created the International Information Centre for Special Needs Education, wanting a new international lobbying base for the further changes needed. For him there was always something important that needed doing.

In his last year, from June 1993 whilst suffering with cancer of the pancreas, he continued to plan changes from his sickbed. With a laptop computer he began work on a new book '*With Love from the D(e)-Streamed*' and a list of priorities to achieve. High on his list was making Tamar promise to continue with her 'community action' poetry and broadcasts on radio – which she did.

For him she also wrote 'We who follow must continue to support the work he has left to us in trust.' He inspired all of us with a wish to communicate. Alan, an artist and special needs teacher, is not averse to using his artistic abilities and love of chess as extracurricular additions to motivate his pupils or making the occasional home visit where necessary, to aid parental co-operation.

Deeply saddened by his inability to give a keynote talk in Hungary in honour of the legendary Dr Buday, he nevertheless managed to finish writing his speech, despite his severe deterioration, and it was translated into Hungarian. At his memorial meeting at Ravenswood Village, a spokesman from the Hungarian Embassy presented my mother with an award for him. He greatly appreciated the friendship of colleagues and, in his last months, was moved to tears on knowing that Professor Mittler, Christiana Horrocks, Professor Davie, Lady Plowden, Baroness Warnock, Professor Corbett, Professor Russell and Peggy Jay had agreed to speak at an event to honour his life. As he deteriorated he knew that he would not be able to attend and the occasion would become a memorial. He was deeply grateful to Professor Mittler for undertaking the project of this book and to all those who visited him or wrote to him in his last months.

Only two days before he died he was wondering how he could achieve an international award for Siyazama parents who run a project to improve conditions for South African township disabled children. His ability to be passionately committed continued throughout his life and his dying. In this he was aided by his wife. When Princess Anne visited Ravenswood she said to my mother, 'When you marry a missionary, you become a missionary's wife.' The 16-year-old girl had recognized in the 17-year-old wise ex-shop steward a level of moral integrity and political leadership whilst he recognized her staunch loyalty, compassion, and enthusiasm.

Together with his strong moral principles, he had a great sense of joy for life. Wherever we lived, a weekend walk was essential and he would point out the moral benefits of there being free parkland as well as the beauty of nature! He and Tamar attended Kenwood concerts all his life and he would sing Italian opera with gusto from the bathroom or the garden! It was his love of life that led to his visual image for the 1990s. Instead of the familiar depressing curve of normal distribution, Stan turned it upside down to provide a wineglass – the bottom of the glass, the container is the brightest and spreading up instead of down are the average and handicapped – a toast! Dad, we drink your health!

Last Speech

My father in bed
completing his last speech
It is a fine one

It is the one he has been living
all his life

My father is writing his last speech
Computer on lap
an auxiliary brain

My father the failing magician
can't keep food in
but can't keep words in either

How they struggle out of their
white life-cells
then pass free onto the luminous screen

As he grows thinner
they assemble for him
they gather the continents
the history the geography
the Wild Boy of Aveyron
the pioneers Itard, Seguin
even his favourite sentence –
the one we laughed at
'The increasing humane consciousness of the British public'

And the words stay
They stay on the disc
They stay on the file
They stay on the printed page

And the words have no cancer of the pancreas
The words have no pain
The words did not lie awake all night
weeping for those they would leave behind
needing morphine a bath a water bottle a pillow

Father in bed
writing his last speech
He's tiring now
suddenly asleep

the computer screen
turning its lights out
to not disturb him

and the words in his head
turning their lights out
one by one

So many fine words
Such a fine speech

Valerie Sinason
Bruises and Light (Karnac Books, 1995)

Index